Sullivan Holman M'Collester

After-Thoughts of Foreign Travel in Historic Lands and Capital Cities

Third Edition

Sullivan Holman M'Collester

After-Thoughts of Foreign Travel in Historic Lands and Capital Cities
Third Edition

ISBN/EAN: 9783337208936

Printed in Europe, USA, Canada, Australia, Japan

Cover: Foto ©Andreas Hilbeck / pixelio.de

More available books at **www.hansebooks.com**

AFTER-THOUGHTS

OF

FOREIGN TRAVEL

IN

Historic Lands and Capital Cities.

BY

SULLIVAN HOLMAN M'COLLESTER.

THIRD EDITION.

BOSTON:
NEW ENGLAND PUBLISHING CO.
16 HAWLEY STREET.
1882.

TO

My Wife,

THE ASSOCIATE OF MY STUDIES AND EXPERIENCES,

AFTER TWENTY-NINE YEARS OF HAPPY COMPANIONSHIP,

This Volume

IS AFFECTIONATELY INSCRIBED.

AUTHOR.

PREFACE.

These After-Thoughts of two and a half years abroad, are not offered as exhaustive essays, but rather suggestive compends of subjects considered. They were first presented at some intervals in lectures, which will account for their variety of style and method. Their aim is to direct special attention to those countries and events, whence has come our civilization. Accordingly, I have gleaned from the places visited and studied, such facts and suggestions, as would naturally induce others to investigate and gather up from foreign lands and men that instruction and knowledge, which tend to hallow the past, enrich the present, and ennoble the future.

We cannot realize too fully, that in the progress of civilization, the good, however antiquated, is sure to survive; that each epoch has not failed to crown its successor; that the Orient has been constantly bestowing upon the Occident. Therefore, in this latest time and far western civilization, we have received inestimable treasures, and ought so to appreciate and use them that we may be able and desirous to give to the world more and better gratuities than we have received.

The present form of these After-Thoughts is a response to the earnest request of many friends who listened to them in the lecture-room. That they may yield pleasure and profit to readers and students of history and character, is the sincere wish of the Author.

CONTENTS.

		PAGE
I.	Scotland and Edinburgh	1
II.	London	33
III.	France and Paris	67
IV.	Spain and Madrid	95
V.	Germany and Berlin	119
VI.	Switzerland and Berne	157
VII.	Florence, the Art City	189
VIII.	Modern and Ancient Rome	211
IX.	Naples and its Buried Cities	248
X.	Greece and Athens	269
XI.	Lower Egypt and Cairo	297
XII.	Modern and Ancient Jerusalem	332

AFTER-THOUGHTS

OF

FOREIGN TRAVEL.

I.

SCOTLAND AND EDINBURGH.

THE traveller, after riding upon the Atlantic for nine days, or more, whether he has enjoyed or disliked the voyage, is quite sure to be delighted as he approaches the coast of Scotland. The islands are so green and the bluffs of the mainland so abrupt, that he can but revel in pleasure and wonderment. If he passes in the daylight Giant's Causeway, or the Isle of Staffa, he can behold the grandest formation of basaltic rock; or, if he can stop, so as to enter Fingal's Cave, he will witness one of the sublimest cathedrals in the world, having old ocean for its flooring, huge crystals of basalt for its walls, and native fretted work for its roofing. As he comes to Iona, he thinks of the long line of Scotch kings buried here, and of the sainted Columba, who, in the sixth century, and in the dim light of Christianity, was wont to teach that Iona is the abode of the blest; or, as his steamer sweeps round the Isle of Arran, he is likely to recall the legend of Robert Bruce, telling how, in 1306, he crossed the sea from Arran to the mountainous coast of Carrick, that he might attack the English forces gathered there, and, if possible, conquer them. Having spent a day in reconnoitring, he lay at night in the barn of a loyal cottager, and in the morning, as he awoke, he saw a spider climbing a beam of the roof. Soon the insect fell to the ground, but immediately it made the second essay to ascend. This attracted the notice of the hero who with regret saw the spider fall the second time. At once, it made the third unsuccessful attempt, and so continued till the twelfth failure; but the thirteenth effort was a success; the spider reached the ridge of the barn, when the king sprung to his feet and exclaimed, "This despicable insect has taught me perseverance: I shall follow its example. Have I not been twelve times defeated by the enemies' superior force? On one fight more hangs the independence of my country." In a few days after, history informs us that his anticipations were fully realized in the glorious victory of Bannockburn.

As the steamer enters the harbor of Greenock, which is at the mouth of the Clyde, there is joy on the part of all passengers, even if the fog is thick and the rain falling fast, as is usually the case. Here it was that the old Scotchman was asked, "Does it always rain here?" "Na," he replied, "it sometimes snaws." The coast, so far as the eye can reach, is bold and picturesque. The situation of Greenock is beautiful, and the town presents an attractive appearance from the sea. But its chief interest springs from the fact that it is the birthplace of James Watt. Here it was that in early life he watched the steam lifting the teakettle lid, and conceived the idea of applying it so as to drive the locomotive. Here, also, John Galt, the novelist, lived and died. What significance noble lives add to the beauties of nature and the works of man!

If the tide is in, the steamer pushes on up the Clyde after inspection. Very soon the foreigner has the opportunity of seeing what Scotch perseverance and industry will do; for the Clyde which was at the beginning of the present century an inferior stream, scarcely navigable for the smallest crafts, has been widened and deepened, so that ships of heavy burdens can pass up its winding course as far as Glasgow. Then, too, its banks for miles are lined with new ships on the stocks in process of completion. As one comes within the sound of the clattering and whacking of ten thousand hammers, as they are welding together the ribs and making tight the keels, he can but imagine that pandemonium is close at hand. At the junction of the Leven and the Clyde, he is surprised at the abrupt rising of the Dumbarton Rock to the height of five hundred- and sixty feet above the surface of the river. The rock measures a mile in circumference, and ends in two peaks. The highest of these is crowned with a tower bearing the name of Wallace's Tower, from the fact that the Scottish hero was confined here. Still higher up the river is a promontory, on which stands the ruins of Dunglas Castle, and under its shadow is an appropriate monument to perpetuate the name of Henry Bell who first introduced steam navigation on the Clyde. Farther on is to be seen a large block of stone, marking the spot where the Earl of Argyle was captured after his unsuccessful expedition from Holland. In half an hour more the steamer reaches Renfrew Ferry, where Somerled, Thane of Argyle and Lord of the Isles, in 1164, fighting against

Malcolm IV., was defeated and killed. Now the country seats multiply fast on either side of the river, and in a little while the steamer is anchored by the wharves of Glasgow. The American, as he enters the streets of this city, is reminded of New York. He soon is made fully aware that he is in a great metropolis. As he walks the streets and examines the buildings, he is impressed with the feeling of durability. As he observes the merchants and bankers behind their counters, and mechanics at their benches, he is quickly persuaded that they are bound to have a good living, if active brains and busy hands can gain it. Glasgow is the third city as to population in the United Kingdom, and is all the while advancing in wealth and population. It is surprising that such a city should have sprung up here on the banks of the little Clyde, twenty miles from the sea; for its natural advantages are surpassed by most other commercial cities. Its climate is temperate, but its atmosphere is excessively humid. Perhaps it could be said of this place with truth, that it has more rainy than fair days during the year; yet it is a healthy town. Possibly the oat-porridge with which the young blood is so generally fed, has something to do with the health of the Scotch people here, as well as elsewhere. The features and physiques of the average man or woman, as seen on the street, in the office, or church, indicate physical and mental strength.

The shrine before which the pilgrim to this city is prone to worship first and last, is its Cathedral. This is a grand old Gothic structure built in the reign of David I. It wears somewhat of a gloomy, yet venerated aspect without, and within it presents in the dim light struggling through the most exquisitely painted windows, curiously sculptured naves, aisles, and tribunes, separated by hugest pillars and stoutest walls. As one studies it, he must be conscious it implies that there is something enduring in religion. The mind that conceived such a temple must have had conceptions of "a building not made with hands."

To the east of the Cathedral, rising above it several hundred feet, is the Necropolis, "the silent city," with its numerous columns and hosts of stones telling where the ashes of the rich and poor, the learned and ignorant, find a common resting-place.

Argyle is the Washington Street, and Buchanan the State Street, of Glasgow. The new Union Depot is a magnificent structure. George's Square is especially interesting, because it is graced with the statues of Scott, Peel, Watt, Burns, Clyde, and Moore.

A foreigner will not be likely to remain long in company with a real Scotchman without hearing the name of Robert Burns tenderly spoken and some of his sweetest lays repeated. In Glasgow we are made to feel, we are quite in the realm of the Ayrshire poet. The people are wont to say, "It is but a little way, only forty miles, to his old home." Taking the train bound for the south, we are soon buzzing through emerald hills and across the greenest meadows. In this autumn season, herds of fattest oxen and flocks of monstrous sheep are feeding in the fields. Frequently we spy humble peasant-homes, and here and there catch glimpses of palaces among grand old elms, beeches, and sycamores, where dukes and nobles live. Before we scarcely dream of it, we are at the station of Ayr. Leaving the train, as we go forth, thinking, walking, looking, we can understand, as never before, the bard's eulogy, —

> "Auld Ayr, wham ne'er a town surpasses
> For honest men and bonnie lasses."

We come to the river whence the town takes its name, and the "Twa Brigs," and the scene of Tam O'Shanter's wonderful experience. These span the river not far apart. The lower one, which was the New Brig in the poet's day, is now used for public travel, while the Old Brig is fast going to decay. The drowsy Dunyon clock has been removed to the Wallace Tower in the centre of the town. Old Simpson's is still at the end of the brig, telling its tale of Tam O'Shanter and Souter Johnny. Having visited the places particularly associated with the life of Burns, we have no desire to tarry longer in Ayr, though it is a pleasant seaport and manufacturing town; and so we hie three miles away to the southward, and we find ourselves in front of a little thatched cottage with the inscription over the central door, "Robert Burns, the Ayrshire Poet, was born under this roof, the 25th of January, A. D. 1759, died A. D. 1796, aged $37\frac{1}{2}$ years." Passing into the room where the poet was born, one can scarcely refrain from asking, is it possible that Scotland's greatest bard first opened his eyes upon the mortal in this humble house and still more humble kitchen? How true are the words of Seneca that "the humble and the lowly born often receive true praise"! The chairs, bed, and hollows in the stone flooring indicate age and long use. On the walls in the square-room, adjoining, are hanging various portraits of the poet, and certain relics made particularly valuable because associated so intimately with his life. The nooks and table are completely covered with signatures. One of the most appropriate and significant memorials on the walls of this room is a poem written by J. G. Whittier, commemorative of the genius and influence of Burns, being neatly framed and placed there by Hon. Israel Washburn. Everything about the old home is expressive of simplicity and prudence, calling up the picture of the youthful mother, when, in the bleak winter with her baby-bard in her arms, she came so near being crushed by the falling in of the roof, and then of being frozen to death, as they were borne through frost and snow in the darkest night to a neighbor's dwelling. Here one is reminded of the fact, how the Burns family passed through the severest buffetings, and could support themselves only by hard labor, practising the most rigid economy.

A short distance from the old home, close upon the banks of the Doon, stands the veritable antique kirk with its strange windows through which Tam O'Shanter stared "at the winsome dancing party and Old Nick as he fiddled." Up in the gable tower still hangs the ancient bell, with its short, rusty chain, dangling so high that even ghosts would find it difficult to toll, as it was tolled in days of long ago. Girdling Kirk Alloway is a neglected "city of the dead," where are to be seen the graves of the poet's father and mother, marked by stones erected by himself, and inscribed with an epitaph written with his own pen, and expressive of the tenderest affection. Not far from the kirk, on a mound stands a modern mausoleum of Ayrshire's bard, in the form of a Grecian temple sixty feet high, having a dome crowned with a tripod and gilded urn. On the flooring is a beautiful bust of the poet cut in the finest marble. On a table near, are the Bible and Testament given by Burns to his Highland Mary at their last parting, and on the fly-leaf of each Burns placed a Masonic sign, adding these texts, "Ye shall not swear by my name falsely; I am the Lord." "Thou shall not forswear thyself, but shall perform unto the Lord thine oaths."

Just under the shadows of the monument is a rustic structure containing the statues of Tam O'Shanter and Souter Johnny; comical characters, indeed! They look as though they were worthy heroes for epic verse. Forty rods from this sacred spot, partly under the hill, is the auld brig over which Tam drove his Meg at full speed, with the witches and warlocks at his heels, till the keystone of the arch rocked, and drenching rain put an end to the furious chase. On the brig may be enjoyed charming views of the

"Banks and braes o' bonnie Doon."

In the summer the shades are so thick, the breezes so cool, the water so clear, the currents so musical, and the birds so merry, how could the poet but sing

"Ye flowery banks o' bonnie Doon,
How can ye bloom sae fresh and fair"?

Go up or down the Doon, follow the roads or ramble across the fields, and you cannot fail to find the scenery most inviting. It was somewhere here that the youth was running his plough afield, and the muse of his native land fired his heart and bid him come and write the songs of his nation. "Were Byron and Burns now alive," said Hawthorne, "the first would come from his ancestral abbey, flinging aside, though unwillingly, the inherited honors of a thousand years, to take the arm of the mighty peasant who grew immortal while he stooped behind the plough." It would seem that

"A heaven-directing voice was near .
That bade him sing, and Scotland cheer;
That muses bounded at his call
And vowed obedience, one and all."

If we think of Chaucer as the poet of manners, Spencer as the poet of romance, Shakespeare as the poet of nature, Milton as the poet of morality, we must think of Burns as the poet of the heart and every-day life. Scotland had been long waiting for just such a bard. Previous to his coming, the land had been swayed by severest passions. Its history had been a bloody one. From earliest times wars had raged; defeats and victories had prevailed. Terrible results were being experienced from contentions between Scots and Picts, barons and menials, Protestants and Papists, Covenanters and Liturgists. The poor were being ground down by the rich, which the clergy and the schools were either unable, or not disposed to remedy. If the Scotch intellect at the middle of the last century had become keen and logical, the heart was cold and untouched. So at this time, just when the Sotch people seemed to be most in need of help, teaching them that all men are equal in the sight of God, so far as they are equally true and noble, whether they be kings or peasants, Robert Burns came from the rustic field and thatched cottage, singing "Bonnie Doon," "Auld Lang Syne," "Scots wha hae," "Cotter's Saturday Night," "Man's a man for a' that," leading oppressed and doubting minds at once upon mounts of fairest vision. With them he weeps, with them he laughs, with them he works, and with them he prays. To the people of Scotland the lays of Burns hold in their hearts a place next to the Bible. His songs have become household words throughout his native land. The humble poet of Ayrshire has risen a star of the first magnitude, to shine forever from the firmament of the past.

> "His resting place is hallowed ground,
> His worth and fame are now unbound;
> Let piles of marble stand or fall,
> His songs will long outlive them all."

Leaving these fairy scenes, by land and sea, by steam and coach, we wander among the Highlands of Scotia. We find the scenery wild and the country sparsely settled. The sides of the mountains are purpled with heather and the valleys are spotted with numerous lakes. The grouse and the deer revel in these romantic lands. The long-haired cattle, shaggy-coated ponies, and dark-nosed sheep, roam at pleasure in many of these rude places. Here once dwelt the warlike Celts and Picts. Their descendants are still possessors of the land. They glory as of old in their stern pedigree and clannish customs. No language to them is so sweet as the Gaelic tongue; no music, so charming as that of the Scotch bagpipe. In the little hamlets and peasant districts the people are poorly housed, scantily fed, and slovenly clothed. At Oban, Inverness, Wick, and other larger towns, an entirely different order of things exists. The people are moved by the spirit of the age. They believe in canals, railroads, and telegraphs, and take a decided interest in schools and churches. Their roads, bridges, and tunnels plainly show that they are enterprising and industrious.

Of all the lakes in Scotland perhaps Lochs Lomond and Katrine take the lead. It is true they are not clothed like Grassmere and Derwentwater with the classic associations of Wordsworth and Southey; or like Leman and Luzerne, with historical pictures of Bonnivard and Tell; or like Como and Maggiore, with luscious vines and marble villas: still they are rich with legends of Rob Roy and Helen McGregor. They are constantly guarded by Bens Nevis, Lomond, and Venue, some of the highest mountains in Great Britain. Here and there jagged rocks and threatening cliffs hang close over the glassy waters. As one is borne on steamer along their winding course, he experiences a strange interchange and commingling of the beautiful and the sublime. The bracing air and stirring views are sure to infuse the heart with fullest life. He can no longer wonder that chiefs and vassals have loved this land, that clans have fought for it, and even died for it. These waters abound in fish, and at seasons are all alive with sea-birds. It is not strange that Scott, with his line, gun, and dogs, should often have been lured hither for sport, and at the same time should have gathered up so many reminiscences of startling events with which to give striking colors to his word-pictures. These lakes are sure to be the summer resort of tourists who are fond of the natural and historic, the placid and the grand.

Aberdeen with its institutions of learning, Dundee with its extensive docks and remarkable bridge across the Tay, Stirling with its lofty castle and hoary abbey, as a central setting in the most enchanting landscape picture, and Melrose with its famous abbey and Eildon Hills, offer special attractions to all who would know the people and the civilization of Scotland; but the city of all others in this robust land is Edinburgh.

It is hard to realize that where now this cultured city stands was once the densest wilderness where the elk sported, the wild boar revelled, and the wolf prowled unmolested. When man first came here is uncertain. No doubt the Castle Rock, towering so high above the surrounding country, first attracted his notice. Here he must have felt that nature had made for him a stronghold on which he could be safe against the attacks of wild beasts and savage men. As early as the eighth century, it is known, there was quite a settlement here, made up of little houses with thatched roofs. It must have been inhabited then by some of the brave old Scots and Picts. The promise must have been slight, indeed, that life would blossom from this pristine rudeness into the fairest fruitage. But in King David's day it had grown into a burgh, and in the time of Robert Bruce it was being regarded a respectable city. About the time Columbus discovered the New World, it became the home of the famous Stuarts, and had grown into a walled town; and before the first settlement had been made in America, it had run up a long line of kings; and before the Pilgrims stepped upon Plymouth shore, it was seemingly regarded a finished city, for its limited enclosure had become crowded with buildings, and the rulings of its Jameses and Charleses were to the end that its walls would not be extended. But its ramparts were at length beaten down, and its boundaries enlarged, so that when Samuel Johnson looked upon it, he pronounced it "an imposing metropolis"; so, too, it looked to Oliver Goldsmith, and afterwards to Robert Burns; and still more striking is its appearance to-day, for it has become a city of two hundred thousand inhabitants, being distinguished for its university, academies, public and charity schools. It appears to be clothed with a classic air. Poets and geniuses have been born and educated here. The whole world has been greatly benefited through its intellectual development. The fact that it has produced and schooled David Hume, Sir Walter Scott, and graduated from its university Thomas Carlyle, is sufficient to render it forever memorable, and a place to be sought after by all who have been blessed by its gifted minds.

The site on which this city stands can scarcely be surpassed, if equalled. The city of the Cæsars crowning the seven hills, or Athens in the time of Pericles and Phidias, belting its Acropolis so graced with temples and art-wonders, or the city of Constantine set upon its many hills, could not have possessed the romance and grandeur of Edinburgh. Here plain, water, hill, valley, cliff, crag, and mountain, are strangely commingled. It is evident that volcanic force, glacial abrasion, and aqueous action, did their utmost to render this place wildly sublime and beautiful. As man has laid claim to it, he has taken advantage of the natural, so as not to mar the gifts of earth, water, and sky, but rather add to their attraction and picturesqueness. It covers over many acres, and would require many ox-hides of Virgil's time, cut into finest strings, to girt its circumference. If its climate is somewhat rigorous, it is bound to improve, and be sought after by the scholar and tourist. To see Edinburgh one must have weeks there, and be all the time astir at that. Looking upon it is like looking through a kaleidoscope,— no two views are ever the same; so that the more it is studied, the more it is wondered at and admired. Calton Hill is the commanding outlook of the new town. This height is verily an acropolis, adorned with its Doric columns and majestic monuments to the noble dead. It rises some three hundred feet above the sea. When the day is clear, it affords an extended view of the Forth, spotted with its sails and smoking stacks; of the hills of Fife, throwing off their constantly varying shadows; far to the north may be caught glimpses of the Grampian Hills, reddened, perchance, with blooming heather; to the west are the Pentlands, in summer green, with smiling fields quite to their summits; while a little to the south rise Salisbury Crags, presenting their formidable breastworks; and a little farther on towers aloft Arthur's seat swaying its sceptre over all below. As one looks from Calton Hill upon the new town, if he has the least bit of poetry in him, he must feel as though he were reading a poem cut in stone. The style of architecture clearly shows that modern minds have been made familiar with the best works of beauty and taste in all the past. The peculiar characteristics of the skilled and cultured Doric and Corinthian, the Roman and Goth, the Norman and Saxon, are repeated here. As the eye runs across from the new to the old town, how the buildings seem to rise and sink and rise! They are singularly lifted one above another, as though they had fallen together by chance, yet in perfect order. Look upon this scene in the evening, after the gas-jets are fired on the streets, and the windows everywhere are flecked with streaming lights. No fairy tale could paint a picture more enchanting than this. Away down in the valley, away up on the hill, because of their distance, lights dimly flicker; and here and there, in large blocks of buildings, rows of wavy tapers will ascend one above another, even eight or nine stories. Let this twinkling field be overhung by an unclouded sky, thickly sown with burning stars reflecting the radiance of heaven, and you have such a picture as is nowhere else to be witnessed and enjoyed.

Walking along Princes Street in warm weather from Calton Hill, the eye is delighted with majestic and beautiful public buildings, hotels, and stores on the right hand, while on the left are unique gardens with greenest plats and walks, bordered with variegated pansies, geraniums, and mignonette. On the mound dividing the gardens stands the Royal Institute, crowded with works of modern and ancient art. The buildings themselves will bear careful study; fashioned after Grecian models, grim-eyed sphinxes are coldly looking from the roof, while on the ridge over the main entrance is a colossal sitting statue of the Queen in her robes of state. In these gardens are statues of Ramsay, the poet; of Wilson, better known as Christopher North; of Black, the Scotch historian; of Livingstone, the African explorer; and the most inviting of all is the crucial Gothic spire, resting on four grand English arches, serving as a canopy to a statue of Sir Walter Scott. Some forty characters described in the great novelist's writings are represented in stone and occupy conspicuous niches in this monument which rises to the height of two hundred feet. Through a deep natural depression in these grounds may be seen, every now and then, whiffs and folds of smoke ascending from the screaming engines as they burst out of the tunnels and rush through the valley. When the sun shines, mingling shadows are incessantly falling upon these gardens from Castle Rock which guards them on the south. Though it rises so abruptly, and its sides are so jagged, yet children play all the day with safety at its base. In spite of the trees hugging its spurs, and mosses sticking in its clefts, it ordinarily presents a cold, barren face to the new city; but as the rains fall and the sun shines, its sides look as though they had been bathed afresh in a sea of emerald.

George Street, running parallel to Princes, forms the ridge of the new town. This is terminated at one end by Charlotte Square which contains the equestrian statue of Prince Albert, grouped about with the royal family. It is a work happily conceived and tastefully executed. On this street, too, stand imposing statues of

Dr. Chalmers, George IV., and William Pitt; and at the other terminus is St. Andrew's Square, from whose centre towers the lofty fluted column of the first Viscount Melville. The new town extends down to the Frith of Forth, spreading over a large area. Here we find the Royal Gymnasium and the Botanic Gardens, which speak well for the city. As we examine the lay of the land, the water, and the buildings, we are reminded, in many regards, of old Athens stretching far away to the Bay of Piræus.

Though the casual observer may be most interested in the new, the lover of history will seek the old town, and especially the street leading from the castle to Holyrood Palace. These extremities are most intimately connected with the life of Mary, Queen of Scots: in the latter she was unfortunately married to Darnley, and in the former she gave birth to James VI. of Scotland. Looking at the castle, it appears as though chiefs and warriors within its walls, with drawbridge up and portcullis down, might frown upon the mightiest external foes with insolence and perfect composure. If David I. did build Holyrood Palace, that it might be a royal place, it nevertheless has been a bloody one. Surely the crowns of kings and the palms of warriors have been thickly set

with thorns. Two centuries ago on this street
dwelt dukes, scholars, and aristocrats. The
buildings remain very much as they were, but
how changed the population! As wealth and
refinement went out, wretchedness and poverty
came in; so that, from the windows thickly
sown all up and down the sides of the buildings,
where beauty and prosperity were almost constantly gazing into this narrow street thronged
with moving crowds, squalidness and adversity
now kill time by viewing all through the day
and far into the night swarms of ragged children, barefooted women, and beer-faced men.
Over the doorways, in the wynds, and on pro-
jections, are to be seen armorials and signs of
olden times and better days. On the upper
part of this street are the Parliament buildings,
full of rich memories and remarkable transactions; at present they are used for the Court of
Sessions and the Supreme Court of the kingdom. In them Argyle and hundreds of other
brave covenanters were consigned to death without any form of trial. Walking through the
halls, many notables of the shadowy past look
out from the marbles, or down from the canvas.
Partly in front of these stands St. Giles'
Church, in which, long ago, John Knox
preached so powerfully that his hearers feared

lest his pulpit should fly in pieces. It was in this church also, not long after, that Jenny Geddes threw her stool at the priest because he was reading his prayers. From this street we can look through the window and see where John Knox sat while he was writing his "History of the Reformation." Through it, Montrose, of aspect proud, and fire flashing from his eyes towards his enemies, was led with a rope round his neck to the place of execution. Hume sought it often while he was writing his history, and Scott loitered about it, that he might secure all the facts of its fossilized history; and still the lover of antiquity can scarcely walk it now-a-days without starting up some new ghost of bygone experience. Near the lower end of this street is the Canongate burial-ground, where may be seen the tombs and graves of Dugald Stewart, Adam Smith, and Robert Ferguson, who have enriched the world with their rhetoric, philosophy, political economy, and poetry.

Under the shadow of the old castle on the south, some four or five hundred feet below, is Grassmarket, where, in the middle of the seventeenth century, a hundred brave covenanters were put to death because they could not submit to the use of a foreign ritual in their worship.

In all other regards they would bow to the rule and dictates of an alien king; but the rights of conscience they would enjoy, if they had to die for them. Still farther to the south and west is Greyfriars Church, around which history lingers with wonder and reverence. It was built in 1612, and it was here in 1663 that the first signatures to the National Covenant were appended. It is surrounded by a churchyard, in which may be seen many a tombstone telling of Scotland's distinguished dead; but the most interesting tomb is that of the martyr-covenanters who were executed in Edinburgh during the reigns of Charles II. and James II. The ivy is likely to flourish here, and pilgrims for the ages to come will visit this sacred shrine and revive the memory of the hundred heroes whose ashes to-day are sacredly guarded.

Not far from Greyfriars is Heriot Hospital which is a great blessing to the city. It is named after George Heriot who was goldsmith to Queen Anne and James VI. When he died he left a large fortune to the city of Edinburgh for the purpose of establishing a school within its limits for educating orphan boys free of expense. The present substantial building was completed in 1659, and a school was opened to receive boys from the ages of seven to ten, that they might enjoy the best educational, social, and religious advantages, till they should become fourteen years of age, when they would be put to some trade, and still the institution would continue to assist them to an apprentice fee of fifty dollars annually for the term of five years. It now supports some four hundred students, and has sent out large numbers in the past well fitted for a successful life-work. The bequest was so invested, as to increase rapidly the yearly revenue, and in 1837 the income was sufficient to support other schools, and several were established in different parts of the city for schooling indigent boys and girls free of tuition; so that now more than four thousand children are being richly blessed by the munificence of George Heriot.

Beyond the confines of the old town to the west, the city is rapidly increasing. In fact, some of the most desirable residences are here to be found. It is delightful about the Meadows. No doubt, the present population have not a little of the old Gothic, Saxon, Norman, and Celtic blood coursing their veins, still they are proud to be known now as Scotchmen. If they are not equal to England numerically, they desire Scotland to be regarded, at least, half of Great Britain, and Edinburgh the light of Scotia and the most attractive city of the world. "They would have it a Weimar without a Goethe, and a Florence without the sunshine of Italy." They are not given to sham, and so they are striving to have a city worthy of lasting fame in the way of classic taste and romantic beauty. As you observe the people on the thoroughfares, you see no rushing and driving, as in New York, but a meditative movement, as though they had just been reading the *Scotsman* and were not altogether absorbed in business. Their men and women, it would seem, intend to spend more or less time each day in the open air. As nature and art have been munificent in scattering gardens, squares, parks, and meadows through the city, they enjoy wonderful advantages of the rural and civic combined. This fact has had much to do, no doubt, in moulding their characters, making them desirous to have a town strong and, at the same time, unique and beautiful. But this must not imply that the Scotch are stylish in their attire, or express special taste in the cut of the coat, or the color of the dress; as a rule, it is quite the contrary. Perhaps they imagine cultivated minds and tastefully adorned physiques are not compatible. In their movements they are far from being awkward; their step is firm, and the swing of the arm direct. In their address they are frank and positive, yet particularly obliging in their intercourse. They have modelled their church-edifices and school buildings after the best Grecian and Gothic patterns externally, but within they have evidently constructed according to their own notions, guarding against comfortable sittings, possibly believing in, and, therefore, wishing to enforce the idea that the way to religion and knowledge is verily hard. Church-going people and students in America would regard it severe treatment to sit on flat, bare boards, as they do here; nevertheless, they do not complain or express a wish to have it otherwise. Those brought up on the Scotch catechism and oatmeal porridge are fitted, perchance, for almost any hardship.

Edinburgh is truly a city of schools. Her citizens regard their University as scarcely second to any other. Its buildings are in the old town and wear a venerable appearance. This institution has made a good record, and is endeavoring to keep pace with the progess of the age. In the departments of theology, art, medicine, and law, it numbers at present more than two thousand students. It is well supplied with museums, libraries, and facilities for illustrating the sciences of chemistry, physics, astronomy, botany, zoölogy, and geology. The present faculty is regarded strong and efficient, still no one professor is singled out as remarkably clever. Its friends glory in its past, and delight in repeating on stone and canvas the illustrious names of those professors who were brilliant lights while living, and, now that they are translated, reflect the radiance of heaven. They seem always pleased to speak the names of Munro, Ferguson, Stewart, Blair, Wilson, Lee, and Sir William Hamilton.

Edinburgh High School has a fame as broad as that of Rugby or Eaton. Academies for both sexes, and public schools of all grades, from the ragged to the high school, are numerous, so that all the children from six to fourteen years old can be accommodated, having room besides for a large number of youths coming from other parts of Scotland, and even from foreign lands, to be educated in this classic city. In the fall and winter, Edinburgh may be called with propriety the city of students. It is a pleasure to see the young men and women, lads and lasses, as they daily crowd the streets on the way to and from their recitations. Their step is quick and elastic, and their faces are blooming with health. Though so full of fresh life and joy, yet they conduct themselves with the utmost propriety.

Probably no other city in the world, according to its population, has so many libraries and books as Edinburgh. The people here are generally given to reading, and in the winter they largely attend lectures, scientific and literary, given before different institutions.

Because of the opportunities for education, this city is much sought after by those desirous of improvement; for this reason many scholars and professional men who can afford it, come here and settle for life. Here they can enjoy the present and the past, the country and the town, as possibly nowhere else. If one is at leisure in this city, he may feel he is gaining information all the while, for the castle is constantly looking down through its gray old history, and Holyrood is always sending up its enchanting messages from long departed kings and queens; the lights and shades of fable are ever floating around Arthur's Seat, and fruitful memories incessantly brood over Calton Hill. If one would have a change, let him ride out a few miles, and he can view the exquisitely beautiful Roslyn Chapel, or the grim, crumbling castle close by; or, let him walk through the labyrinthian paths to Hawthornden, and see where Robert Bruce was secreted, and Drummond courted his muse. Let him sail down the harbor a few miles and he can catch the echoes of the groans of those unfortunate prisoners who were unjustly shut up in the huge Bass Rock; or let him cross to Fife, and he will be able to discover many interesting relics of the Jameses. Let him go to Merchiston and he can learn of Napier while he was inventing his logarithms. Let him take the morning train and ride thirty-eight miles through a most interesting country and stop at Melrose, and he can visit the quaint mouldering abbey there; then riding three miles to Abbotsford, he can look upon the curiously constructed and capacious residence of Sir Walter Scott, shaded by a forest and facing the Tweed. Within he can witness the choice library of the poet and scholar, the table on which the Waverleys were written, the rooms where the great man lived and died, the museum and armory, where are gathered up so many treasures speaking of the good man's life. Then he can roam through the fields, the woods, and along the banks of the Tweed where Sir Walter was wont to tread, thinking, admiring, and enjoying so much the works of nature, and communion with the Maker of them all. After this he can ride four or five miles to Dryburgh Abbey, and examine those ivied ruins in which sleep the ashes of Edinburgh's most honored and beloved son. From this sacred tomb he can return to the station and to the city the same day. So let one turn in whatsoever way he will in this town, matters of interest are sure to come up. If he should prefer to remain indoors, and he is in a mood for solid reading, the *North British Review*, *Blackwood's Magazine* and Chambers's Works, may be dropped at his door, fresh from the Edinburgh press. Edinburgh is the Athens of modern Europe.

II.

LONDON.

AT the time Athens was in a decline, Jerusalem apparently strong, Alexandria flourishing, and Rome mighty, a rude and inferior city was standing on the river Thames, about sixty miles from the sea. It was inhabited by Britons; whence this rude people came, it can only be conjectured. However, the prevailing opinion is that they early emigrated from the land of the Norsemen. Whatever may have been their origin, they were a brave and vigorous race.

Half a century before the Christian era, as Rome was fast becoming "mistress of the world," Julius Cæsar with eight thousand soldiers landed on British soil. The great general was not a welcome visitor to this land; and, on account of severe hostilities, he soon withdrew from it. But a year afterwards, with greatly increased forces, he entered it, expecting to find "rivers of pearls" and richest treasures;

still, in all this he was sadly disappointed, and soon left the country in troubled disgust.

During this time the Roman power was waxing strong and still more ambitious. So, some five decades after the stars had shone strangely bright upon the Judæan hills, and prophecy had been fulfilled, once more the Romans entered this land and subdued the hardy Britons, capturing their Lon-Lyn, signifying City of Ships.

Only in imagination can we picture that ancient town, made up of wooden huts and mud hovels, without any walls, bank, court-house, church, or school-edifice. The people were clad in skins and the crudest materials, living upon the wild productions of the country. Their ships were no more than rafts and log canoes. Such was London when the Romans captured it.

The old, how unlike the new! The London of to-day, who can fathom it, or describe it? One might as consistently undertake to exhibit the Atlantic Ocean from top to bottom. It is the largest city the world has ever seen, already swarming with nearly four millions of human souls, and constantly increasing in population. It occupies an area of a hundred and fifty square miles, having a circumference of more than forty miles. It numbers some four hundred thousand houses; it has nine thousand streets and lanes, about twelve thousand policemen, some eight thousand surgeons and physicians, nine hundred preachers, seven thousand barristers and attorneys, more than a hundred and twenty thousand shopkeepers who carry on more than two thousand different kinds of business. It is estimated that a hundred thousand people enter the city every morning and leave it every night. It seems almost a mystery how such a city should have sprung up on an island situated so far north, with a soil and climate uninviting. Still, on examination it becomes evident, London enjoys not a few natural advantages Its temperature does not vary to extreme heat or cold. It stands upon a site slightly diversified as to surface, gradually inclining to the Thames, having a loose soil, so that it is readily drained. The Thames with the flow and ebb of the tide affords good opportunities for commerce. Comparing its mortality with that of other large cities, it ranks as one of the most healthy. It is true, it has suffered at several different periods from destructive plagues; the same is true of Rome, Paris, and New York. It is said, there is a tonic in the atmosphere of England the year round. No doubt the robustness and activity of the people are due in no small degree to this fact. Certainly something has stimulated them in body and mind, so that they have been able to do more for modern civilization than any other nation. For the past two centuries all must admit that they have taken the lead in literature, science, and mechanical invention; and in saying this, I do not feel, I am speaking disparagingly of any other country. We Americans are their descendants, and it is expected the children will surpass their parents when they shall have fully reached their maturity. The English are beginning to feel and admit this time has already come to us. The old folks usually at first find it pretty hard to give up to their children, and, no doubt, ours across the Atlantic are having such an experience. Rome delighted to be the "mistress of the world," and it would not be at all strange, if England should be as much pleased to be the "queen" of the world. If we are slow to allow she is that now in arms, I think we must grant she is swaying the mightiest intellectual sceptre at the present time. A nation that has produced Shakespeare, Milton, and Bacon, has the right to mental supremacy, till some other shall have produced greater intellectual heroes. Now it is a fact that almost every English name of any note has had more or less to do with its metropolis. So London's chief attractions do not come so much from elegant buildings and beautiful works of art, as from the haunts and corners where poets, divines, philosophers, and scholars, have lived and wrought out thoughts which are quickening minds everywhere. Londoners have long believed in free trade in its widest sense. They have been anxious to send out cotton and woollen goods of their own make, and have been still more desirous that the works of their best authors should reach the remotest dwellers beyond the seas. Their intellectual productions have been sown broadcast, so that to-day who is there that does not know something of London and the noted men who have lived there? Nearly every foreigner visiting the city for the first time, has some spots specially marked. Some things are sure to have prominence and deep historical significance. The stranger is certain to give precedence to such matters. So, on entering the city, he naturally turns his steps as soon as convenient to London Tower. This is to be expected, especially, if he is interested in military exploits, or tragic acts. Probably no other memorial of the city reaches so far into the past. There are hints that Vespasian of Roman rule had a fortification here. It is known for certainty that William the Conqueror built a portion of the visible structure. The present buildings cover over several acres, encircled by a moat. As we pass over its drawbridge and under its portcullis, the most daring and cruel scenes of English history rise before us. Its very stones breathe of blood and saddest story. Here brave Wallace pined for his beloved Scotland; here Catherine Howard, Sir Thomas More, Cranmer, Lady Jane Grey, and the Earl of Essex, perished; here Anne Boleyn placed her white hands round her delicate neck, as she stooped over the block, saying, "The headsman would have little trouble"; here many subjects of kings and kingly subjects have been tortured to death. Here Walter Raleigh was unjustly confined for long years, during which time he wrote his "History of the World"; here many Puritans, Cavaliers, and Jacobites, have sighed and died for liberty.

Leaving the crimsoned prison and hideous implements of torture, as the guide leads the way, we catch a sparkle and a brilliant glimmer of the royal jewels. The crown, sceptres, and swords, quite blind the eyes to behold them.

Passing to the Equestrian Armory, we can see numerous suits of mail worn by kings and knights in the days when they fought with blade and lance. We can scarcely conceive how the warriors endured these bands, chains, and mail, of steel and bronze. In another apartment we witness the Oriental weapons and arms captured during the English campaigns in Asia. But time forbids our tarrying long at the Tower. In our modern civilization, it does not command the attention it did, when the greatest glory was to be found on the battle-field.

The next object in order of antiquity, and of the greatest interest, is Westminster Abbey. Tradition says, from the night St. Peter came over from Lambeth in a fisherman's boat, and chose a site for the abbey, it has been a sacred spot where the pilgrim has delighted to linger. It was built by Edward the Confessor, and in it William the Conqueror was crowned. It is burdened with deeds of royal splendor, and works of darkest shade. But we cannot stop to trace out its full history, or learn all the particulars, while it was under Catholic sway; or why the Jews were nearly beaten to death for attending the coronation of Richard I.; or why Edward I. was so attentively watching the Stone of Scone which had been placed under his chair; or how Henry VI. came to select here a place for his interment; or how Henry VIII. was the last

English king crowned by popish hands; or in what manner Charles I. was buried out of sight and Cromwell was throned a king. It seems fitting that all the kings and queens of England should have been crowned here. No Norman ruler has a final resting-place in Westminster Abbey, and hereafter no more monarchs are to be buried in its cloisters. On approaching the abbey, if the sunshine is dimly struggling through the commonly murky atmosphere, we can scarcely refrain from experiencing a silent charm stealing through our very being, not because of light, joyous spires and airy traceries, towering aloft, like those on the cathedral of Milan. From its architecture nothing is seen to remind one of branching forests or fir-tree cones; nevertheless, its snow-shaped roof and stony battlements speak of broad crags and ledgy crests that have fought the ages and so far won the victory.

Now entering under the low stooping arch of the north door, and being fairly within this mausoleum, we are first struck with the light reflected from the windows in the distance high above us. They cast upon us the glow of the morning, the noon, and the evening; the purple of the heather, the gold of the broom, the azure of the bluebell, the crimson and scarlet of rose and dahlia. Now, as we walk from cloister to chapel, noting the tombs of kings and queens, the erect statue of Chatham by the northern entrance, the almost speaking image of Pitt guarding the western door, the graceful Shakespeare, the acknowledged sovereign in the Poets' Corner, and the commanding Wolfe in the chapel of St. John, all seem to say this place is sacred, not so much because monarchs have been crowned and buried here, not so much because of its school, its monastery, and religious services, as for this reason, it is the resting-place of the noble dead of every rank and genius. It is more than the Pantheon of France, or the Valhalla of Germany, or the Santa Croce of Italy. Its very atmosphere seems solemnly peaceful. Parties who were at fearful variance while living, here rest in apparent concord. Even bloody Mary and turbulent Queen Elizabeth sleep in the same vault, and across the aisle repose the ashes of poor Mary, Queen of Scots. Our own Motley is buried here, who has built for himself the most enduring monument through his classic histories. As we stand by the tombs of Newton, Burke, Peel, Cobden, Thackeray, Macaulay, Dickens, Maurice, and Kingsley, we are reminded of those who lived to honor and ennoble the race. Their mantle has fallen, not upon one, but all the nations, not for tyranny, but for freedom. Americans can but be happily and gratefully impressed in Westminster Abbey as they recall how Lord Chatham, Fox, and others spoke bold and encouraging words to our people when liberty was threatened and likely to be crushed, bidding them march on in the van of human rights, led by Washington, Franklin, Jefferson, and Adams, our peerless and sainted heroes. We find some monuments here of departed worthies, whose mortality sleeps far away. Well it is thus; for they belonged not to London, or England, but to the world. So Pope chose to be interred in the parish church of Twickenham; Gray, in the cemetery of Stoke Pogis; Burns, at Dumfries; Scott, in Dryburgh Abbey; and Shakespeare, in the humble church of Stratford-on-Avon. This abbey, what a legacy to London and the world, with its memories of eight centuries, quickening every phase of the past, making us feel the whole human family is one brotherhood, and that, if the body dies, genius, love, and true nobility, live forever!

Of the modern works the most prominent and distinguished object is St. Paul's. It is not yet two centuries since it was completed. On its foundation it is in the form of a Roman cross, five hundred feet long and three hundred and seventy feet high, built of stone, mostly marble. By far it is the grandest cathedral in Great Britain, yet it might be placed inside of St. Peter's at Rome. Approaching it from whatever direction possible, it presents an imposing appearance. It is a spot around which Londoners appear bound to huddle and crowd; so merchants and business men have kept pushing up their stores and shops towards it, until it is closely cramped and shut in, and yet there are those who would like to get up still nearer, and would pay for the land at the rate of five millions of dollars an acre.

Its style of architecture is English and Roman, being the embodied thought of Christopher Wren. Entering it we are struck with a sense of vastness; especially is this the case standing under the dome. Walking about it, we have the feeling, it is not sufficiently occupied, presenting too much open space, though it contains already many tablets and monuments of England's heroes and celebrities. Some of the works of art are extremely fine. We can but admire the statue of John Howard; it does honor to the celebrated philanthropist; that of Dr. Johnson will bear careful inspection; and that of Joshua Reynolds is regarded by the English a masterpiece of its kind. Here are elaborate memorials over the ashes of Lord Nelson and the Duke of Wellington, England's greatest military heroes, the one upon the sea, and the other upon the land. Here, too, Wren rests from his labors, with the inscription over the choir to his memory, "*si monumentum quaeris circumspice.*" Yes, this cathedral, the outcome of thirty-five years and more of earnest thinking and toiling, is his monument. Thus it is, one's life-work, whatever it may be, is really his monument; if this is of harmonious proportions and expressive of goodness, it is enough: men and angels will delight to behold it.

For the antiquarian and historian the place of greatest attraction in London is the British Museum. The external appearance does not indicate its vastness and valuable possessions, which surpass those of any other institution of the kind in the world. On entering it, we are first introduced to large tombs, huge winged lions, gigantic man-headed bulls, massive sphinxes brought from Abyssinia, Egypt, and other Eastern lands, having been cut out of sienite and the very hardest stone, eight or nine centuries before the Christian era. But we leave these monsters to view the Elgin Marbles from old Athens. These were taken from the ruins of the Acropolis, and many of them are the actual sculptures from the Parthenon and other temples which adorned that height. Through these works we can form an acquaintance with Phidias, whose chisel must have been guided by zeal, genius, and refined skill. Surely beauty must have been the highest ideal of the Greek mind. In connection with these are sculptures from the temple of Diana, which was so magnificent at the time St. Paul looked upon it. Passing on, we actually walk among the ruins of Thebes, Karnack, and Memphis. Here the antiquarian can find hieroglyphics and inscriptions, which would fill volumes, should they be deciphered and written out.

On the flooring above, it would seem, we can walk for miles through corridor after corridor containing mounted quadrupeds, mummies, Indian relics, minerals, and botanic specimens. But the most striking feature of the museum is the library, placed under its lofty dome a hundred and forty-five feet in diameter, containing about a million of books. From its centre under the glass dome radiate tables and seats sufficient to accommodate at the same time five hundred readers. Any one being properly recommended can occupy a seat and order what books he may wish, and they will soon be laid upon the table before him. It is open every day of the week, except

Sundays and holidays, from six to eight hours. Around the room on shelves are forty thousand reference books, which the readers can consult at their pleasure. It is stated, there are more American books in this library than are to be found in any one library in our own country. It contains sixteen hundred different copies of the Bible. All communications are carried on in it so as not to disturb the quiet of the place. This is, verily, a great mental workshop. Ministers, lawyers, doctors, artists, and searchers after knowledge, are here every day it is open. The amount of good this library is doing cannot be estimated. It is the great central library of the world, from which are constantly flowing currents of thought and information to replenish periodicals, newspapers, and supply matter for new books. When the great libraries of Cordova and Alexandria were destroyed, the world met with an irreparable loss; but it would be a far greater one, if the library of the London Museum should be consigned to the flames. Its friends look upon it as sacred, and guard it with the utmost precaution.

A supplement to this institution is the Kensington Museum, which seems intended more especially to meet the wants of students in art and science. This already occupies some twelve

acres of ground, much more than the British
Museum, and is about to be greatly enlarged.
On entering the main building, the architectural
room gives us the first welcome. As we look
round we realize, if the old Jew expressed in
his work only one idea, which was theocracy,
the ancient Greek but one, which was beauty,
and the pagan Roman simply one, which was
Rome, we find great diversity here. The Trajan Column, the Apprentice Pillar, the arches,
friezes, and portals, are expressive of varied
taste and beauty. In the Oriental court, as we
examine the ancient wares, so nicely shaped and
exquisitely colored, we are ready to admit,
" some arts have been lost." But the collection
of special interest here is that of Dr. Schliemann from the ruins of old Troy. This consists of numerous vases, pitchers, jars, stone
implements, vessels of copper and silver, gold
rings, bracelets and frontlets for the head, and
a tablet inscribed with Greek characters, revealing the fact that it stood near the Scæan gate
of ancient Troy, thereby making the old city,
concerning which Homer so thrillingly sung, a
reality. Now Agamemnon, Hector, and Achilles, are veritable characters. We can now almost see those old Greeks and Trojans fighting
on the plains, and around the walls of Troy,

and, finally getting into the city by stealth, wreaking vengeance on the parties that had stolen away Menelaus' fair and betrothed Helen. All honor is due Dr. Schliemann for his untiring labors in making these great discoveries which must tend to increase faith in the gifted bard, causing more poets to court his muse and rhetoricians to study his style.

On the walls of this court are a score and a half of alcoves containing full-sized mosaic portraits of eminent artists of all ages. Accordingly, Phidias, Apelles, Raphael, and Angelo, are there. In the Italian court the statues of Moses and David are colossal. In the picture gallery we become interested at once in the cartoons of Raphael, and a copy of his Transfiguration Scene which was his last work, and which was borne in the procession at his funeral. Here we also find many paintings of Landseer and Turner. We are soon captivated by those of Landseer, for they seem to express living characters; as we look at them, the animals appear to move; the "old dog" is so sad over the remains of his dead master, and the "twa dogs" are so funny, we are ready very soon to award the palm to Landseer, as the chief among artists in painting animals. In an adjoining building are the patents and models of the most remarkable machinery of the country; and these are so adjusted that they can be carefully examined. But the oldest things here are the newest. The original spinning and carding machine of Arkwright is a curiosity, and the first locomotive, "Travitick's," is a marvel. After looking over the curiosities the most conservative must admit the world does move.

In another apartment we can witness the chemical analysis of many vegetables and organized bodies. The forty elements which enter into the composition of the human system, are all parcelled out in exact proportions. Of course the power which put these things together so as to form a man, is not exhibited. Evolution, or chemistry, has not as yet discovered vital forces. If theories alone were sufficient, these would have been portrayed and made perfectly plain long ago.

But the most interesting feature of this institution, is the fact of its instruction which is given in art and science at so small expense that it is within the reach of the humblest. So large numbers of both sexes are being led forward in these departments of learning by able and experienced professors; and, furthermore, they have free access to a large library containing all the different works published, treating of art and science. Add to the London and Kensington Museums the Kew Gardens which are doing so much for the science of botany, and "such a trio" is formed for enlightening and spreading knowledge broadcast as nowhere else can be found. Thus they become stronger bulwarks to Great Britain than her strongest military fortifications. Their elevating power is extending to the remotest corners of the earth, teaching men how to think and do. What greater charity, or good, is possible to human souls?

In an immense city like London, the questions force themselves upon us, "Whence comes the money to carry on this endless traffic? How are these multitudes fed and clothed?" Well, as we go to the Bank of England, the largest monetary establishment in the world, covering over eight acres of ground and employing a thousand clerks, we readily begin to understand whence, at least, a portion of the money comes which propels this ponderous machinery of trade. The bank has a capital of more than seventy millions of dollars, and notes in circulation exceeding ninety millions of our currency. All the printing of the bank is done within its own limits. Its notes are never reissued, and those returned are registered, filed, cancelled, and preserved for seven years, that the bank may guard against all possible mistakes, and be prepared to meet any fraud that may chance to arise. Obtaining an order from the manager of the bank, we are permitted to go through its different departments. In the bullion office we observe an ingenious apparatus for weighing gold, and capable of testing thirty-five thousand coins a day. As the pieces are running through it, if one varies in the least from the standard, it is spitefully snapped out, as having no right there, until it shall have been recast. The steam machine, for printing the notes and marking them with microscopic writing, seems almost to surpass intelligence itself, as it does its work.

Just across the street on Cornhill is the Royal Exchange, a massive and substantial structure, with lofty Corinthian columns in front. From ten to three o'clock, six days of the week, this is a busy place. Bankers and merchants rush in and out, as though life was at stake. As we watch the business we are impressed with the feeling that important transactions are going on, and large sums of money are continually changing hands. After this observation we can but have some definite conception, as to the source of the money which is constantly circulating through the numberless financial channels of this vast metropolis.

Facing these two buildings across Cheapside is the Mansion House, the official residence of the Lord Mayor. This is another stanch edifice. Looking upon these three buildings and others near them, it would seem as though they must stand while the earth lasts.

If the House of Parliament is, like Westminster Abbey, in a sunken part of the city, still it is made prominent by its magnificence and purely Gothic style of architecture. It covers over some eight acres of ground. It has eleven hundred apartments, one hundred staircases, two miles of corridors, is warmed by sixteen miles of steam pipes, and the gas to light it costs eighteen thousand dollars per year. It is made out of limestone, and the expense of building it, exceeded two millions sterling. Chief among the many objects of interest in this stupendous building are the Chambers and Houses of Peers and Commons. But to see them when most inviting, we should visit them while Parliament is in session; and should we be so fortunate as to be there when Hon. Stafford H. Northcote and Prime Minister Gladstone are to make speeches on important national questions, it will be all the more exciting. Mr. Northcote will be pert, sharp, and somewhat verbose, and sure, before he closes, to glorify John Bull; but Mr. Gladstone will foretoken the true orator in rising from his seat, and, as he utters his first sentence, he looks manly, his language is classic, and his manner natural. What he says and what he does show that he is familiar with the highest culture of the ages. He makes a daily study of Homer and other old authors. He believes in progress and Divine justice. It is worth more to an American to hear one speech from Mr. Gladstone than to visit a hundred Parliament Houses, though they be adorned by a Victoria Tower, five hundred and fifty stone statues, and many superior paintings.

Lovers of art are not likely to remain long in London before visiting the National Gallery. This has one of the finest situations in the city, occupying the highest part of Trafalgar Square, which consists of a large open space decorated with a lofty column guarded by four monstrous stone lions, and surrounded by fountains constantly jetting forth water. These works are a testimony to Lord Nelson. The front of the gallery does not present a harmonious and pleasant appearance; it is too much broken up. Within, however, are to be seen most choice paintings, still by no means so many as are to be found in several galleries on the Continent; but most of the different painters of the different schools and ages are represented here. Turner's collection was a valuable gift, and is a precious treasure to the English nation. Some of Landseer's best works are in this gallery. Turner excels in depicting landscapes; and Landseer, animals. Ward's and Cooper's paintings are of a high order, and Reynolds's portraits are true to life. None should fail to notice particularly Murillo's "Holy Family," Rubens' "Judgment of Paris," Raphael's "St. Catherine," Perugino's "Virgin and Child," Rembrandt's "Woman taken in Adultery," and Correggio's "Ecce Homo." Three days of the week this gallery is free to the public.

The parks of London form one of its most striking characteristics. There are half a dozen of these right in the heart of the city, each embracing from ninety to four hundred and seventy acres. These have been justly called the lungs of London. St. James's is particularly noted for its palaces and daily military displays. This was a favorite resort for Charles II.; he enjoyed hunting after his ducks in the reservoir, or playing pall-mall in the open ground. Regent is the largest, and so laid out as to combine garden, lake, meadow, and woodland.

In connection with this is the London Zoölogical Garden, which is, no doubt, the finest of the kind in the world. Here one can see the elephant, and ride upon his back, if he may wish. If present at the appointed time, he can witness the feeding of the ferocious creatures, and hear the roar of the lion and the frightful shrieks of the tigers and cats, or enjoy the wonderful feats of the sea-lions, as they leap out of the water to catch their food, as it is hurled at them; or he can watch the beavers, as long as he will, while they are so busily engaged in cutting up logs and dragging them away for the purpose of building dams.

Hyde Park is the place of special resort for the *elite* and nobility of the city. On almost any pleasant afternoon may be seen a rich display of the extravagances and follies of many generations. Should we judge from the thousands of richly attired gentlemen and ladies walking or riding here, we would draw the conclusion, there can be little poverty in London. Rotten Row, which is the southern part of this park, is devoted to horseback riding, and is made a lively place by those who are fond of equestrian sports and exercise. Kensington Gardens, so famous for their history, as well as for their beauty and elegance, join this on the west. The walks, flowers, shrubbery, and grand old oaks, elms, and sycamores, are truly inviting, and render the gardens almost enchanted grounds. Close by we see the palace in which once dwelt William of Orange and his fair queen. In this mansion Prince George of Denmark and George II. breathed their last. On the borders of this garden stands also the house in which the wise Newton lived. Here, too, is the Holland house, in which Tom More so much enjoyed his Whig coteries. Near by, also, Addison dwelt to regret his marriage to a lady of rank and extreme fashion.

In addition to these parks, as we wander through the city, we find numerous squares and circles of various dimensions from one to five acres, laid out with taste and in many different styles. These open and beautiful places must serve to improve the æsthetic natures of all coming in contact with them, as well as have a decided sanitary influence.

Of the many public monuments scattered through the city, the latest erected is the oldest, Cleopatra's Needle, which has been brought but recently from Egypt. This takes us far back to the splendid city of Heliopolis where it was first set up, and then to Alexandria where it assisted in adorning a magnificent city, and now it serves to grace the largest city ever known. It certainly is a significant memorial, uniting the past to the present. But the monument which signifies the most to the English people is that of Prince Albert. This consists of a colossal statue of the Prince seated beneath a beautiful shrine and surrounded by sculptures illustrating those arts and sciences which he fostered, and the many improvements which he originated. About it are elaborate groups of statuary, representing astronomy, chemistry, geology, and geometry; rhetoric, medicine, philosophy, and physiology; faith, hope, and charity; fortitude, prudence, justice, and temperance; painting, sculpture, architecture, poetry, and music; Europe, Asia, Africa, and America. It is worthy the distinguished dead it commemorates and the city it adorns.

Walking the principal streets of London, we are impressed by the thronging multitudes with a sense of its vastness, opulence, and intense activity. Standing on the London Bridge, for instance, at mid-day, we should find it difficult to count the numbers hurrying to and fro. It is estimated that a hundred thousand people pass over it daily. Sailing up or down from this bridge, we have the like impression of great wealth and multitudes of moving beings.

As we witness the forests of masts, the Thames does not appear to be an insignificant river, as it is sometimes represented. Here are steamers constantly coming in and going out to different parts of the world. The tunnel under the Thames, of which we heard so much some years ago, has proved a decided failure; but the underground railroads which coil around beneath nearly all sections of the city, are a success and a great convenience.

The streets and houses of London are encrusted as thick with marvellous feats, anecdotes, legends, and traditions, as are the hulls of old ships with barnacles. These sights have a kind of charm to the foreigner, familiar with history, for he has read and dreamed of them, and longed to look upon the places whence have come mental forces that have stirred the world.

By the central milestone on Cannon Street, brave Romans were wont to meet and talk of Cæsar and his legions. Their roads are now buried ten or fifteen feet beneath the foundations of the city. From the deep excavations made every year, many relics are being discovered. A piece of Temple Bar which is the only remnant left of the ancient walls is now the centre of historical London. In Charles II.'s time this bar was completely bestudded with the heads of the Rye conspirators; and still later it was thickly set with the heads of Jacobites. To the Temple hard by, long ago warlike templars were wont to come in their white cloaks and red crosses from the fields of strife, to do service in the name of the Most High. Afterwards, the Knights of St. John frequented it, to show reverence to their Supreme Worshipful Master. Still later, the lawyers came hither to find a sacred shrine. The Temple is still standing, and lawyers still control it and worship in it on the Sabbath. The best music of the city may be heard in this quaint old house of praise. We are disposed somehow to linger about this place. There is a uniqueness in the Temple itself; then, too, Dr. Johnson, Goldsmith, Lamb, Jeffries, Cooper, Butler, Sheridan, and Tom More, used to drink ofttimes at the pretty fountain, and celebrate in the sacred courts praise to their Maker.

Fleet Street, which passes the Bar, is full of memorials. Richard II. rode along here to St. Paul's with his party-colored robes jingling with golden bells. Elizabeth, beruffled and gorgeously decked, passed over this street in her cumbrous-plumed coach to thank God for the scattering of the Armada. Here Cromwell, a king in all but a name, and more than a king by nature, returned the keys of the city, as he went on his way to Guildhall to preside at the banquet of the obsequious mayor. William of Orange and Queen Anne were borne over these pavements to return thanks for victories over the French. The old printers strode this street who first published the plays of Shakespeare and the epics of Milton. Over it also passed the early bankers who laid the foundation of permanent wealth.

If Fleet Street is so full of interest, we shall find the closes and alleys leading from it equally so. The scholars, poets, and literati of every description chose to be removed from the din and whirl of business. So in Shire Lane we come upon the Kit-Cat Club, where Addison, Steele, and Congreve, were wont to disport. Izaac Walton dwelt here, and Hazlitt resided, when he fell in love with the tailor's daughter and wrote the "New Pigmalion." In Fetter Lane, we find the house of Dryden, where the poet was often favored with the company of Otway and Baxter. In Crane Court the Royal Society held its first meeting, in which the great Newton was its central figure. As we enter Whitefriars, we recall the time when this was inhabited by actors; and as we pass into Blackfriars, we wonder that it should once have been the retreat for players and painters; here it was that Shakespeare lived while he was in London. Ludgate was a debtors' prison, which was enlarged by a widow of Stephen Foster in the reign of Henry VII. who himself, tradition says, had been a prisoner there, till a rich widow seeing his face through the grates, secured his pardon and married him, and ever after took a deep interest in that prison. At St. Dunstan, we can see where good Romaine and the pious Baxter preached; and at Murray's old shop, where Byron often loitered with his cane in hand at the shelves of many books.

The chief feature of Cheapside is Guildhall, which is just as lively now and popular as ever. Here Lady Jane Grey and her husband were tried; here the Lords and Parliament declared in favor of the Prince of Orange. On this street stands the new Bow Church, from whose tower Wren projected a balcony for the royal family to occupy on state occasions, to enjoy the most favorable view of splendid pageants as they should pass. In this tower hang the old Bow Bells which used to strike long ago the death knell of so many sentenced to die, and now they give voice to a clock that also jets from the church over the crowded thoroughfare. Bread Street leading from Cheapside enjoys the honor of having been the birthplace of Milton, and a short distance away, in St. Giles's Church, he lies buried.

Smithfield, once so renowned for its jousts and tournaments, is the place where the noble Wallace was executed like a robber, and the gentle Mortimer was led to a shameful death. But in spite of its dark side, it has some bright spots; for somewhere here Chaucer, the father of English poetry; Spenser, the author of "The Faerie Queene"; and Hogarth, the pictorial satirist, were born. As we visit King's Street, we learn how Spenser died there for the want of bread. Near Great Tower Hill, our Penn was born. In Covent Gardens, which are so attractive because of their fruits and flowers, Lady Mary Wortley Montagu had her advent into this world. On the site of the Durham House Sir Walter Raleigh lived. On Cornhill the poet Gray opened his baby eyes upon mortal things; and here Johnson and Boswell met for the first time.

The scholar visiting London will not fail to seek out Paternoster Row, the great mart for booksellers; and, if he has not been apprised beforehand of its narrowness and gloomy aspects, he will be disappointed as he enters it, and almost sure to feel, this narrow street, barely wide enough for a wagon to squeeze through, cannot be Paternoster Row. But as he reads the names on either side as he passes along, which have become so familiar to him by seeing them on the title-pages of books, he becomes satisfied this can be no other than the most bookish street in the world.

Among the elegant buildings in the city are the club-houses. Nearly all the different professions, parties, and trades, have their houses provided with spacious apartments for eating, reading, talking, and sporting. These clubs really have much to do in controlling civil and secular affairs.

To see special display of merchandise and aristocratic buyers and sellers, we must go upon Oxford and Regent Streets. The meanest shops and poorest wretches, we will find in Drury Lane and at the Seven Dials. The palace and the hut are common in London. Here we will often meet with excessive wealth and excessive poverty. The mansions are many, but the hovels are still more. The pauper rates now are exceedingly heavy, yet there are hosts crying for bread and clothing. If the city does pay some fifteen thousand dollars per day to provide for the needy, still there is indescribable suffering among the poor. Their numerous hospitals and infirmaries, though on a grand scale, are crowded to overflowing. The English people, as a whole, are very kind-hearted and generous towards the unfortunate. Frequent public appeals are made in their churches in behalf of their poor, and bountiful collections are taken up.

Among the higher and middle classes a good degree of interest is felt for the cause of education. The several denominational colleges and many private schools are well sustained. But if the law does require that every healthy child from six years of age to fourteen shall be in school some forty weeks during the year, and if in the permanent schools there are five hundred thousand scholars, yet large numbers remain untaught. The staff of instruction in these schools consists of some two thousand adult teachers and as many more pupil assistants. The schools generally in London will not bear a favorable comparison with those of Boston, Berlin, or Edinburgh.

The general quietness in this city on Sunday morning impresses the Christian stranger with the feeling, London is a religious city; and then, when the bells from the nine hundred places of worship send out their calls, and the streets become alive with men, women, and children, pressing their way to the different churches, he can but feel, it is truly a Christian city. As we listen to Spurgeon, Martineau, Canon Farrer, Parker, Baldwin Brown, and Stopford Brooke, we are ready to allow that London has its great preachers. If it is asked how its pulpit compares with that of New York City, as to eloquence and cultured thought, the answer must be given that the former falls far below the latter. The preachers lack vivacity and positive expression. Of course there are many exceptions, and particularly, among the Dissenters. The people at large are becoming satisfied a state church, in the long run, is a hindrance to real progress, and they seem bound, as soon as possible, to hasten the disestablishment of the English Church. The religious bodies manifest but little interest in the Sabbath-school work and general reform movements compared with what is expressed in most of our churches; still there is an awakening going on now; they are becoming alarmed at the present state of social life; they are realizing they must bestir themselves and stem the tide of intemperance and profligacy, or their ruin is inevitable.

But London with all its wickedness is a well-regulated city. Its policemen are most efficient and faithful. Their vigilance is felt and trusted by day and night. Perhaps there is no other place where their power is more signally expressed than in the main thoroughfares which are usually so crowded when they become blocked up with omnibuses, hacks, freight-wagons, and footmen; now these throngs are not boisterous or demonstrative, for they are aware the policemen are sure to be round, and should there be any abuse to man or beast, the violator would be certain to answer to the extent of the law for his misdemeanor; and so quietly the Gordian knot becomes unloosed and all go on their way, as though nothing had happened out of the common order of things. This shows there is a wholesome moral and restraining power in this vast metropolis, and that in spite of its rampant passions and dens of iniquity, there are good men enough in it, as yet, to save it; and so, as we traverse its streets and witness its substantial buildings, and look upon the internal working of its civil, educational, and religious institutions, we can but feel, London is still to be for the ages to come. It is worthy to live. Though it is the greatest city, may it become greater; though it has done so much for civilization, may it do still more; and as the loftiest beacon along the shores of civilization, may it rise still higher, sending benignest radiance far out upon the vasty deep, to guide countless hosts into the fairest havens!

III.

FRANCE AND PARIS.

WHEN Nineveh and Babylon had fallen, Sidon and Tyre had passed their zenith, the glory of Athens and Ephesus was fading, and Alexandria and Rome were enjoying their fullest prosperity, there was an extensive country occupying the north and western part of Europe, inhabited by people known as Gauls, or Celts. Its surface was diversified with hills and vales, plains and mountains, rivers and sea-coast. Its soil was light and naturally productive; its climate was temperate and salubrious. Along the rivers and the sea-coast, the Celts had established many settlements. They dearly loved the land, and often desperately fought in its defence. As a people, the Celts were active and brave. Their complexion was fair, their eyes light, and their hair blond. They were sprightly and fond of the beautiful. They were religious, and worshipped on the tops of the mountains under the open sky, or in grottos roofed by giant trees. It would seem they had

advanced as far as possible without foreign aid.
So when Rome had developed a high state of
civilization, having received the best blood and
life from Oriental nations that had risen, flourished, and fallen, when she had learned how to
build large towns and extended roads, being
ambitious to possess great territory, she sent
her Cæsar with a vast army over the Alps into
the lands of the Gauls, who were inhabiting
what is now Switzerland, Spain, and France.
The Romans were victorious over the Gauls.
Those known as Celts yielded to the invading
foe. It would appear they were at once interested in the general advancement and superiority of the Romans, readily accepting their
customs and adopting their manners and language. The Celts who were afterwards called
by the Romans Franks, and known to us as
French, were very receptive and much given to
æsthetic taste and expression. It was not so
with their German neighbors; these were particularly fond of red hair, and practised dyeing
it with woad to heighten their favorite color, and
when it was twisted into a war-knot upon the
top of their heads, they were satisfied, — their
beau-ideal was reached; they cared not for the
advanced civilization of the Romans, and resisted
and beat them back, as they attempted to invade

their country. So the mighty Cæsar was unable to subdue the brave people beyond the Rhine. They held themselves intact, till they went forth from their own borders in the course of time to subdue and conquer.

Accordingly, the Celtic towns soon changed, as Roman colonies settled in their country. The latter found, as they entered the land, a little city where now stands the imposing capital of the French Republic. It was confined to the small island of the Seine. It then contained no magnificent buildings as now. It was not connected by any grand bridges, as at present, with the mainland. But they were easily infused with the spirit of the Romans who believed in large towns and great roads ; and so their little city began to spread itself first on the right bank, and afterwards upon the left, and was called Lutetia Parisiosum. After Christianity was introduced into the country, this became the headquarters of the church. Early its Notre Dame was consecrated, and nearly every street had its chapel, whose altar was dedicated to some St. Geneviève of blessed memory. During the Christian centuries, with a diversified fortune of good and ill, the city has gradually advanced. Though having been subjected to the rule of more than forty different kings, emperors, and presidents, prompted more or less by false ambition and vainglory, still Paris has become the most beautiful city in the world. With its history will be associated the names of Charlemagne, Louis XII., Napoleon I. and III., Louis Philippe, and Gambetta.

Six hundred years ago Paris had its "Twelve Masters" who were held in as high esteem by its citizens, as were the Seven Wise Men of Greece by the Athenians. Its University for more than a century has done much to give it fame abroad and prosperity at home. Its free lectures upon all subjects connected with literature, science, philosophy, and art, given by the most eminent scholars of the country, have created and fostered a spirit of growing enterprise which has blossomed into noble ideals of liberty and patriotism. The teachings of Cuvier, Guizot, Thiers, Mignet, Victor Hugo, and Lamartine, have lent a potent influence to inspire the people with high aspirations to preserve and ennoble their land. Here, I feel, may be discovered the power which has preserved and revived the city and the country after having passed through fiery ordeals, and sometimes so crippled, it would seem, they could never rise again. It is marvellous how soon the scars of the Revolution of 1848 were abraded, and how the ravages of the war of 1870–1 should have nearly all disappeared at the time of their great Exposition in 1878; and at no previous period was it ever more hopeful than now. The city is possessed of wonderful vivaciousness and industry. It is a lively town; how could it well be otherwise, being filled with nearly two millions of human souls? It occupies an area of thirty square miles, and is twenty-one miles in circumference, having three thousand streets ornamented with ten thousand trees. It contains sixty-five thousand houses, eighty churches, forty theatres, two thousand schools, and the largest library in the world.

To obtain the finest and most comprehensive view of Paris, let one in midsummer, when the day is fair, ascend to the top of the Arc de l'Etoile which stands upon high ground near the western limits of the city. From this height, as he looks eastward, he will be almost sure to exclaim, "The most magnificent picture of a city I have been permitted to look upon." The city is quite circular in form, and almost entirely surrounded by a range of hills, green with grass and woodland. The distance across from hill to hill must be some eight or ten miles. So within this gently sloping valley is to be seen the greatest mass of the cleanest and handsomest buildings of the whole world, irregularly divided by the serpentine course of the Seine, spotted here and there by beautiful parks, and dotted off into sections by rows of emerald trees. From all over the city comes up the sound of busy, humming life. As the eye passes to the westward, just without the outer wall, it discovers the inviting residences of Neuilly; a little farther on, and to the south, may be seen the Bois de Boulogne, looking so cool and refreshing, and still beyond are visible the park and village of St. Cloud. This is one of the landscape pictures which will bear to be studied, and the more it is scrutinized, the more it must be admired. The Triumphal Arch itself is a work deserving to be carefully scanned. It was intended to be the grandest one ever built. It is of pleasing proportions, a hundred and fifty feet high, adorned with statues and reliefs intended to make prominent the brave deeds of Frenchmen, and, especially, the great deeds of Napoleon I. Its foundation-stone was laid to mark his birthday, which occurred on the 15th of August, 1806. It has already cost a million and a half of dollars.

From this arch extends into the city direct to Place de la Concorde, the broadest, finest, and most frequented street of Europe. On a pleasant afternoon it would be difficult to count the carriages constantly passing to and fro. The equipages for the most part are costly and elegant. The political economist, as he should behold all this display, would be forced to the conclusion that many in the by-places of the city must suffer, because of such extravagance and waste. On either side of this street the houses are lofty and airy. Bordering it are the Champs Elysées, or Elysian Fields; and truly, judging from outward appearance, the last part of the day and late into the night, it is the abode of the blest. Hosts are certain to be here, and all given to merry-making. Such gentility, such activity, such laughing, such looking, such knacking and sporting, can nowhere else be experienced. By this street stands the house of Francis I., which was built more than three centuries ago in the forests of Fontainebleau, and in this century was removed to its present site. Looking upon this thoroughfare is also the Palais de l'Elysée, which has been occupied by King Murat, Emperor of Russia, Duke of Wellington, Napoleon III., and President MacMahon. On the south side of the Champs Elysées is the Palace of Industry, which was built for the Exposition held here in 1855. It is a massive structure of stone, iron, and glass, and is now used for fairs and public exhibitions of art and agricultural works.

The gardens and groves of the Champs Elysées are just what and where they should be. It would be difficult to conceive of a more enchanting place than this among temporal things. It must serve to cultivate a love for the beautiful in nature. Leaving the happy fields we come to the Place de la Concorde which has been called the grandest and most inspiring open space in any city. Its history is freighted with the most thrilling and horrible deeds. It was first called Place Louis Quinze; then Place de la Revolution; and finally, Place de la Concorde. Here it was that twelve hundred persons lost their lives during a display of fire-works in honor of the marriage of the Dauphin, afterwards Louis XVI., with Marie Antoinette. In 1793, the guillotine was erected here for the execution of Louis XVI., and here it remained till many hundreds suffered death upon it. Here the fair and innocent Marie Antoinette ended her days, and Madame Rowland breathed her last, uttering the words, "O Liberty, what crimes are committed in thy name!" And, finally, Robespierre, with a hundred of his associates, chiefly judges, jurors, and officers, who had constituted the Tribunal and Commune of Paris, causing such an effusion of innocent gore, terminated their bloody career here. In 1814, the Prussian and Russian armies, and in 1815, the British, were encamped here; and after the Restoration, it was proposed that a fountain should be established upon the ground where the scaffold had stood, but Chateaubriand opposed the project, saying, "All the water in the world could not wash away the stains of blood shed there." Now it is marked by an obelisk, which once stood before the great temple of ancient Thebes, and afterwards adorned the city of Alexandria. To the north and south of the monolith are now two magnificent fountains, with granite basins ornamented with bronze statues representing the seas and rivers of France. The limits of the Place de la Concorde are defined by eight grand statues emblematical of the leading cities of the Republic. From the centre of these grounds we have to the west, a fine view of the Triumphal Arch; to the east, of the Tuileries; to the south, of the Legislative Palace; and to the north, of the Madeleine. These views alone are well worth the trouble and expense of journeying from foreign lands to enjoy them.

Approaching the Tuileries we are struck with

the palatial appearance of the buildings. They receive their name, it is said, from the fact, the grounds which they occupy, were once used as tile-fields. An extensive area in their front is planted out with trees and ornamented with flowers and fountains, affording favorite resorts for all classes. One portion seems to be consecrated to the welfare of little children. At times they are numberless. Happier and more charming faces are nowhere else to be seen.

The palaces were greatly damaged by the communists in their recent war; but they are being restored, and it is intended to make them more beautiful than ever. The architecture in Paris is sufficient to prove that the French people are natural artists.

Joining the Tuileries is the Louvre, consisting of a square of palaces, whose perimeter must measure more than half a mile, having an extensive court in the centre. Looking at these stately and harmonious buildings, it hardly seems possible that, where they now stand, there was once a marshy swamp infested with wolves; but such being the fact, the origin of the name Louvre is readily perceived. These palaces were built at different periods and occupied by different royal personages. But the Louvre is now devoted almost exclusively to works of art. The ground flooring is occupied with sculptures gathered from all parts of the world. In the Egyptian Hall are to be seen sphinxes, colossal statues, and sarcophagi, which were chiselled and polished two thousand years before the dawn of Christianity. In the Assyrian rooms are huge sculptures taken from the ruins of Nineveh, bass-reliefs brought from Pergamos, and some beautiful relics found at Athens. In the museum of the Middle Ages are collected treasures from all the different countries which gave any attention to art-works during the Renaissance period. In the rooms of the modern sculptures there is many a statue that breathes out an enchantment, and is sure to hold the inspector spellbound. Their conception and execution are just what they should be. They are full of poetry, history, and inspiration. Ascending to the next story, we have before us in the different halls seven miles of pictures. As we enter the collection of the old masters, and scrutinize carefully the paintings of Raphael, Correggio, Rubens, Leonardo da Vinci, and Murillo, we are not disposed to wonder that this should be called the "Unrivalled Art Gallery." Weeks are required to see them all; and then, after one has discovered his favorites, he requires weeks more to study these in order to catch the inspiration that burned in the hearts of those who were called to blend colors, so as to give real expression to the soul of saint and sinner. Then, too, it is interesting to observe the artists who are at work in these rooms, copying the pictures which they most admire. Here are the young, the middle aged, and the old, apparently all absorbed in using the pencil and brush. For centuries the French artists followed altogether in the footsteps of others, creating no school of their own, being no more than apprentices to the Italian and Spanish masters. It is true, they early distinguished themselves in architecture, leading the nations in some regards in this department of art. To a large extent they invented and developed the Gothic style. By nature they are inclined to be artists, but not, till within the past century have they become eminent as painters, establishing a school of their own. But now, as we study the works of Claude Lorraine, Horace Vernet, Poussin, and Desportes, we cannot doubt that they are producing some of the best art-works, and give promise of excelling all other schools on the Continent. The French people take a deep interest in these galleries, making them free to all a portion of each day; so the poor can enjoy them as well as the rich.

It is a fact that most of their leading artists at the present time have sprung from the common, or lower classes. Besides the Louvre, Paris has several other public as well as many private galleries. At the Luxemburg Palace are a few of the finest art-treasures in the city. The sculptures and paintings are mostly modern and of the French school. The palace itself with its gardens is a marvellous work of art.

Not only do the fine arts occupy a conspicuous place in this city, but arts of all kinds. At the Conservatory of measures are collected numerous models of mechanical and school apparatus. Here the farmer has the opportunity of examining the most improved plough or pump; the mechanic, the best water-wheels and steam-engines; the miner, the most approved drills and lifters for quarrying coal; the potter and glass-maker, fine illustrations of the beginning and progress of their works in France; and the educator, the latest styles of furniture and apparatus for the school-room.

In the Hotel de Cluny the antiquarian and the lover of the ancient can find many things to gratify their taste. The building itself is one of the oldest in the city. Parts of it were built by the Romans as far back as the third century, while the remainder was erected in the early reign of the Goths. It is a quaint and curious old structure. Within are treasured odd and grotesque works in wood, ivory, cloth, iron, precious stones, and metals, many thousands in all. The Roman altar, with an inscription to Augustus Cæsar, is the oldest Parisian monument in existence. Here it was Julian, was proclaimed emperor by his soldiers in the three hundred and sixteenth year of the Christian era; and here the first Frankish monarchs resided, till they changed their seat of government to the island of the Seine. In the Cluny the oldest things are the newest at the present day.

At the Hotel des Invalides the soldier, and those fond of military arts, can be gratified and instructed, for in its museum are to be seen, it would seem, all the different kinds of weapons ever invented for destroying human life; at least, there are enough of them, being more than four thousand specimens. This museum occupies but a small part of the building which is mostly devoted to the needs of soldiers who have been disabled, or of those who having served their country long, have become superannuated and deserve a pleasant home in their old age. In its halls during the day may be seen many veterans who bear scars of hard service in defence of their country. Louis XIV. was prompted by noble motives when he, in 1670, founded such an institution capable of affording a home to five thousand invalid soldiers. In front of these buildings are extensive parade grounds which are rendered lively all hours of the day, when the weather will permit, by the feats and manœuvres of soldiers. The French believe in military science, and endeavor to put it in practice. In time of peace they prepare for war.

In the rear of this institution is the tomb of Napoleon I. This is a grand structure of marble and granite, sustaining a lofty dome. Its style, gilt and polish within and without, make it a splendid work. In an open circular crypt, directly under the dome, rests on the mosaic pavement a vast sarcophagus of red Finland sandstone, containing the ashes of the great warrior. It is a fitting monument for such a character. A life full of display and self-aggrandizement would be quite sure to covet just such a final resting-place. It was made to extol the man. How unlike the tomb of Washington, and yet how much more sacred is the latter than the former! The one is visited mostly out of curiosity, the other out of grateful remembrance. The glory of the one dims with age, that of the other brightens. It is safe to point the young to the last as worthy of imitation, but it is hazardous to emphasize the life of the first. The one seemed to lose sight of self in struggling for God and country, while the other, in his endeavors, appeared to magnify himself above God and country. The one asked not that his deeds should be displayed upon miles of canvas or extravagant triumphal arches, the other craved this world's pageantry. This tomb ought to signify to every observer of its splendor, that true goodness alone can produce true greatness. Anything short of this cannot build for immortality.

The church edifices of Paris are few, according to the population, compared with most other civilized countries. It is evident why this should be so, when we consider how France in the time of the Reformation threw her influence in favor of Rome, not from conviction of duty, but from policy, thinking to gain thereby more temporal power and emolument. The reformers were driven from her cities, and hollow-hearted priests were suffered to have control of her religious affairs. In the course of time these became, as might be naturally expected, the butts of ridicule, because of their ignorance and hypocrisy; and the masses in Paris particularly rejected their foolish teachings, saying, if they were the representatives of Christianity, they would have nothing to do with it. So Paine, Voltaire, Diderot, and others led off into infidelity and the severest scepticism. It was not very long before a large majority of the people came to feel, there was no reality in religion; soon Sunday with them was turned into a holiday; its old churches were almost deserted, and scarcely any new ones were built during the seventeenth and eighteenth centuries. This will show why, with a population of nearly two millions, the city should have only some eighty church-edifices.

The Notre Dame, the cathedral of the city, is well worth a careful examination, being of the purest Gothic style, and built in 1163 on the site of a church of the fourth century. During the period of the Revolution, this venerable pile was doomed to destruction; but the decree was afterwards withdrawn, and the sculptures only were demolished. The building was then converted into a Temple of Reason, and the statue of the Virgin was replaced by one of Liberty; and in the choir, where had been chanted for ages sacred music, martial strains were made to resound. On a mound in the centre the torch of Truth was lighted, over which rose an emblem of philosophy after the manner of the

Greeks, ornamented with the busts of Voltaire and Rousseau; thus it continued till it was reopened as a place of divine service in the present century. Its carvings over the central entrance, representing the last judgment, with the figure of Christ in the centre, and the portals on either side ornamented with figures of saints and their attendants, must have required great skill and patience in their elaboration. The interior, like other Gothic cathedrals, has its high nave and side-aisles supported by huge columns. Its large circular windows are called in Paris the finest and richest in the world. All who examine them must admit they are beautiful.

The perfect gem of a little church is the St. Chapelle, connected with the Palace of Justice. It is really the climax of Gothic architecture. Its decorations are exceedingly rich and handsome; its altars, pillars, and windows, are exquisitely fine. It is now used but once a year for religious service, which is the annual "Mass of the Holy Ghost," observed by the lawyers at the reopening of their courts after the autumn vacation. So we are to infer that the lawyers of Paris do have a religious turn of mind, at least, once a year. It was built, it is said, in the thirteenth century, for the purpose of receiving and retaining the Lord's crown and the true cross, which were purchased by St. Louis and conveyed to the chapel through the streets by the barefooted king. These relics are reported to have cost four hundred thousand dollars, and the building one hundred and sixty thousand more. During the revolutions, it has suffered severe damages, so that four hundred thousand dollars in addition have been expended in repairing and restoring it.

The Pantheon is the most conspicuous church in the city. Standing upon elevated ground, with its lofty dome, it overtops all the other buildings. It resembles St. Paul's in London and St. Peter's in Rome, but is inferior in size, still well proportioned throughout. Within, it seems more like a memorial hall than a church. In the last century it was converted into a Pantheon to perpetuate the memory of illustrious citizens. Accordingly, in its vaults and arcades, Voltaire, Rousseau, Lagrange, and many more have been entombed.

But the church of all others in Paris is the Madeleine. It occupies the most frequented part of the city. Though a modern work, it is purely classical. It was patterned after the Parthenon of ancient Athens. Its portico, extending round the building, is supported by fifty-two Doric columns, some fifty feet high, and six feet in diameter. It is constructed entirely of marble. Its pediments, cornice, and frieze, are magnificently illustrated by sacred scenes. Its bronze doors are carved with bass-reliefs representing the delivery of the Commandments. The interior is one vast nave, lighted from above through four spacious domes. This is gorgeously gilded and decorated with paintings and marbles. It is difficult to make this building seem like a Christian church. It was commenced before the Revolution of 1789. In Napoleon's reign the work was renewed with the view of making it a temple of glory. Under Louis Philippe it was completed and converted into a church. Though it contains a mixture of classic and Renaissance details, and has often been on this account criticised, still it is difficult to conceive how it could be improved. It is a work to be admired, in spite of all criticism.

The main streets of Paris are called boulevards, for the reason, the oldest occupy the site of the fortifications in the time of Louis XIV., which then surrounded the city. These are so roomy, so clean, so spotted with trees, and lined with elegant blocks of buildings, that they proffer to the traveller striking attractions. On these are to be found the principal hotels, stores, cafés, shops, and costly residences. Along these are passing at all hours of the day and night as well, an innumerable number of omnibuses, tramways, and hacks. These are verily thoroughfares. Were they compressed, as the streets of London, they would appear as crowded; as they are, they can be passed over without difficulty. No other city is better supplied with conveniences of easy traffic. Everything is so systematized and placed under efficient police control, that even the stranger can enter the city for the first time, and be conveyed to any place within its limits without inconvenience or imposition. No cattle or sheep are ever seen on the streets or within the city walls. The fattened animals are slaughtered outside of the city, and conveyed to the markets, for the most part, by under-ground railroads. All produce, and, in fact, everything before it can be brought into the city, must be inspected. The entrances are so guarded that this is readily done. No other metropolis does more for the welfare of its citizens than Paris. Its sanitary regulations are quite complete, and for this reason, no doubt, it ranks as one of the healthiest cities. Paris, being built on sandy soil and out of light-colored stone, having generally a clear and bright atmosphere, is externally cheery and beautiful.

Paris has some thirty libraries. The largest of these is the National Bibliotheque, which contains three millions of books and one hundred and fifty thousand manuscripts. It is estimated that, if the cases containing them should be placed in a continuous row, they would reach the distance of thirty miles. Most of the books are of the choicest editions. In connection with this library, there is a large reading-room which will accommodate four hundred readers at the same time, with chairs, desks, and attendants sufficient to furnish at short notice any book wanted. It is open six days of the week for six hours per day. It affords a great resort to scholars of all professions.

The Arsenal Library contains one hundred and eighty thousand volumes; the Louvre, one hundred thousand; the Hotel de Ville, eighty thousand; the Institute Library, fifty thousand. In all the different libraries of Paris there are more than four million volumes. So it is apparent that this city is abundantly supplied with reading matter which is placed within the reach of all; and, when we add to the multiplicity of books, seven hundred and fifty newspapers and periodicals published in Paris, we can but infer that the Parisians are a reading people. It is true, much of their literature is of a light order, still their papers and works on science, philosophy, and art, are numerous and of a high order.

The French people are expressing special interest in the cause of education. Their school system is divided into three grades, denominated superior, secondary, and primary. The first is especially devoted to mathematical and physical science, and is not inferior to that of any other country. This is carried on by the means of lectures before certain established institutions. The best talent of the land is employed in giving instruction. The College of France, which is established in Paris, has a corps of thirty-nine professors, and the University has thirty-seven. In Paris there are several other schools of this order. Before these, from three to five lectures are given daily. They are well patronized by men and women of all ages. The gray heads are numerous in these audiences, and many of those advanced in years are intently engaged in taking notes. The lecturers themselves are masters of their subjects and enter into them with great enthusiasm. Seldom will the auditors become inattentive, even when the lectures are protracted to an hour and a half in length. It is surprising, as well as gratifying, to find so many attending these lectures, treating of political economy, poetry, tragedy, medicine, art, history, electricity, geography, and, in short, all the different branches of learning. If a people were not fond of study and interested in investigating, they would not voluntarily patronize such institutions.

The secondary grade of instruction comprises about the same course of study pursued in our colleges; however, instead of recitations, the teaching is given in lectures. The students are divided into classes according to rank and studies. In Paris the largest number of students is found in the department of law; in that of medicine next; in science next; and the least number in theology.

The primary grade answers to our public schools. Elementary education was almost entirely neglected from the time of the Revolution of 1793 to the accession of Louis Philippe to the throne; but the efforts of this monarch, aided by Guizot and Cousin, soon wrought a great change, and ever since, the progress of primary education has continued to advance, till now the Republic and the metropolis are well supplied with schools. The school-rooms and methods of instruction are subject to criticism; the former are not in keeping with the views of ancient Speusippus who said that the young in their course of education should be surrounded with an abundance of pure air and clear light and a plenty of beautiful pictures. The instruction appeals more to memory than to the understanding, in imitation of Jacotot's system.

The charity and reformatory schools in this country are usually conducted in keeping with the most improved methods; particularly is this the case with the institutes for the blind, the deaf and dumb, and wayward youths. The people here generally believe in education, and so public opinion tends to force the children into the schools. It is seldom that you here meet youths who are unable to read and write. The children, as a rule, are bright and apt to learn. Only let them be properly trained and they are certain to develop into the noblest maturity. The government of France is now manifesting more interest in the cause of education than ever before. The result of the national exhibitions has served to stimulate the masses in this direction. Then, too, her present form of government can be sustained, she feels, only by an educated people. In the past, she has been greatly embarrassed by Church and State in her school work. Emperors and priests are hostile to free-thinking subjects; they believe in the education of the few, not the masses. At their hands France has suffered more than language can tell. Could she have been wise and strong enough in the sixteenth century to have chosen the better part, and broken away from Rome, and held fast to the Bible, she would have been saved, undoubtedly, from so many dramas deepening into tragedies, and would have held no second place among civilized nations. But alas! she let slip her golden opportunity, and, accordingly, has been tossed to and fro, alternately glorified and despised. It seems strange she has not been crushed into the dust. She would have perished, had there not been a marvellous recuperative energy and national tenacity in her people. Nature has been most propitious to them in the bestowment of real genius, astute mental qualities, and stirring temperaments. For this reason they have revelled in all conditions of life, from that of secluded peace to the wildest wars. They have been the gayest of the gay, and the gravest of the grave. At one moment they have been the slaves of base prejudice, and the next they have launched into the most extravagant speculations. In matters of taste they have been as inexorable, as they have been lax in matters of morality. Their sentiments have been as changeable as an April sky. Their national existence has been more theatrical than real. Their medal has always had a reverse side. Over against the glory of letters has been set the gloom of heart-crushing atheism; and over against the splendors of the battle-field have hung the horrors of revolutionary massacres and the wretchedness of domestic infidelity. But shall it continue to be thus? Present indications declare it far otherwise. The severe ordeals through which the nation has recently passed, have not crushed their spirits, but served to sober and make them feel more dependent upon some power higher than themselves. This is made evident from the fact that the people are more interested in national and religious affairs than ever in the past. Sunday is no longer a holiday to the extent it was a decade ago. Sabbath morning their churches are well filled; especially is this true of all dissenters from the Catholics. The Protestants now in Paris number more than sixty thousand, and are rapidly increasing. The missionaries sent from England and America, are being greatly encouraged in their labors. Let the Parisians become thoroughly Christian in their homes and every-day life, and their city would become more beautiful and enduring. Then they would be able to lead, not only in matters of taste, but in the highest forms of æsthetic culture. Their "Liberty, Equality, and Fraternity," inscribed upon so many public buildings, would have more than a humanitarian significance. Their works of art would receive higher tints and touches; their philosophy and literature would become broader and deeper; and their lives would adorn their city with grander attractions than triumphal arches, with more satisfying results than the finest galleries of art, and with more instructive treasures than the largest libraries.

IV.

SPAIN AND MADRID.

THE history of Spain is more than a drama; it is a tragedy. Looking upon its physical features, we discover it is favorably situated; but few countries possess such maritime advantages, being washed on two sides, and more, by navigable waters; then, too, its latitude and great diversity of surface are propitious to the growth of almost every variety of vegetation. The grape, olive, mulberry, orange, and lemon, seem to spring spontaneously from the soil. The numerous mountains are unfailing reservoirs to the brooks and rivers running through the valleys and across the plains. Spain is a land of beauty and sublimity. Its highest summits covered with lasting snows, its towering hills waving with oak and pine, its lofty crags, deep dells, cerulean skies, and salubrious climate, all serve to render it exceedingly attractive to man. Its first inhabitants of whom history makes any mention were Celts. Rudely did they live and delight in the land, the waters and forests supplying and satisfying their wants; but it was not always to be thus.

Before the light of Christianity shone upon the world, there were civilized nations dwelling along the shores of the Mediterranean. They were given to adventure and discovery. In the course of events they sent explorers to Iberia, as Spain was then called, who found it rich in mineral wealth; and this opened a field for Grecian, Carthaginian, and Roman settlements. These were adventurers, the same as the first settlers in Virginia. But circumstances so ruled, that many of them became permanent dwellers along the southern borders of this delightful land. No doubt, they introduced the advantages and comforts of their own civilization.

In the reign of Julius Cæsar, Rome was holding supreme power among the nations. She had already extended her rule far to the east, and still prompted by an unbounded ambition, she felt her sceptre must sway over the regions of the far west; so her forces penetrated into this distant land, conquered it, and changed its name to Hesperia. They soon built large towns and great roads. They worked the mines extensively, and returned immense treasures of wealth to Rome. For centuries they possessed the land. But nations have their fall, as well as their rise. If Rome had been the mistress of the world, in the fourth century she had her decline; and with her fall, sooner or later, passed from her grasp all her possessions. The Ostrogoths from the north swept over Italy, laying claim to all her lands and cities; about the same time, the Visigoths came down from Scandinavia upon Spain, subduing the Romans there, claiming the country as their own. Though conquerors, they adopted the language of their subjects. There were good reasons for this; the Romans were more cultivated than the Goths. It was might that gave them rights, making the former slaves. For about four hundred years the Goths ruled this land. Under their sway it did not advance; in fact, it lost ground.

At this time the Arabs were taking high rank among the civilized powers. They were ambitious to gain new territory, that they might spread their religion. They believed this was to be done by the sword; accordingly, they became skilful warriors for those times. They had captured many countries in Asia and Africa, and now they were anxious to obtain footing in Europe, that they might set up the standard of the Prophet there. In 711, from Northern

Africa they crossed into Spain, and in a great battle fought at Xeres, they gained the victory, and at length were able to plant Mohammedanism throughout most of Spain. The Moors, as these Arabs were denominated here, were skilled craftsmen and adepts in many branches of learning. They selected Córdova as the capital of their European possessions. Here they built a superb mosque, whose splendid relics remain to this day. It was supported by three hundred and sixty-five marble columns, had nineteen bronze doors of curious workmanship, and was lighted by forty-seven hundred lamps, kept constantly burning. Here they early established a university, whose portals were thronged with students long before the colleges of Oxford and Cambridge were dreamed of. Here was a library containing six hundred thousand volumes long before printing had been discovered.

The Moors were an industrious people and fond of agriculture. They introduced to the country plantations of sugar, rice, and cotton, and transplanted from Africa palm-trees which have continued to flourish ever since. Many branches of learning received their special attention. This was true of chemistry, botany, astronomy, philosophy, and medicine. They borrowed and transmitted to us our numerals.

They were the first to manufacture carpets, silks, gold and silver embroidery, and paper, in Europe. Their schools were so far superior to those of surrounding nations that many Christians patronized them. In many of their leading towns, academies and libraries were founded; their literature was heralded abroad; for centuries their march was onward. Their kingdom became the most opulent and influential; their rulers dwelt in gorgeous palaces and indulged in sumptuous feasts; their artists, poets, and philosophers, were counted by hundreds. But during these mediæval ages wars were almost constantly occurring in this land. The Goths, who had been driven into the mountains of the north and east, but not conquered, were frequently making attacks upon their neighboring enemies, and by degrees kept regaining their lost territory, and thereby forcing the Moors into closer quarters. There is an element of tenacity in the Gothic nature, as dogged as that in the Jew; at least, it never gives up. They had not been lying simply on their arms in these mountain passes, but had made the most possible out of the Saracen civilization, so that as fast as they captured Moorish towns, they were prepared to render them still more prosperous. Many of their governors were men of marked ability, and so ruled as to become influential at home and abroad. The Spaniards had now become famous for their enterprise and national growth; their commerce was entering the most distant ports; they had vessels exploring for new discoveries.

Now the Moorish star of empire was fast declining, and the Spanish waxing bright; and, in 1492, the final blow was struck, and the last vestige of Mohammedan tyranny abraded; and through the means of that brave little fleet which sailed out from Palos the same year, Spain was greatly enlarged and enriched. Christopher Columbus had proved himself a genius and a hero. No wonder that, as he presented the title of the West Indies to the Spanish Court, bells should ring; guns, be fired; bonfires, kindled; and Columbus, hailed as a nobleman of the first rank! All this was justly due the self-sacrificing man. But it is sad that afterwards, enemies should have robbed him of his just reward, and that King Ferdinand should have suffered him in his old age to pass his last days in poverty and disgrace.

Spain at this period was the wealthiest and most prosperous nation of the world. Its fields were the best cultivated; its ports the most thronged. It was then renowned for the corn of its plains, the wine and oil upon its hillsides, the milk and wool of its pastures, the timber from its mountains, the marbles from its quarries, and the treasures from its mines. Spring and summer were never absent from its valleys, though perpetual winter brooded over its mountain-tops. A halo of glory seemed to be spanning Spain. The light which had long since been extinguished in Alexandria, Athens, and Rome, had blazed out anew in this land. The union of the glowing imagination of the East with the strong intellect of the West, was promising the happiest results. A new mental life appeared to be rising from the sepulchre of antiquity. Illustrious scholars and finished writers were everywhere becoming common within its borders.

Such was Spain three centuries ago, but now how changed! Its bright luminaries have passed away. The monk, the matadore, and the brigand, have taken their place. The school has been supplanted by the bull-ring; the pen, by the stiletto. Much of its surface has been shorn of its beauty, and left desolate and ugly. Large tracts of arable land are lying perfect wastes. The forests are nearly all gone; the rivers have ceased to whirl saws and spindles; its commerce has disappeared; its pruning-hooks have been beaten into swords, and its ploughshares into spears; and ninety thousand laborers have been converted into ninety thousand warriors. The people at large are badly housed, scantily fed, and meanly clad; the villages and cities swarm with beggars. Surely a blight has come upon Spain. Why should the finest country in Europe become so desolate? Why should a people, naturally talented and noble, become so degenerate? Three hundred years ago, when Martin Luther tore off the monkish cowl, and laid bare popish wickedness and priestly iniquities, Germany felt the shock and broke allegiance with Catholicism; the little country of Holland, which had fought so desperately against the encroachments of tide and sea, was ready, at once, to resist unto death the religious inroads of Romanism; the tiny Republic of Geneva raised its battlements high against the invasion of the monster, and became the cradle of a great liberty; England and Scotland sprung to arms and beat the foe from their borders; but France, Italy, and Spain, ran to the rescue of Rome, and Spain became the most desperate foe to the Reformation. No sooner had it made this decision than its decadence began. This step, however, was taken against the will and wishes of the best minds of the country; from multitudes we might select Carlos de Sesso, Augustin Cazalla, Constantin Ponce de la Puente, Ponce de Leon, Antonio Herezuelo, Christobel Losada, and Juan Gonzalez, whose names will live and be loved. Even the Reformation was hailed at the very steps of the throne; Don Carlos, the heir-apparent, was moved by its spirit, and for this reason Philip II. caused him one day to be seated with sawdust scattered profusely round, and ordered an executioner to separate his head from his body; and so a father, because of bigotry, murdered his son.

The Reformation found numerous friends in New Castile, in the cities of Seville and Toledo, in the towns of Granada and Valentia, in Saragossa and Barcelona. Its light was penetrating even to the convents and monasteries. As Philip II. saw the progress it was making, he joined hands with the Pontificate of Rome, determined it should be levelled to the dust and destroyed. So in one single night eight hundred Protestants were put into chains and thrown into prison at Seville. The Inquisition was revived, and thousands of lives were sacrificed at the stake and on the block. In ten short years, from 1560 to 1570, the Reformation was exterminated from Spain. Is it strange that darkness should come over that fair land, having brutally murdered so many of its noblest characters? The calamity was not merely upon the surface; it sank into the very vitals of society. The merchants and artisans of the cities, the peasants of the rural districts, the shepherds on the mountains, the rich and the poor, the wise and the ignorant, all were shocked and paralyzed by the terrible blow. Liberty, morality, and manhood, were hurled into the grave which Catholicism had dug. A little while before, Spain, of all countries, would have been the last one selected to do such bloody work for the purpose of burying freedom of conscience in the dust.

But Philip could not be content in wreaking his vengeance upon Spain; he must be one of the instigators of the horrible Bartholomew massacre; he must attempt the downfall of Holland and the overthrow of England. An inferior man physically, but of tremendous will, he was bound that Catholicism should be nourished by the blood and ashes of Protestantism. While he sat upon the throne, he wielded the mightiest power for the wrong. He struck death-blows at conscience, reason, and humanity. Knowing these facts, we need no longer wonder that, in the course of a few centuries, Spain should become prostrate and the most degraded among European realms — a land without any well-organized school system, with a bull-ring and cock-pit instituted in every city of any considerable size, which are sure to be open on Sundays the year round, and are patronized by all classes; even the poorest wretches will sell the rags from their backs for the sake of obtaining admittance into these barbarous exhibitions. To-day Spain is a military despotism; small in area, with a population of twenty-three millions, it has ninety thousand soldiers; these are finely clad and sumptuously fed. The people stand in awe of the soldier; he commands, and they obey. The military expenditures and waste force upon the citizens enormous taxation; but they have no means of remedying this injustice; so every year the country is becoming more reduced and impoverished. Their king, Alphonso XII., is a mere tool in the hands of the military rulers.

Another incubus, to drag Spain down, is the priesthood. The priests are very numerous wherever there is anything to give them good support, for, like the soldier, they believe in elegant attire and dainty living. The country is becoming reduced so fast that it is evident, if there is not some unforeseen change for the better, the time cannot be far distant when this country will be as desolate as the Trojan plain, or the Carthaginian fields. Had it not been for foreign aid, Spain would have had no railroads; and were it not for foreign assistance, they would not be running at present.

In passing from France into Spain the contrast is very striking; the former is characterized by thrift, order, and industry; the latter, by neglect, confusion, and indolence: the one has the promise of a bright future; the other seems bound to an inevitable death. Were it not for its past the traveller would not be very much inclined to seek this country, and much less, to spend time in it under the present order of things; for wherever he goes, whether it be by rail, or boat, or carriage, or on foot, he is subject to more or less inconvenience, and all the time feels anxious; brigands are on every hand; robberies and murders are incessantly occurring; and the chances for redress and justice in case of misfortune, are rare indeed. But, despite all the discomfitures, asssociation and nature render Spain most inviting to the seeker after knowledge, and to the lover of natural beauty and human antiquities. These are to be met with on every hand.

At Burgos stands a magnificent Gothic cathedral of the mediæval ages. It really consists of a cluster of churches. The mind that conceived them must have been gifted, and the hands which piled them up must have been skilled and strong. There, too, in the Town House, may be seen the tomb containing the ashes of the heroic Cid who has figured so strangely in Spanish history.

At Valladolid which was once the capital of Spain, may be witnessed the palace in which Philip II. was born, the house in which Columbus died, the home of Cervantes while he was publishing his marvellous "Don Quixote," and the spot where the first *auto-de-fé* was kindled, that Romano might atone for becoming a Protestant.

At Seville may be visited another grand cathedral of the fourteenth and fifteenth centuries, containing the tomb in which the remains of Columbus were first deposited, and where his son Ferdinand lies buried. This is also the birthplace of Velasquez and Murillo. All who have looked upon their paintings, can but feel an interest in their nativity and the places associated with their lives. In the sixth century Seville was the favorite city of the Moors, and still later it was the residence of many Spanish monarchs. Here the first court of the Inquisition in Spain was instituted in 1481. Its object then was to force the Jews to become Christians; and all who refused and did not flee the country, were sentenced to be burned alive, and generally many of them, at the same time, and on some great holiday. The unfortunate victims were usually followed to their funeral pyre by trains of priests chanting hymns, and processions of magistrates and judges clothed in their robes of office. The king was wont to be present and sit with his hat off by the side of the grand inquisitor, approving of the revolting scene, called by the Spaniards *auto-de-fé*, or act of faith.

At Cordova are to be found many Roman and Moorish antiquities. It is claimed to have been founded by Marcellus, and that here the Romans established their first colony in the land. It also boasts of having given birth to the two Senecas, the poet Lucan, and many other famous characters. For a long time it was the Oxford or Cambridge of Spain.

At Grenada is the noted Alhambra, an ancient palace of the Moorish kings, built about six hundred years ago, and yet, in a good state of preservation. The style of architecture, ornaments, and inscriptions, is unique and wholly Arabic. It would be difficult to conceive of a structure more airy, graceful, and beautiful. Besides this there are whole ranges of palaces, towers, and castles, which once belonged to the Moors. Grenada also contains a fine old Gothic cathedral. It has, moreover, been the birthplace of many illustrious men: among others were Alonzo Cano, the Michael Angelo of Spain; Rueda, the Spanish Thespis; and Luis de Grenada, the Hesperian Demosthenes.

Thirty miles from Madrid, at the foot of the Sierra Guadarama, stands one of the largest granite structures of the world in one of the most barren and solitary places of Spain. This is the Escurial, an immense palace containing eighty staircases, seventy-three fountains, eighteen hundred and sixty rooms, and twelve thousand windows and doors. It was erected by Philip II. at a cost of seventy-five millions of dollars. But why should it have been placed in such a dreary wilderness, since Spain furnishes so many spots of loveliness and grandeur, where the orange gives its perfume and the palm its fruit? From all these Philip II. turned away, preferring this place because he desired to commemorate a victory gained over the French by the Spaniards, and still more, to make a votive offering to San Lorenzo who, a saint according to the legend, was martyred here upon a gridiron; and so in the shape of a gridiron was this monstrous pile of stone built; and here Philip II. came to live, as king and monk, where he could hear only the tempest's howl and the thunder of the avalanche, as it rushed down the mountain-side. Here lived the man of peering eye, narrow forehead, and protruding jaw, who swayed the mightiest sceptre at the time of the Reformation. In this palace were written those terrible decrees, — and out of these gates they were despatched, — which caused the soil of Holland and the Netherlands, of Italy and Germany, to be dyed with the blood of martyrs. The chair is to be seen in which he sat when he plotted the assassination of the Prince of Orange, and the desk is, as it was, on which he wrote the mandate that launched the Armada. The room is pointed out where the wretched man being devoured by worms, died, participating in mass which was being performed in his behalf before the great altar of his gilded and elaborately decorated church. Not far from the chapel is the descent into the gorgeous tomb in the form of the Pantheon at Rome, where may be seen the black marble urn containing the dust of Philip II. In this tomb are thirty-six sarcophagi, holding the ashes of Spanish kings and royal personages. Philip intended this tomb to be a mausoleum which would surpass in beauty and grandeur that of the Medici at Florence. But, if Philip caused the civilized world to be ransacked for designs and models in order that the Escurial might be the most imposing work of man; if he sought marbles from the mountains of Sierra; jaspers and agates from Sicily and Sardinia; sculptures of mantels and altars from Madrid, Florence, and Milan; gratings and gates of brass from Cuenca and Saragossa; candelabra and bells from Toledo and Seville; pictures and statues from Italy; gold and gems from the Indies; the rare woods from the New World; the tapestries from Flanders; and sacerdotal vestments from the nunneries of Europe, — after all this painstaking, his palace is a splendid failure, ugly in its outward and inward aspects, wanting proportion and harmony, — a fit emblem truly of his own life.

At the present time it feigns to be a university; but its students are few and of inferior quality. So there it stands, in the mountain wilderness, as a lasting monument of Philip's folly, cruel bigotry, and excessive sensuality.

But the Spaniards' favorite city, as it should be, is Madrid. This is their Paris or Washington. They regard it one of the most beautiful capital cities on the eastern continent. Its position is, like the Escurial, very extraordinary. It stands twenty-four hundred and fifty feet above the sea, with a broad, naked plain belting it, and the snowy mountains to the north and east, miles away, keeping constant watch over it. It would seem, a more unfavorable spot nowhere else in Spain could have been found. It was established there by Charles V. and Philip II., because they thought its site was the centre of the country. They allowed the forests to be cut from the plains, and soon the hot suns burned up the smaller vegetation and baked hard the surface; such is the setting of Madrid, overhung with the perpetual frost-work of the Guadarama. So its climate is constantly varying: one hour, the chilly blasts of the north are beating down upon it; the next hour, the hot winds from the south are sweeping it; one side of the street may have an arctic temperature, while the other is burning with torrid heat. These frequent changes render it a most unhealthy city; still, in spite of all obstacles, it has continued to grow, till now it has a population of nearly four hundred thousand, having a circumference of eight miles, containing eight thousand houses, one hundred and forty-six churches, eighteen hospitals, thirteen colleges, fifteen academies, fifteen libraries, a grand palace, a beautiful park, and one elegant street. The buildings are made of brick and stone, and generally, high and crowded together; the streets are narrow and badly paved. The chief business of the city apparently is the parading of soldiers and the promenading and loitering of the citizens in public places. The people differ very much as to their size, appearance, and temperament. Many faces are exceedingly handsome, and others emphatically ugly. As they are carefully studied, evident traces can be discovered of the Celt, the Greek, the Roman, the Moor, the Jew, and the Ostrogoth. The people are social and very fond of show. In the afternoon of each day, when the weather is favorable, on the part of the higher classes, there is sure to be a display in the public places of silk trailing-dresses and costly bonnets, broadcloth cloaks and fur hats. In airy styles they far outdo Paris or New York. The taste of the lower classes appears to run to patchwork and party-colors. It is amusing to see the poor creatures in their diversified costumes. Trade and work here have nothing the snap of Chicago or Liverpool. With the Spaniards it is play or begging first, and then work. Their mercantile establishments and show-windows would not compare favorably with those of Edinburgh or Boston. The greatest display of articles for sale consists of war implements and dirk-knives. The highest ambition of the young men is to become matadores and picadors. Their idea of a real hero is a man who can strike down a furious bull at one thrust of the lance.

In the schools, there is the greatest lack of system and thought. In fact Spain has no well-organized school system; their government is too unstable for that. The king, to-day, does not know that he will be king to-morrow. The people may support certain political measures this week, and reverse them the next. There is a constant unrest, or fluctuation, throughout the land, unless it be while the people are asleep, which is usually the last part of the night and the hottest portion of the day. Little assistance is received from their religion, for it is mainly confined to the lips and gestures. The ranks of the priesthood are crowded; for they insure respectability and ample support.

The institution which has the strongest hold upon the people of Madrid is the bull-ring. A low class of theatres is well patronized, but the bull-fights move and bring together the masses. These are advertised on the largest placards posted in conspicuous places, giving the number of animals to be slain and the names of the actors who are to contend in the arena. Every Sunday, and often on Monday, these cruel exhibitions take place, except a little while during the very coldest weather. The ring at Madrid is similar to the Colosseum at Rome, and is capable of seating some eight thousand spectators. As the matadores and picadors enter the ring, attired in rich and gaudy costumes, the excitement and cheers begin; then, as the door opens and the wild animal springs into the arena, men, women, and children, are mad with excitement, and delighted to see the horrible contest go on; the more enraged the animal, and the more cruel the strife, the better they enjoy it. The matadores and picadors who make successful thrusts are honored with the greatest applause; the crowd salute them, and some of the women of the higher ranks show them special deference, frequently making feasts for them at their homes. Often the king and queen are in attendance at these barbarous exhibitions; they have a special box fitted up and kept for their convenience. Public opinion seems to be decidedly in favor of these amusements; even many of the most intelligent Spaniards will not only patronize them, but will argue in their favor and claim for them beneficial results. Is it strange that a people in such a condition are subject to repeated revolutions, that their king's, or queen's life, is in constant jeopardy, and that murders and robberies are of frequent occurrence? The mystery is, how the government can be sustained for any length of time.

The most inviting place in Madrid is the museum containing a few rare marbles and more than two thousand pictures. It is worthy every way to be classed among the first galleries of Europe. Some two hundred and fifty of the best paintings were produced by Spanish artists in the sixteenth and seventeenth centuries. These works represent what Spain was in its palmiest days. Its modern paintings are few and of scarcely any note. So in the line of art, Spain is living upon the past; but it is far otherwise with France, Germany, and England; however, it is fortunate indeed, it has this boon; it is like a spring in a parched desert; it is like manna in the wilderness; it is like good news in a far-off country: we cannot stand before these noble works without being helped and inspired with the loftiest sentiments. We must feel happy emotions, as we look upon Murillo's "Holy Family," his "Rebecca at the Well," his "Adoration of the Shepherds," his "Child, St.

John"; or Velasquez' "Adoration of the Kings," his "Christ on the Cross," and his "Rome"; or Rubens' "Judgment of Paris," his "Garden of Love," and his "Peasant's Dance"; or Titian's "Adam and Eve," his "Ecce Homo," and his "Christ bearing the Cross"; or Raphael's "Holy Family"; or Van Dyck's "Crowning with Thorns"; and many other pictures of very great merit. Ah! the influence of the fine arts is benign and redeeming.

The art galleries of Spain are about her only saving agents. It is true, that in Madrid and other cities, Protestantism has a slight footing, but missionaries, as preachers, can do little in such a country. What she needs most are missionaries, as teachers, who will instruct the young to think and exercise conscience aright; some of her towns are ripe for such a work. But where are the laborers? Who will support them? The Spaniards cannot, if they had the will, for they have not the means with which to do it. Alas! the mendicants are countless now, and are becoming more numerous every day; piteously and importunately they are begging for bread. The soldiers and priests heed not their cry, but, by their fast living, impoverish them all the more. It would seem Spain is as low as she can be. We can but hope some Columbus, or Vasco de Gama, or Tell, or Bruce, or Lincoln, or Garibaldi, will come forth to her rescue, who will be able to break her fetters and enable the people to help themselves. What a blessing to the nations, it would be, if Spain again could shed the light she did three centuries ago! What a blessing it would be, if she should become truly Christian! So favorably situated, her light would shine over the Mediterranean, casting a halo around Egypt, Palestine, Greece, and Italy; over the Pyrenees her light would travel to France, Switzerland, Germany, and the Netherlands, across the Atlantic to England and America, making millions of hearts rejoice and be glad that Spain was henceforth to be the home of the Christian, the scholar, and artist.

V.

GERMANY AND BERLIN.

IF the traveller enters Germany by the way of Belgium and Holland, he soon discovers that he is in a low country, and learns the full significance of the term Low Dutch, if he never comprehended it before. He can scarcely fail of surprise, as he finds large tracts of land occupied by cities, villages, or farms, situated several feet below the surface of the North Sea, and which would surely be submerged, were it not for the artificial dikes that have been built and are kept in repair at great expense and unyielding industry. This land is the gift of the sea and the river. Most of the country north of France, and along the sea-coast of Prussia, is fenced off by canals. The wind-mills are rising conspicuously on every hand, and are doing faithful service in lifting the water from the lower to higher canals, that fields may be drained and soils redeemed from the aqueous element, so as to grow corn and wheat in abundance, and furnish the greenest pastures for droves of handsome horses, herds of thriving cattle, and flocks of valuable sheep.

In the central part of Germany, table-lands abound. These are diversified with undulating surfaces and smooth-sided hills. The soil is usually well adapted to tillage, and the lands are thickly cut up into farms and dotted over with cottages and barns. The vines drop luscious grapes by the river-sides, and maize ripens on the terraces. The peach reaches perfection by the Rhine. The chestnut and walnut flourish in certain districts. The oak and beech crown the hills, and the elm and poplar border the streams.

In the south of Germany are Alpine heights, where the Rhine and Danube take their rise. In a few instances the mountains ascend so high, as to be covered with lasting snows; however, for the most part, the land here is arable. Broad plains stretch out from Lake Constance and the rivers. Forests of evergreens are growing on the highlands, and orchards of apples and plums, on the plains.

In area Germany now is larger than California, but smaller than Texas, having a population of more than forty-two millions.

As we travel in this enlightened country at the present day, feeling the influence of its schools and religious institutions, we can but recall the time when barbarians held the sway here, and Goths and Huns were lords of these realms. Through the dim light of history, we catch glimpses of tribes, as the country was becoming thickly populated, emigrating to other lands. The fierce Vandals were foremost in leaving their native country, taking up their abode in Spain for a while, and finally pushing their way into Africa. The Visigoths afterwards followed in their wake, settling in Southern France and in portions of Spain. Then the Ostrogoths pushed over the Alps and subdued Italy. Then the Franks crossed the Rhine and took possession of what is now France. At length the Saxons went over the sea and captured Britain. We can readily see how these Gothic tribes should bear away with them similar characteristics. They were impatient of restraint, fond of war, abhorred indolence, delighted in excitement, craved independence, and respected woman. The Allemanni, or Germans, who remained in the country, were never conquered. The Romans found in them a power sufficient to withstand their severest attacks. They were surprised to find that people of light-blue eyes, fair complexion, and medium stature, more than their equals. Julius

Cæsar himself bears testimony of their valor, and extols their indefatigable bravery. We read how they believed in self-government, and early held local courts which were presided over by magistrates chosen by the people. Their leaders were elected from chiefs most distinguished for brave deeds. Their towns were not walled, but they so lived that each man could enjoy his own family and homestead. They delighted to till the soil, herd cattle, hunt and fish.

Such were the Germans whence came the Anglicans and Saxons in the fifth century of our era, who settled in England and caused that country to become great and prosperous, and whose descendants afterwards came to America and established our institutions of freedom and culture.

In sailing up or down the Rhine, or wandering in other parts of this land, we can scarcely fail of becoming deeply interested in the ruined castles which cap many hills and guard mountain-sides; for they are clothed with stirring legends and thrilling adventures. These take us back to the feudal ages, and are quite certain to revive scenes of daring knights, courtly nobles, and lordly priests. Let fancy picture a scene of those old times. Yonder on the summit of rising ground stands a castle. It presents, somehow, a strange and formidable appearance. At once it begets within us a sense of awe. It seems to look down upon the surrounding country with a lordly supremacy. As we approach it, we find it is girdled by a winding moat. The drawbridge down, we cross to its only entrance which is guarded by two lofty towers united by a heavy arch. Under this are to be seen in the yawning opening the iron teeth of the portcullis, ready to devour any foes attempting to force their way into the castle. When fairly within the walls, there rises before us the lofty keep which is the residence of the feudal owner and his family. It does not bear the marks of beauty, but of strength and security. Within, it is cut up into many apartments which are small and comfortless. The light struggles into it through the smallest loopholes. The furniture is meagre and rude. The great hall is the chief room, where the baron seated on his dias at the upper end is wont to preside at the table with his family, and sometimes entertains guests at banquets and festivities. Within the stone fastnesses the feudal owner enjoys a good degree of safety. Powder has not yet been invented, and cannon has not demolished the hugest breastworks of solid masonry. With drawbridge up and portcullis down, the inmates have nothing to fear from spear, battle-axe, or catapult.

Let us now ascend the battlements of the tower and have a survey of the country round. The landscape is spotted far and wide with meadows, woodland, lake and river. Now and then may be seen residences of knights and nobles; here and there dwellings of villeins; and still farther on, the huts of serfs. While gazing, we descry among the trees bordering the way to the barbican, or entrance to the castle, glistening of spears and mailed armor. This is the lord and his retinue returning from his sovereign's court, where he has been doing homage to his barony. Having laid aside his sword and spurs, with hands laid in those of his monarch, he swears to serve him with life and limb loyally forever. Upon this he is clothed with new investiture, showing fullest title to his castle and realm. With great joy he returns to his feudal home, conscious that he has added strength to his government, and will receive increased homage from his subjects.

Really, there is much to be admired in this old feudal system. It had its mission to fulfil in the march of civilization. It certainly did serve to nurture fidelity and gratitude, chastity and virtue. In the castle, at least, it did tend to cultivate respect for woman. The sweet charities of home were often made to blossom out from its grimy walls. Still, as a political system, it savored not of democracy; it left almost everything to the mercy of the chief. It favored aristocracy, but not the commonality. On the whole, it was a severe order of discipline; but, like the storms and snows of winter, it was making ready for the bloom of springtime.

In this land many evidences and relics serve to show that the Germans were early devoted to religious thought and worship. The names which we apply to the days of the week, are of Saxon origin, and plainly indicate divinities which they adored. On the first day of the week they worshipped the sun, and so they called it Sun's daeg, and we have changed it to Sunday; on the second day of the week they served the moon, and so it was named Moon's daeg, and we have contracted it to Monday. So their old cathedrals are the outcome and expression of their religious fervor. These are grand testimonies of religious enthusiasm and spiritual aspiration. In fact, Gothic architecture took its rise here, and in France and England about the same time; and, too, when the northern nations of Europe were inflamed to a red heat with religious excitement. It was during the Crusades which had their origin the last of the eleventh century that hosts from Germany and France went forth to fight for the restoration of the cross in the Holy Land. In works of art, the Greeks had borrowed from the Egyptians, the Romans from the Greeks, and now the Germans from the Romans. Still there was something peculiar to this land and people; and though they borrowed in art-works from the past, yet they so remodelled as to fashion anew; and hence the outcome of the Gothic style, which, all must admit, is the expression of profound religious conviction.

As we stand near the banks of the Rhine and look at the cathedral of Cologne, we can scarcely fail of being convinced that that structure is deserving to be called the St. Peter's of Gothic architecture. If the name of its designer has been lost, nevertheless, it testifies concerning a genius of taste and sublimity, out of whose conception sprung surfaces, columns, arches, and towers, crystallizing into solid stone and fairest beauty. Though commenced five hundred years ago, yet it is but recently that it received its finishing touch. Walk within, and its nave, aisles, vaults, pillars, transepts, and windows, can but impress you with a sense of deep religious awe. As fact rises above fact, we cannot doubt that its plan originated in one man, whose soul was that of a poet and prophet, and who, by his works, like Angelo and Raphael, was beckoning humanity heavenward.

As we take a position in front of Strasburg Cathedral, where we can have a good view of the noble Vosges and the Black Forest, separated by the most picturesque river of Europe, be it at mid-day, or when the stars are lustrous and the moon is radiant, that lofty structure seems a glorious work of beauty and grandeur. It appears like a masterpiece of strength and light, almost worthy to have been dropped from Paradise. It is the highest human structure in the world. Should it be placed beside the pyramid of Cheops, it would tower above it by twenty-four feet; though the cross of St. Peter's is lifted so high into the sky, still the spire of Strasburg Cathedral rises forty feet higher. Prospecting from the plats below, the whole structure is clothed with an airy, celestial appearance, yet firm, broad, and easy. The union of façade, tower, and spire, is harmonious and complete. Passing within, we are struck with its massiveness of outline and solidity of proportions, its height and breadth, and its rich yellowish tinge. Its astronomical clock and monuments are matters of interest; but these are trifles compared with the building itself: this speaks of the loftiness of the mind, the divinity of the soul, and the expectancy of the heart, to dwell in the temple not made with hands.

The cathedral at Mayence of red sandstone and quaint style; the one at Ulm, with its grotesque shapes without, and extraordinary magnitude within; the one at Ratisbon, which King Ludwig caused to be renewed and refurnished; and the one at Magdeburg, with the figures of saints cut into its walls, — all are expressive of religious fervor, assuring us, if minds and hearts had not been devoted to prayer and praise, these wondrous expressions of Gothic architecture would not have been conceived, and much less built into such sublime forms of grandeur and beauty.

From these hoary structures, it is evident that Gothic architecture is the outcome of religious enthusiasm which signally prevailed from the eleventh to the fourteenth century. But from the dawn of the Reformation, art-inspiration began to wane. If dogmas were changed for the better, and society was improved, it is certain there was a decrease of religious sensibility. The currents of thought were turned from the ideal to the actual, from the spiritual to the visible. The Reformers were disposed at first to reject even the good in Romanism. Protestantism, as yet, has not given to the world a great genius in art. The last of the heroic artists were Rubens and Vandyke, who were Catholics; however, art to-day finds some of its best patrons and most appreciative admirers among Protestants. Cultivated religion is bound to worship in grand temples and beautiful churches. However much we may admire these old cathedrals, there are other objects of still greater interest to the scholar and Christian, as they journey through this land.

In the town of Wittenberg, which is small and evidently becoming less, is the house of Martin Luther, which is a humble structure situated in the outskirts of the little city. From its outward appearance we certainly should not be drawn towards it, yet somehow, it does allure and at once almost fascinates; it stirs innerly and takes hold of the heart. The very walls seem to say, "We hold the secrets of a great man." We pass within to the low-roofed chamber where Luther was wont to think and study. It is pretty much as the famous occupant left it. The masonry, the frame-work, round-paned windows, the oaken table, the "professor's chair," some needle-work of his beloved Catherine de Bora, his beer-cup, psalter, and other relics, remain quite where Luther last used them. It is true, coveting hands and blades have clipped away from the table and woodwork bits of remembrances. We cannot think, this is wrong; for it is the result of love and goodwill. It is natural to feel that a great man belongs to the world, and the things which he handled, after his death, become common property. In this room the great reformer's soul was so disciplined, he dared to do for the right. Perhaps, over that heavy table, he finished his translation of the Bible, which he commenced while in exile at Wartburg. No doubt he often bent over it in prayer, and so became strong for action. Here he prepared those theological lectures which, when he delivered them in the university, shook the whole of Germany and the Christian world. Here he tore in pieces the sophisms of Aristotle, fashioned a new grammar for his nation, and composed those theses which demolished the indulgence theory and the infallibility of the pope. A chamber in which such work has been done, ought to be remembered and kept sacred for all time.

In another part of the city is the university,

to which Luther was called from the cloisters of Erfurt to the chair of philosophy when but twenty-five years old. As he began to lecture and preach before the students, his tongue stammered and his heart quailed; but as he was consecrated to duty, it was not long before the youthful monk was surprising the most learned scholars with his eloquence and new doctrines. Soon he was promoted and appointed Biblical Baccalaureate and lecturer on theology. In this new position, he surpassed the highest expectations, and his fame quickly became far-reaching; students were drawn to Wittenberg from Prague, Leipsic, Heidelberg, and the farthest points of Europe. If the old university is no longer crowded with students, it is full of the richest memories.

In the Palace Church situated in the southern extremity of the town, are the graves of Luther and Melancthon. On the walls hang life-size pictures of the two reformers. On the oak door of this church Luther nailed his ninety-five Latin theses which were like bombs hurled into the religious camp, blowing priestly creeds and superstitions into flitters. Only a little way off from the church, just outside the Elster gate, on the banks of the Elbe, stands a thrifty oak, marking the spot where Luther, in the presence of his students, burned the Papal bull which set on fire the Romanish Church. Surely Wittenberg in its wasting condition, is all alive with the inspiring associations of the reformer, poet, musician, and tremendous actor.

If the traveller is interested in the Reformation, he cannot afford to fail of visiting the small town of Worms, which is situated near the banks of the Rhine. It is an ancient town, having existed before the Romans invaded the country, and was afterwards an imperial city. It was a favorite resort for Charlemagne; but it is especially noted for the diet of Worms, which was in session on the 17th of April, 1521. This was an august assembly, composed of the young emperor, Charles the Fifth, with all the priests, papal nuncios, and Catholic dignitaries of Germany. Before this body Luther had been summoned to appear, that he might recant, or receive condemnation. Hosts of Protestants were in the city, fearing and dreading consequences. As they recalled the fate of Huss, they felt Luther ought not to enter that diet; and so, on his approach, a party went forth to meet him, hoping they should be able to turn him back. But to their entreaties he replied, "Were there as many devils in Worms as there are roof-tiles, I would on." As he went to the hall of the diet, many hearts prayed that he might be sustained, and others that he might be speedily crushed to the earth. The reformer was lost in the sense of duty, and for two hours he fearlessly faced king and priest, declaiming for freedom of conscience and liberation from superstition. "Here stand I," he said; "I can do no other. God assist me!"

This is the most signal event of modern history. It was a new birth of civil and religious liberty. The very dust of Worms now cries aloud in praise of the brave man who dared to strike religious tyranny to the earth, and raise conscience into the sunlight of Christian liberty.

Still another old town, to which we are drawn by the force of the Reformation, is Augsburg, occupying a broad, open plain close upon the waters of the Danube. This was once an imperial town, but its ancient splendors have passed away, and its principal streets are now almost as still in the day as in the silence of night; yet there are witnesses here and there of its vanished greatness. Verily, a halo of glory broods around its time-worn towers. As we walk its streets, we are reminded of the 15th of June, 1530, when the emperor,

Charles the Fifth, was approaching this city. The mass of the people went forth to greet him. The king was kingly in his bearing. His countenance was stern and grave. The procession conducted him up the Maximilian Strasse to the cathedral, where a Te Deum was sung, and the Romanish Legate Campeggio pronounced the benediction. On the next day followed the festival of the Holy Body of Christ, and all persons in Augsburg were required by imperial command to observe the day and take part in the services at the cathedral. Of course the Protestants could not submit, and Margrave George, of Brandenburg, told the emperor, "Before he would so betray God and his gospel, he would kneel down before his majesty and suffer his head to be hewn from his body." This was significant, and plainly indicated that something remedial must be done on the part of emperor and priest. Protestantism was no longer to submit to the edict of Worms, which condemned Luther and repressed his writings; so on the 25th of June, 1530, it was reluctantly decided that the Protestant Confession should be read publicly in the cathedral. At the appointed meeting, Charles was seated on a raised dias, surrounded by his Catholic princes and clergy. Opposite sat the nobles and doctors of the Protestant party. Luther was not there; he had voluntarily remained behind at Coburg; but his place was filled by a worthy and competent representative who was of small stature, with a high forehead, pleasant blue eye, and mild, contemplative face. Such was Philip Melancthon outwardly, but innerly he was scholarly, spiritual, and profound. He was present with a Confession of Faith, which he had carefully prepared, and which must be regarded as the first full statement and intelligent digest of Protestant belief ever published to the world. When it was sent to Luther, and he read it, he said, "This is sufficient." As it was read in that imposing assembly at Augsburg, king and sympathizer were so overwhelmed that they dared not undertake to suppress it; and so Protestantism for the first time was publicly acknowledged a fact in Augsburg, and its old church was crowned with the lasting honor of witnessing the first victory of the reformer over the pope.

Over all the face of Germany the legendary light flickers, and sprites haunt the groves, and fairy creatures sing by the streams. The Germans remind us in many ways of the nature-loving Greeks. They have their retired and bosky retreats, their naiads and fauns, their Pan and Bacchus. Their scholars, dramatists, orators, poets, and artists, are wont to cluster together, as did the old Athenians. Their centre, or meeting-place, must be where nature is unique and varied; where the day smiles and the night is propitious; where fountains sparkle and flowers bloom; where birds sing and winds regale. Such a place is Weimar. Nature has done much to render it attractive, but man, more. Its buildings, occupied by its few thousand inhabitants, are mainly inviting in form and style; but these do little towards making the town enticing to the pilgrim stranger, compared with the gifted minds that dwelt here for a series of years. Here lived Goethe, the prophet of the philosophical and the profound; Schiller, the poet of the people, and their sparkling genius; Herder, the myriad-minded student and scholar; and Wieland, the translator and publisher. Were not these talented souls enough to create a modern Athens? What thrilling associations and touching beauties hover around spots where such men wrought! Trees may decay and rocks may crumble away; but moral worth and intellectual greatness are constantly accumulating and towering.

The house of Schiller continues nearly the same as he left it. It is a small two-story building. The rooms are quaint and simple. In one of these we can see his library which is not large but composed of choice books, the desk and table on which he penned thoughts that live and burn, and his harp and piano whose chords and keys he would touch, to woo the muses to his aid.

The houses of the other gifted ones are not exhibited to strangers. The ducal palace and park, the grand ducal library of a hundred and forty thousand volumes, the theatre which was under the superintendence of Goethe and Schiller, and the cemetery where rests the mortal of these immortals, are favorite resorts to strangers who have been stirred by "Faust" and thrilled by "William Tell." The Germans hold Goethe in holy reverence at a distance; but Schiller they clasp to their hearts in tenderest love. The former was born at Frankfort-on-the-Main, and the latter at Gohlis. Whatever they touched, or looked upon, at least, savors of the divine. Their monuments already are many, which have sprung up almost by magic from the soil and the hearts that they have touched; and they are certain to multiply as the world shall grow into their acquaintance. Noble characters progress through the ages.

The Germans not only love poetry and honor

their poets, but, during the present century, they have been passionately inspired by gifted minds with a fondness for science and the facts of this world. This intensity of thought, if it was not first kindled in Potsdam, received largely fuel and renewed ignition from that city which is a few miles from Berlin, and one of the finest and most regularly built towns in Germany. Its royal castle, and new buildings ornamented with statuary, render it notable; but the fact of its being the birthplace of Alexander von Humboldt makes it a Mecca to all travellers interested in science and natural history. Not far from the town is the chateau of Tegee, where, on the 14th of September, 1769, the child Humboldt first made his appearance among mortal things. Here it was that Alexander and his brother William played, and here he listened to the glowing narration of George Foster, concerning the wonders of foreign lands, and his heart was fired with a desire to become a naturalist. In the right way he went to work, disciplining his mind during long years in the schools under the tuition of the best minds. At length, being well equipped, he went forth to gather up from the lands of the earth inestimable treasures of geology, ethnography, and geography. As he returned from his explorations, honored men flocked to hear and see him. He wrought with scholars who were foremost in the march of science. Gay Lussac, Leopold de Buch, and Arago, soon acknowledged him a mental prince. Monarchs delighted to confer upon him honors of knighthood. As the evening of life came upon him, calmly we see him in his adopted city, with his mind full of pictures of the natural world, and his heart flush with love to God, engaged in a colossal enterprise, — one too daring, it would seem, for the most talented when the currents of life run swiftest; but Humboldt felt, we judge, as did Dryden,

> " A setting sun
> Should leave a track of glory in the skies."

His track of glory is the "Cosmos." In this work he passes in review the vastest amount of human knowledge. In it he has wedded the exactness of mathematics and the ideal of poetry. The "Cosmos" is the "Iliad" of this modern Homer. See him, eighty-seven years old, penning out its immortal lines; or observe him on his way to the court of the king. He is somewhat stooping, slow but firm of step, very simply dressed, carrying, perchance, a pamphlet in his hand. All in Berlin, or Potsdam, know him, as he is passing, and reverently say to each other, "There goes Humboldt."

So the great man worked on till the 5th of May, 1860. As the sun of an afternoon was shining into his room, he was translated while exclaiming, "How glorious are these rays; they seem to call the earth to heaven." Tenderly, kings, scholars, and commonalties, bore his remains to his native city, and there sacredly entombed them. Thus a sweet, fruitful, and beneficent character passed to the immortal. It does us good to review it, and look on those things which Humboldt touched, and realize that he thought the earth, sea, and sky, were richer than bankers' vaults, or sovereigns' jewels. To remember and ponder such a life cannot fail of producing more life.

The lover of music will count it among his fortunate experiences to have heard some of the compositions of the great masters of melody performed in their responsive land. He will rank it with seeing the high Alps, or the mighty pyramids. In German music there is a mingling of soul and passion; however, the intellectual outweighs the emotional. This is not the case in Italy; the feeling there controls the mental. As one listens to some of Mozart's exquisite instrumental pieces, it seems as though two opposing forces were contending for the mastery. The one is storming, thundering, trampling, and overcoming; while the other is soothing, entreating, winning, and finally gains the victory of love and truth. Or let one listen to a composition of Beethoven: for instance, the piece composed as he felt deafness coming upon himself. It opens with a stroke of horror and dismay. For some time, it appears as though there could be no submission to the misfortune. The wailing and resisting are frightful; but at length, glimmering, tremulous hopes begin to express themselves. By-and-by, the soul is cheered with the reflection that music is from within, and that when the ear shall be deaf, the soul can draw melodies altogether from the spiritual; that when the groans of mortality can no longer be heard, the harmonies of angels will swell the heart.

Another striking characteristic in German music is its dramatic quality. As we listened to the "Trial Scene," as it was brought out by the orchestra at Dresden, it was wild and furious in action at times. When the words "Crucify Him" were reached, the notes jarred, roared, and thundered, filling the very air with consternation. So it was with "The Creation," as we heard it expressed in Berlin. Its effects, however, were not depressing but full of encouragement. Particularly was this the case as the orchestra came to the word "light." Surely there was light then; and the heavens were radiant with glory. No wonder that Haydn, its composer, while once listening to it, as it was being successfully performed, with streaming eyes and uplifted hands, should exclaim, "Not from me, — it came from heaven."

Leipsic at the present time is the musical centre of Germany. Here some of the best talent of the world is earnestly at work, further developing the science and perfecting the art of music. Certainly since, and, possibly, before, Luther composed his "Choral" on the way to the diet of Worms, music in this land has been regarded, at least, one of the divine arts. Let Germany lead on in this noble cause, and she will be likely to add to her galaxy of illustrious musical names others as brilliant as those of Luther, Mozart, Haydn, and Beethoven.

Art in this country is loved and really worshipped. The rich and poor are attracted towards the artist. All delight to do homage at his shrine. He is honored in the palace and in the public square. His studio is the pride of the city and the country. His pictures, or statues, are more precious than gold or rubies;

so the people generally take pride in exhibiting the works of their artists, which are numerous in their own and in foreign countries. With special satisfaction they point to the productions of Durer, Holbein, Rembrandt, Van Dyck, and Rubens. After seeing Rubens' "Descent from the Cross," Van Dyck's portraits, Rembrandt's "Sacrifice of Isaac," Holbein's altarpieces, and Durer's "Adoration of the kings," we cannot think strange that the Germans should cling fondly to these geniuses, as well as hundreds of others.

In the Pinakothek of Munich there are eighty-eight pictures of Rubens, which comprise but a small part of all he painted. As we study them, we can scarcely conceive how it was possible for one man to illumine the canvas with such an amount of striking colors. Rubens is truly the Titian of the North.

Rembrandt known as the King of Shadows, has nineteen pictures in this gallery. Standing before them, we discover supernatural gleams and lustrous glooms; figure after figure emerges from its shadowy background, as though they grew out of the canvas while we gaze. We are often led to wonder whether these are actual, or the creations of fancy. Here, too, is Van Dyck in his regal splendor, being represented by thirty-nine of his paintings. Here, also, is Albert Durer looking down from the walls. As we compare his portrait by himself with that of Raphael by himself, and one of Giorgione by himself, it loses nothing by the comparison. Certainly Durer's is beautiful, while Raphael's is saintly, and Giorgione's is sublime.

In this gallery, as well as in most of the others of Germany, there are many first-class pictures. The building itself, its rooms and adjustments, are expressive of art.

But the gallery which is far-famed above all others is the one at Dresden; and its attraction is mainly due to the fact that it contains Raphael's "Madonna del Sisto." Well, this is enough to immortalize one gallery. As we stand in front of the picture, contemplating its perfection, we feel like holding profoundest silence. It appears too ineffable and divine to be talked about. Its power, like the still small voice of God, is to be felt. Looking upon it day after day, it keeps growing in our admiration, as though it were a work let fall from heaven, all the while being lighted up with fresh celestial beauties. Those features of the Madonna, so placid yet full of significance; those eyes, so radiant with internal light; that attitude, so graceful; that Christ-child, so tenderly and sweetly embraced, as though just descended from on high; that face of St. Barbara, implying she is taking her last look of the mortal; that expression of St. Sixtus is laden with faith, hope, and charity; and lastly, those cherubs below are the types of childish rapture and sweetest inspiration. The whole is harmonious and complete, the perfection of the real and ideal, the union of heaven with earth.

The Germans display as much love for sculptures as paintings. In the Glyptothek at Munich, we discover more than a small vatican of marbles. Truly this city reminds us of ancient Greece, as to its style of architecture and taste for art-works. So King Ludwig ransacked Grecian hills and plains, and delved into the ruins of their wasted cities, disclosing immortal marbles with which to adorn his native city. Accordingly, the Glyptothek was constructed with its appropriate halls having floors of marble, walls of variegated stucco, and ceilings ornamented with mythical figures and paintings showing the rise, progress, and decline of sculpture. In one hall we see the restored Ilioneus, the perfection of blooming youth and unspeakable beauty and innocence; in another apartment, we witness the sculptures, that once decorated the temple of Minerva at Ægina. They still breathe out thrilling inspiration, asserting themselves as the enduring heroes of the "Iliad." Æneas, Paris, Hector, Ajax, and Laomedon, are apparently all ready for duty. Had not the Grecian sculptors been poets and creators, the marble never would have grown divine under their hands.

As we come to the statue of Leucothea, embracing the child Bacchus, we no longer think it strange that so many have been entranced, while gazing upon its naturalness and perfection of every part. This work alone is sufficient to crown Phidias as the champion with the chisel and mallet.

Besides many modern sculptures in this gallery, there are a hundred and forty-seven rare specimens of ancient art.

Another exhibition of statuary, which the traveller cannot afford to miss, is the museum connected with the bronze foundry of Munich. Here are to be seen the models of most of the metal statuary of the civilized world, which is gracing doors, squares, commons, and pinnacles. Here is an opportunity to contrast the representatives and ideals of different nationalities. Our Lincoln, Washington, Mann, and Webster, hold prominent positions among these artworks.

The statue of Bavaria, which stands just outside of the city in a beautiful meadow, is the largest bronze statue ever cast. Its height is eighty-four feet. The Rumshall, a Doric portico resembling the Propylæa of ancient Athens, encircling the huge statue in part, is becoming filled with statues and busts, to perpetuate the fame of this country.

So it is, in most of the German cities are to be seen beautiful specimens of statuary, plainly showing that the people believe in their nationality and noble characters, and aim to hold them in lasting remembrance. Evidently this is the only way for a nation to build securely. If the virtues of the wise and good are not handed down in every possible way from generation to generation, civilization will of necessity wane. It is plain the Germans understand this fact, and, therefore, are making the most possible out of their works of art. These cannot fail to impress favorably the truly enlightened who examine them.

Education in Germany is now a ruling passion. All healthy children from six to fourteen years old are required by law to be in school most of the time. On graduating from the grammar schools, perhaps the majority of the boys advance into the gymnasia, where they study, from four to eight years, the ancient classics, mathematics, German literature, history, and some modern language. Having completed this course the average student ranks, as to culture, about the same as our college junior. On leaving the gymnasium, if one decides to follow a profession for a life-work, he must go to the university, to receive special training for his selected vocation. Here he must remain four or more years before he can be crowned with his degree and the right to follow a profession. The university gives instruction altogether by lectures. Degrees are conferred on passing in oral examination, and the reading of an elaborate thesis, except in theology, where the degree is purely honorary. After a student becomes fully matriculated into any one of the universities of Germany, the privilege is granted him of attending lectures at any university within the realm, according as his wishes and taste may decide. The object seems to be, to encourage students to do the best possible work. So, as the scholar comes out of the university hall, with his doctorate in hand, his head is likely to be silvered with gray, and his eye somewhat dimmed with hard usage. He is certain to be profoundly learned; but what is he really fitted to do? He is not prepared to teach young and inexperienced minds, for he has been grappling with the strongest scholars and mightiest thoughts. He has had no experience in imparting knowledge. He cannot preach, for he has cultivated no habit of expression. He is simply a scholar, and must find a scholar's position, if that is possible where so many others are waiting for a similar chance. If he fails, he is likely to reap at length the bitterest poverty, or at best the meagre rewards of scholarship in Germany.

Unquestionably the leading university of this country now is that of Berlin, conceived by Humboldt and founded by Frederick William only some seventy years ago. Its aim and ambition were to become at once a power in the land. It seemed to leap into life fully matured, astonishing the world with the mental strength of Hegel, Schleiermacher, and Neander, and is now one of the leading educational institutions of the world. Its number of students and professors reminds us of the palmy days of Alexandria, Athens, Padua, Cordova, and Prague. In law, theology, medicine, and philosophy, it claims the profoundest scholarship, and does lead civilization, at least, in certain departments of learning. If Halle contests the honors with Berlin in the soundness of its theology, and

Heidelberg in the development of its legal principles, and Göttengen in its natural sciences, and Jena in some departments of philosophy, still not even Leipsic can vie with Berlin in philological researches. Böchle, with many others following in his gilded track, is letting his light so shine as to reveal, as nowhere else, the hidden laws of language.

Though Germany, with its twenty-two universities and learned faculties, shuns and abhors superficialness, yet it does often fail in practicalness, and comes short of making its deep intellectual thought felt in every-day life. So, if Germany excels in fine scholarship and theory, it lacks in mental appliances and practice. Is not this a natural result of the lecture system? Let the Socratic method be combined with this, so that there should be a mingling of lectures and discussions, and German education would be more signal than it is at present.

The state supports mainly the university, as well as the public school and the gymnasium, so that all who will, can enjoy its advantages. Its educational work has been signal, placing its schools, as beacons upon the loftiest heights, to shed light and glory upon the world.

If Germany forces her children in the public schools to learn the catechism by heart, and is intent upon cramming the youthful mind with Scripture texts and hymns, yet there is no religious awakening in the country. The majority of the educated are rationalists, rejecting all the Christian creeds. The boy at fifteen is almost certain to disbelieve the texts which he was required to learn at ten. The majority profess to have faith in God and immortality. But for the most part they look upon religious ceremony as trifling, prayer as a pagan rite, and worship as the offshoot of heathenish weakness and fear.

It is true, there are districts in which Christian orthodoxy prevails; but these are exceptions. Germany can no longer be called Christian, as it was known to Luther and defined by Leo X. Roman Catholicism has here become deprived of its pristine authority, and the Augsburg Confession has become of small account. The dogmatism of Athanasius and the statutes of the Council of Nice, which once dominated here, are lifeless. The mass are considering Christianity as an Asiatic religion, speedily doomed to oblivion. The comparatively few who are in the ranks of the clergy, are being looked upon as wild enthusiasts or vile hypocrites, who are seeking most for an easy mode of living. The mass boldly declare that human reason is sufficient to establish all needed religious axioms for human guidance. They judge it a grave duty to make this loftiest use of reason. So latitudinarianism is really holding sway. Sunday is generally treated as a holiday. Accordingly, the churches on that day are generally empty, but the beer-gardens are crowded to overflowing. The Bible, they feel, through moral, historical, and scientific criticism, has been exploded. They claim that their extreme rationalism is working good moral results upon their nation; and they hesitate not to compare their average society with that of the most orthodox communities. They judge their honor and integrity will vie favorably with these virtues as expressed in any other country. They say let Goethe, Schiller, and Von Humboldt, be carefully studied, and they have no fear for the welfare of their nation. Reason is their talisman; criticism, their delight; and scepticism, their special forte. What the result of their extreme rationalism will be, remains to be seen. It is certain that Christianity, at present, is but a small factor in Germany.

Berlin, now the capital of the whole of Germany, is one of the largest cities of Europe. We can hardly imagine how and why such a city should chance to spring up in the central part of an extended and naturally barren plain. It is evidently a comparatively modern city; however, it is known that a portion of its present site was inhabited as far back as the thirteenth century.* Its very name is supposed to imply a settlement on a sandy plain. The present city is divided by the Spree which is an exceedingly sluggish stream. In fact the land on which the city stands is so level that it affords no drainage. It is fortunate the soil is loose and gravelly, or otherwise the people could not long survive here. The city is considerably spread out, surrounded by a wall ten and a half miles in length. The buildings are constructed of brick, and plastered or stuccoed outside. These soon acquire a faded appearance. For beauty of situation and style of architecture, Berlin will not compare favorably with Munich or Dresden, the former guarding the rapid Iser, and the latter spanning the clear Elbe. These by nature and art possess peculiar charms; but Berlin is the "city of the plain." It is but slightly elevated above the level of the sea. Its winters are long and usually severe. Its summers are hot and arid. Yet, in spite of all disadvantages, it has become a magnificent city. Its Under den Linden, which is its principal street and fashionable promenade, is in design and in many regards the handsomest street in Europe. This is lined with rows of lime-trees, which extend from the stately Brandenburg gate, and is flanked on either side by many of the finest structures of the city. Here are the spacious opera house, the Royal Palace with its six hundred rooms and saloons, the Armory having weapons sufficient to equip one hundred and fifty thousand men, the University, the Academy of Arts, and the Equestrian Statue of Frederick the Great. The leading external sights of this city can be readily and quickly seen because of their compactness. Berlin owes its growth and renown mainly to the Fredericks. This has been a beloved city to them, and they have striven to give it life, — life internal and external.

If level districts and countries are not prone to produce poets and philosophers, this city has been prolific in producing scholars. For decades a presiding intellectual genius has seemed to hold sway over it, and every now and then has called forth a gifted soul to march on in the van of aggressive thought and civilization.

The Berliners are renowned for their quick and sharp wit and humor, their literary and artistic tastes, their general intelligence and passionate fondness for music. They pride themselves on their schools, from the primary to the university. They delight to exhibit these to foreigners, and to learn all that is possible as to the educational work which is going on in other countries. They do their best to induce students from abroad to come to their city to study. Accordingly, in their gymnasia, university, and schools of art and music, are to be seen young men and women from distant lands. Undoubtedly, the strongest attractions to this city are on the side of its educational advantages. Though it is Protestant, still it has but few church-edifices, compared with its population; not more than one third what there should be, to accommodate the masses, should they attend worship on Sunday. The average German prizes highly his physical and intellectual tastes. He cannot dispense with his beer or book; so his Sabbaths are likely to be spent at the beer-garden, or in the library-room. So, while the German is developing body and mind most fully, it is a question yet to be decided, as to what extent he is developing his spiritual nature. His career thus far has been marvellous. He has brought forth some of the richest treasures from the mines of the earth, and revealed out of the arcana of philosophy countless new and wonderful truths.

Berlin is intellectually great, and her mental splendors gild the uttermost parts of the earth. It is the northern Mecca of scholars whose beacons are brilliant with the lights of its Humboldts, Hegels, and Neanders. As the centre of the most perfect system of education, it is a city of which every German, or foreign scholar, may well be proud.

VI.

SWITZERLAND AND BERNE.

THIS is a prominent country in several senses. Though small in area, yet it towers above all other lands in Europe. It will not average more than two hundred and ten miles east and west, and about one hundred and thirty north and south. Its lower portions are twelve hundred feet above the level of the sea, and one thousand feet higher than the average surface of Italy. Like a towering giant it sways its snowy sceptre over land and sea, far, far away. It is a land of lofty peaks and deep-cut vales; of eternal snows and perpetual spring; of fertile soils and barren rocks; of beautiful lakes and angry glaciers; of sunny nooks and bleakest heights. It is rich in mines of iron, coal, lead, and rock-salt. Its waters abound in carp, perch, and salmon. The hare, squirrel, and partridge, sport among its beech, birch, oak, and chestnut trees. Bears and wolves infest the regions of the pine and spruce. Chamois and gazelles leap from cliff to cliff. Eagles and vultures sail among the loftiest heights.

Early man sought this romantic and sublime region. Whence he came, history is unable to decide. The relics of the Lacustrine villages show that human beings were here during the stone and bronze ages, reaching back, from three to seven thousand years. Some two hundred of these lake settlements have already been discovered. So these facts place this picturesque land among the pre-historic countries. But long after these Palifits had sunk into their watery graves, the Celts, or Cimmerians came hither. As they took up their abode here, it would seem as though Cimmerian darkness for centuries brooded over this realm. While the people along the shores of the Mediterranean were advancing in civilization, the inhabitants among these Alpine fastnesses were rude and barbarous. History presents this Celtic people to us about a century before the Christian era, under the name of the Helvetians. Cæsar informs us that they were strong and warlike. He speaks of Divico as their bravest chieftain and Orgetorix as their most eloquent advocate. After a while, the Roman legions invaded their territory and subdued them, reducing them to a state of slavery; but at the fall of their empire, fresh tribes from the north came seeking homes among the hills, and becoming ancestors of a patriotic and valorous race. The Burgundians came from the Baltic shores, settling around Lake Geneva and the river Aar; then came the Alamanni from the Main on the Rhine, taking possession of the country about Lake Constance; then came the Ostrogoths from Scandinavia, settling in the Rhætian Alps; and finally came the Franks in large numbers, so that at the end of the sixth century, all Helvetia was subject to Frankish sway. The Franks brought with them the rudiments of their feudal system. Their king must be a feudal sovereign, their judge must be a feudal baron, and their soldier must be a feudal vassal. They were pagans and slaves of superstition. They worshipped the sun, moon, stars, sylphs, and shadowy deities. Just the date when Christianity was introduced among them is unknown. We read of Beatus in the first century, and Lucius in the second, as teachers of the Christian religion in Helvetia. A legend states that in the seventh century, it was introduced to the land in a pure form from Ireland by a disciple of Columba, the illustrious founder of the Scottish monastery in the island of Iona. As evidence of this, the fact is cited that bell-towers originated with this monastery; and, as these are numerous among the memorials between the Rhætian Alps and Cologne, along the banks of the Rhine, it is believed they took their origin from Iona and were introduced here by missionaries.

During the reign of Charlemagne, it is proper to say, this territory was subject to his authority, and was greatly improved during his administration. He lent his influence to encourage agriculture, increase manufactures, and establish schools.

But from the beginning of the ninth to the close of the thirteenth century, this land, for the most part, was groaning under feudal despotism. The castle tyranny weighed heavily upon the masses, and it would seem almost strange that it did not crush out all the hopes and courage of these early Swiss mountaineers. The lords, at times, were cruelly jealous and revengeful, as shown by a legend of Tohenberg, which tells us of Count Henry who had a beautiful wife, named Ida. She one day chanced to lay her wedding ring close to the window of her chamber. A tame raven soon after seizing it, bore it off and dropped it into the street. It was picked up by one of the Count's slaves, who at once put it on his finger. The Count, dis covering it on his menial's hand, accused Ida of infidelity, and then, refusing to hear any explanation, hurled the unfortunate wife from the highest castle window down among the rocks, and then caused the servant to be tied to the switch of a wild horse and dragged to death.

Still, in spite of vassalage and persecution, the fire of patriotism and love of freedom were burning in the hearts of these invincible mountaineers; and, as we sail across the waters of Lake Luzerne, and walk the streets of Altorf, we are reminded of King Albert's reign, and his determination to crush out the seeds of liberty which had begun to germinate among the Alps. Accordingly, he sent from his Austrian home, as the current story relates, two hard-hearted men, Gessler and Beringer, to levy tolls, exact dues, and punish with severity any indications of insubordination. Many a sad tale is rife among the Swiss at this day, showing how they were oppressed by these officers of the king. "Is this to be endured," asked Gessler, as he looked at the new house of a farmer, "that clownish peasants should erect such handsome dwellings?" One day, a man committed some slight offence, and Beringer seized his oxen, remarking, as he unyoked them, that "boors might draw their own ploughs"; and because resistance was offered, the man lost his own eyes. Was it to be supposed that these highland foresters would long endure such treatment? Is it to be wondered that their brave wives asked, "How long shall arrogance triumph, and humility weep? Shall foreigners become masters of the land, and kings of our property? What avails it that our mountains are inhabited by men? Are we mothers to suckle sons doomed to become beggars, and bring up our daughters to be slaves to foreigners? This cannot be." After being moved by such interrogations, no wonder three resolute and patriotic men should meet on the Rutli, and resolve that their land should become free. As they made known their aims to their neighbors, they were encouraged, and on Martinmas eve, 1307, these three men met once more on this trysting meadow, and each was accompanied with ten confederates; and here, under the gracious stars shining propitiously upon grass, lake, and mountain, they solemnly swore to live or die for their beloved land, to resist the oppression of the house of Hapsburg, and expel from their realm the domineering Gessler and Beringer. Soon after this followed the daring episode of William Tell. He was one of the thirty-three who had so solemnly pledged themselves on the Rutli. Gessler, it is related, among other expedients for subduing the Swiss, set up in the market-place of Altorf a pole with Duke Albert's hat fixed on the top, to which all passers-by were required to make obeisance. This act of homage Tell refused to render; and, therefore, followed the merciless sentence of Gessler upon Tell, to shoot an apple, many paces off, from the head of his son. Being successful in this, and because an extra arrow was discovered on his person, he is soon after put in chains and placed in a boat, to be borne across Lake Luzerne and confined in a castle. But a furious storm arose before they had advanced far, and Gessler was frightened, and ordered Tell to be unbound, that he might put his skilled hands to the oars, and, if possible, save the imperilled bark. Complying with the command, the hero guided the boat along shore, and as soon as an opportunity was presented, he leaped upon the solid rocks, leaving his oppressors and associates to battle, as best they could, against the threatening elements. A little chapel now marks the spot where Tell sprang ashore; it is really the Mecca of the Swiss. The place is said to have been consecrated in 1388, by those who had been personally acquainted with the heroic act. On Sunday after Ascension day, may be seen numerous boats coming from all directions, decorated with flags and mottoes, in honor of their brave leader, tending to this chapel, where mass is performed, and a patriotic sermon is preached.

Tradition says, Tell on his liberation climbed over the Axenberg and hastened to the lane leading to Gessler's castle, and there watched the approach of his adversary and shot him dead. On the same day, it is said, a party went to Landenberg where Beringer dwelt, stormed his castle and drove him from the country.

If the stories of these olden times have been criticised and doubted, still it is plain, there must have been some reality for their foundation; for it does not appear possible that mere fables should have gained such credence and produced such national results. At the present day, in all parts of the country, the names of these heroes are dearly cherished. The tales of their adventures are related in the chalets, on diligences, and in cars. Their figures are in churches, and on gables of houses. They are commemorated in the songs and the religious rites of the people. The hearts of the Swiss declare to-day that such cruel tyrants did formerly smite their land, and such brave heroes did once save it. Mere fabrication could not have produced such deep-seated hatred and such profound respect.

As we are crossing Albis, from Zurich to Zug, we notice a stone monument by the wayside where Zwingle fell. Here, again, emotional thoughts crowd the mind. History repeats afresh the story of that famous son who reared in this free mountain air, longed for spiritual, as well as civil, liberty. At length, with a warm heart, a resolute will, and a cultivated mind, in 1516, he stepped forth to proclaim boldly against the sale of indulgences, which was being carried on by Tetzel in Germany, and by Samson in Switzerland. He felt the church was enslaving, as the state never had. It was making money, not repentance, the means of salvation; it was saying, "Let those pass first who have wealth; see, they fly!" pretending that those who bought indulgences could witness the souls of the departed escaping from purgatory to heaven. Catholicism had already gained a strong hold in this land; and as Zwingle began to expose the false dogma of indulgences, fiery opposition expressed itself on every hand. But the reformer, by his logic and eloquence, soon gained a large following on the part of the populace. Most of the cities soon became Protestant, while the highland villages remained Catholic. So the bitterest jealousies sprung up, which at length resulted in wars; and in the battle of Cappel, Zwingle was captured by the Romanists and commanded "to call upon the saints and confess to the priests." As he kept his silence, Feckinger cried out, " Vile heretic !" and plunged his sword into the reformer's throat. As Zwingle fell bleeding, he said, " They may kill the body, they cannot kill the soul." Thus the preacher, the shepherd, and adviser, went out of this world glorified. Now, whenever we visit the place where he fell, and look at the mountains towering majestically above, and enjoy the summer air, we can but feel it is consecrated ground, and fittingly emblematical of a noble character. After the death of Zwingle, the famous Ferel kindled the Protestant fires in the city of Geneva, which soon flamed out and consumed the Roman altars and images there. As his light was reaching its zenith, John Calvin, the most illustrious reformer of all, in point of scholarship and enduring industry, took up his abode in Geneva. He dealt heavy blows against Romanism. Elijah-like he fought for what he believed to be right. His influence soon became potent in his adopted city. By lake and mountain, he created a force which has greatly moved and swayed the Protestant world.

At Basle, Berne, Lausanne, and Luzerne, we learn how the wars of religion continued till 1712, when there came an interregnum of peace. During this period, various forms of republican government were tried in different cantons, or divisions. But from 1792 till the Congress of Vienna in 1815, the Swiss were frequently disturbed by foreign nations, and their country invaded by French and Austrian soldiers. However, for some reason the Swiss were never really conquered, or certainly not subdued. By nature they are strongly fortified, and by nature they are truly heroic. Now, for two-score years and more, they have been prospered, proving to the world that their republic is a success.

Let one enter this land from any quarter for the first time, and he is quite sure to be surprised. The mind and heart cannot keep cool. Every turn brings new scenes to light. He is surprised that the hills are so steep, the mountains so abrupt, the grass so green, and the trees so thrifty. If whirled on by the iron horse, how the shelving rocks, the deep gorges, and the towering cliffs rush together. If penetrating the country by the way of Basle and

Luzerne, it is not long before the train is flying along the shore of Sempach, so renowned for the battle fought on its margin, the 9th of July, 1386, when Arnold von Winkleried threw himself on the lances of the Austrians, and thereby effected the defeat of Leopold II., and established freedom in this part of Switzerland. Leaving this body of water, the Bernese and Oberland Alps present their numerous peaks capped with granite and snow; close to the right is the ragged Pilatus, and to the left, the beautiful Rigi; and soon the train halts in the city of Luzerne, just on the shore of one of the most enchanting lakes of the world. This is a city of considerable importance, and especially noted for its fine and commodious hotels. It is belted on three sides with diversified farming lands. Late into the autumn, vegetation is of the liveliest green. All up the sides of the mountains, plateaus rise one above another. These are dotted with little chalets, and occasionally with clusters of diminutive wooden houses. Strange that human beings should delight to dwell where it would seem to be alone the rightful haunts of the eagle and chamois. The common farm-house here is not likely to satisfy the taste of the American or Englishman, who is accustomed to commodious buildings; for, frequently it serves for both house and barn. Neither will he be likely to admire the compost heaps which are smoking in almost every front yard. These are so placed, it is said, for the health of the inmates; but at times it is severe medicine for the olfactories. The average Swiss home is comfortable, but not neat and well regulated. Little cooking is done in the family; the bread, wine, and beer, are bought ready for the table; the butter and cheese are made high on the mountain-sides, where the goats and cows are pastured. It is plain to be seen that the peasant women do not spend much time at their toilet, or in striving to keep pace with the fashions. It would seem that most of them believe in large styles, as to hats and shoes, wearing broad brims and expanded soles. As these women are seen at work with the men, hoeing, shovelling, mowing, raking, bearing heavy burdens, it is difficult to make this mode of living, by any kind of human logic, just or right. As we witness their brawny, sunburnt faces, and their large, stiff hands, we can but rejoice that the women of our country, as a rule, do not attempt to be men in manual labor. We would say, let them exercise very much in the open air; let them teach; let them trade; let them preach; let them vote, if they will; but never let them be forced to dig potatoes and lug produce to market for a living.

On examining their farming tools, they are not found to be light and finished as to style. Their carts, ploughs, hoes, shovels, and forks, are heavy; and their harrows are made entirely of wood. Their horses, oxen, and cows, are worked on their farms, and usually, each separately.

The art-work of special attraction in Luzerne, is the lion cut into the natural rock in the immediate vicinity of the city, after a model by Thorwaldsen, in honor of twenty-six officers and many soldiers of the Swiss Guards, who were cruelly massacred in defence of the Tuileries, Aug. 10, 1792. The dying lion reclines in a grotto, having his body transfixed by a broken lance, and his paw sheltering a Bourbon lily. It is a natural and imposing work.

A ride of a few miles on a steamer from Luzerne, takes one to Weggis, a little village at the foot of the Rigi, which is the usual starting-place of travellers ascending this mountain from the west. Close by the landing-place is a little saw-mill, which is quite likely to allure the notice of foreign mechanics by the slow strokes of the saw and the method of running back the carriage by hand. As the man in charge is asked, if there are any gang-saws in Switzerland, he is nonplussed. In making little trinkets and filigree work the Swiss may excel, but cannot display great ingenuity in manufacturing on a large scale. They may justly be called cute in using the jack-knife. They are certain to keep doing, until what they do, is well done. Their stone bridges and superior roads are sufficient proof of this. They probably have the best highways in the world, though built over the most difficult places.

In ascending to the summit of the Rigi, which is some six thousand feet above the sea-level, a great variety of flora is to be seen. At the base are apple and cherry trees; higher up are oaks and walnuts; and still higher are pines and spruces. The ledges cropping out are composed of granite and conglomerates. In the summer, the traveller, in ascending or descending, is sure to have his attention arrested by the echo of the Alpine horns, the dingle of the cow-bells, the twittering of birds, the chattering of squirrels, the cawing of crows, and the whistling of hawks. Frequently, he will fall in with monks wearing long faces, and brown-hooded gowns, girdled with hempen cords dragging on the ground, intended to be symbolical of their willingness to suffer death, if need be, for the sake of their religion. At almost every turn in the path are to be seen rude crucifixes and pictures of the Virgin, before which every disciple bows as he passes. If travellers are met who have been favored with fair skies, and splendid sunrises and sunsets, they are sure to be lavish with their praises and almost ready to adore the glories of the Rigi; but, if they have struggled to the top, costing much bone and muscle, or have been transported thither by the power of steam, and then have been shut in by the thickest fog and darkness for twenty-four hours, or more, they will be ready to heap anathemas upon the mountain that has scarcely a rival in the wide world for beauty, serenity, and grandeur of scenery. How much conditions of mind have to do in rendering this world pleasant and satisfying! What surprises one most in this country is the fact of so many deep valleys and lofty heights in so small an area. Even a footman in a day can enjoy a marvellous variety of climate, soil, and surface. To get the most possible out of sight-seeing in this land, the travelling should be mainly done on foot. This is practicable, for hotels so abound along the passes and throughout the country, that one can journey a long, or short, distance during the day and be sure of finding good accommodations at nightfall. Probably no other country is so highly favored with good hotels and pensions as Switzerland. They are quite certain to be well supplied with pleasant rooms, clean beds, good bread, tender meats, rich milk, sweet honey, delicious vegetables, and purest water.

The highways run for the most part through deep valleys and over dizzy heights. It is marvellous that good roads should have been built over the Tyrol, the Splugen, St. Gothard, Mount Cenis, and Simplon Passes, reaching at the highest altitude more than six thousand feet above the sea. To build the Simplon, which is forty-two miles in length, required the labor of three thousand men fourteen years. It has six hundred and eleven bridges, and many thousand feet of arches and terraces. It cost at the rate of twenty-five thousand dollars per mile. Napoleon I. conceived and caused this road to be built. Whatever may have been his motives, the design of it is sublime, and its accomplishment grand. Alexander and the Cæsars performed great deeds; the Assyrians raised lofty towers; the Greeks piled up the Acropolis and Colossus; the Romans constructed the Colosseum and the Appian Way; but Napoleon did a nobler work than all these in opening a highway for the nations over Alpine heights.

The waterfalls of the Alps are among the

striking attractions to the traveller. He can but have feelings of awe, as he stands before the lower Reichenbach and gazes at the water as it pitches down more than a hundred feet into a yawning abyss of boiling, rushing, leaping currents. At the upper Reichenbach he cannot fail to experience sublime emotions, as he witnesses a large body of water breaking over the brink and descending two hundred feet without interruption, and disappearing among the gorges below. He will be filled with delight as he looks upon the Giesbach Falls, being so completely invested with the brightest emerald colors, as the water comes sparkling and springing down the steep rocks for many hundred feet. In the sunlight these falls are constantly arched with countless rainbows. As he comes to the Staubbach Falls, if he is a lover of nature, he will be enchanted, as he looks at these in the clear noonday light. High over a shelving rock, aqueous currents fall thick and fast, separating at length into silvery trails, and finally dissolving into sparkling mist. While he sits on the green lawn, admiring the watery lace-work of Staubbach, as he chances to peer on and to the south, lo! there stands out in boldest relief against the dark sky, frowning Jungfrau, hurling from his lofty crest avalanches of snow into the depths, hiding with its frosty vapors the rugged rocks below. As he marks the contrast, he can but feel, here is the most perfect illustration of beauty, there of sublimity; this soothes, that overpowers; this speaks of God's tenderest love, that of his almighty power.

Glacial action is to be seen almost everywhere among the Alps, even where no glaciers now exist. At the present they number some six hundred, covering a surface of nine hundred square miles, giving rise to several of the largest rivers in Europe. They are, no doubt, the leading wonders among these lofty mountains. Perhaps, the most favorable view-point for surveying some of these gigantic agencies, is from the summit of Montanvert. Here we take our stand eight thousand feet above the valley of Chamouni, whose village is under the shadows of glaciers. We catch fine glimpses, as we stand here, of Mont Blanc towering so kingly above hundreds of lofty mountains. Watching as the flying clouds part, we behold almost fairy-like scenes. One moment a silvery or golden crown rests upon its brow, or at another we are reminded of a magnificent rose nodding and swaying in the wind. At one instant we seem to be in the most profound silence; in the next we discover far above us a wake, and then vast folds of fleecy smoke, and soon peals out the thunder of a tremendous avalanche. As we are held spellbound and wondering, we can but ask, why do not the constantly accumulating snows pile themselves high out of the reach of mortal ken? But science comes to our relief, saying that the force of gravity is incessantly drawing them from their volatile regions, and before they have descended five thousand feet, they are converted into solid ice.

Not far from us, but a little farther on, is the Jardin, a green oasis in the midst of eternal snows. Here the gazelle and antelope may be seen leaping from rock to rock; and just under the drippings of avalanches may be plucked violets, daisies, and buttercups at nearly all seasons of the year. How do we account for this garden in the presence of abiding snows? On examination it is found to be so situated as to catch the reflected sunlight on all sides, thereby waking up green mosses and delicate flowers the year round.

As we turn in another direction, we can see three wide-spreading glaciers crowding and grinding down through the gorges into the valleys. The nearest one is the Mer de Glace, being some twelve miles in length and three in width. Looking off upon the surface, we are reminded of a lake's being frozen over while the waves are swelling and throwing spray. Its depth we cannot sound; undoubtedly in places it is a thousand feet in thickness. Every few moments a deep resonance vibrates from some quarter, giving assurance that the vast body of ice is in motion. Now as we attempt to cross it, no difficulty appears to be in the way; still we do not advance far before we find the undertaking hazardous. An innumerable number of seams and yawnings beset us on every side; some of them a little child could easily step across, while others are sufficiently large to swallow up a long train of cars. We are obliged to select our course with caution and courage. Now and then, we must cross ridges so narrow that the least mishap would precipitate us down, down, we can scarcely guess where, or how deep.

In some of these gulfs, and also above the general surface, may be seen massive bowlders which have been broken off and brought from the solid rocks, high up the mountain-sides. Frequently travellers lose their lives in their adventures upon this uncertain sea.

Taking advantage of a favorable opportunity, we descend into one of these chasms. When fifty feet below the surface, as the sunlight plays through the crystal mirror, a strange mingling of indescribable colors greets the eye. Topaz, ruby, amethyst, and sapphire, blend so as to reflect celestial coloring. Descending towards the valley, the openings grow broader and deeper, until the ice is divided into transparent stalagmites and the grandest pyramids which are constantly falling in pieces and unloosing huge bowlders from their wintry chains, while beneath roars and plunges into the valley below a turbid river. Observing the glacier at its terminus, we cannot doubt that it is incessantly in motion; for it would recede, or cease to break in pieces, were it not descending all the while.

The Alps are now lofty, but we can readily understand how this glacier with hundreds of others in the ages to come, will grind them down, and the rivers will bear them on to the seas. Still now it would seem, no other land can be so crowded with the beautiful, the picturesque, and the sublime, as Switzerland. It has treasures for the soul of more than fairy things. The granite pinnacles, so tall, so exquisitely traced; the glistening columns of whitest snow; the azure-tinted glaciers; the deep, sunny vales; the evergreen-mantled hills;

the silvery lakes; the leaping rills; the roaring cataracts; the crash of avalanches; the aurora of the morning; the glow of the evening; all these and inexpressibly more, will long continue to offer real pictures to the painter, ideal inspiration to the poet, and sublimest conceptions to the scholar.

The most classic spots of this marvellous country, are about Lake Leman. Looking upon its waters now in the summer time, one can scarcely guess that it was once unruffled by the boatman's oar and the wheel of the steamship; that the trout and whitefish ruled supreme in its waters; that its shores were desolate wastes, and haunts only of bears, wolves, and chamois. He can hardly realize now that it was formerly thus, as he sees numerous boats skimming its surface, and heavy steamers ploughing its depths, while its shores are fringed with a great variety of vegetation, and speckled with attractive villages. It is singular why its waters should look so cerulean, and in places when the weather is fair, why its surface should be elevated several feet, and thus remain for some time before subsiding; and why this phenomenon should occur oftener in the night than in the day. Science, as yet, has not been able to solve the mystery.

Around the shores of this lake, when Rome was mistress of the world, dwelt the heroic Helvetians who delighted to follow the commands of the brave Divico, and be most attentive to the eloquent words of Orgetorix. Here Cæsar's legions fought against them in bloody battles; here Cæcina was unmerciful to the vanquished, and spurned the earnest entreaties of Alpinula to spare the life of her noble father. In later times courageous men were more successful in wrenching it from the hands of tyrants, causing it to blossom with freedom and prosperity. Here Calvin struck heavy blows in behalf of the Reformation; here Madame de Staël developed her exalted womanhood; here Byron found a muse to sing some of his sweetest carols; and here Gibbon rounded his periods and gave the finishing touches to his word-pictures of Rome.

At the lower end of the lake stands the city of Geneva. It combines the old and the new; broad thoroughfares and narrow streets; spacious buildings and huddled houses; beauty of style and quaintness of form. The centre of attraction in the old city is its cathedral in which John Calvin used to preach. The canopy over the pulpit is the same as when the great reformer stood under it. The building itself dates as far back as 1024. What associations cluster around this structure! What a power Calvin sent forth from it into the world! He dared to do what he felt to be right. Though his doctrines may not be accepted, yet the man can but be honored. The college of Geneva was founded by him, which has added not a little to the character of the city. Its curriculum now embraces nine courses of study. It has some twenty-five professors connected with it, and a library of sixty thousand volumes with all the writings of Calvin, carefully preserved. It has a museum containing a valuable collection of animals and minerals. This is very systematically arranged, showing the regular gradation from the inorganic to the organic, from the lowest to the highest forms of life. In the Botanic Garden, overhung by the walls of the city on one side, and by a grove of stately elms on the other, there is manifested the same system as in the museum.

Rousseau's Garden which stands quite in the current of the Rhone on leaving the lake, is a favorite spot to the Genevese. They delight to visit the place where the author of "Abelard" and "The Confessions," used to spend much of his leisure time. It is now graced with a fair statue of their honored citizen.

The people here are deeply interested in the

cause of education. They believe in having good schools for all classes, and furnish the best advantages for studying French and German. For this reason, and because of the healthfulness of the city, many students come here from abroad to pursue these languages.

The Genevese are a busy people. Idlers are scarce in the streets or public places. Thousands of men and women are engaged in manufacturing watches, pocket-knives, and silk fabrics. Many of the shops and stores present a rich display of jewelry and silks.

In the time of the Reformation, Geneva was a refuge for the oppressed and persecuted. During that period a new translation of the Bible was brought out here. Then the city was strongly Protestant; now nearly half of the population is Catholic. Whatever sect may control this city, it is bound to be famous, because of its beauty of scenery and richness of association. It will be sought after, being the birthplace of Bossuet and Saussure as naturalists; DeCandolle and Boissier as botanists; Riva and Pictet as philosophers; Sismondi and Madame de Staël as historians. These characters alone are sufficient to render a city forever memorable.

Along the shore of the lake for miles are

rich fields and pleasant chateaus. Studying the natural attractions of land, water, and sky about the little village of Coppet, three leagues from Geneva, one can readily understand why Madame de Staël should have chosen a home here, while doing her best work, as an author. Here she lived and enjoyed the influence of her father Necker, the distinguished financier and minister of Louis XVI. On the walls of the ancient chateau still hang the portraits of father and daughter. Here remains her study still furnished with the books of her choice, and the table on which she wrote some of her imperishable works. A short distance from the house is the chapel in which rest the ashes of Necker and Madame de Staël in the midst of a thick beech grove encompassed by a strong wall. How beauty of scenery is enhanced by nobility of soul!

At Lausanne, which stands on ground rising abruptly from the shore of the lake, Gibbon caught inspiration, as he sat in the open air, beholding the wondrous picture which the Great Artist had spread out, enabling him to round his periods and complete his great history of Rome. Since that event Lausanne has been a favorite resort of literary pilgrims to this land. Does not this show, however exalted the natural may be, it is possible for the mental and spiritual to crown it with still brighter glories?

Near the upper end of the lake, rises above the water the Castle of Chillon. It was built in the thirteenth century to command the pass of the mountains from Valais to Vaud. It is an enormous structure of stone and stucco, surmounted with a half-dozen Gothic towers. Tradition and history tell us this has been the seat of the direst cruelty and bloodshed. Here Bonnivard, the patriot and native of Geneva, because he espoused the cause of his republican city and defended its rights, was imprisoned by the Duke of Savoy. Here for six dreary years he was chained in a damp dungeon to a stone column which now bears record of the awful deed. The grooves are evident where his bare feet wore into the solid rock as he paced back and forth the length of his four-foot chain.

> " Let none these marks efface;
> For they appeal from tyranny to God."

If Bonnivard could endure all this, why need any be crushed by trials, or burdens? If he could hope for deliverance, why should any despair of freedom? In 1536 his shackles were broken from his limbs by patriotic soldiers of his native city, and he went forth doing his best for liberty of conscience and religious freedom. His was a noble and consecrated life. His name will be lovingly spoken when the last vestige of the old castle shall have fallen beneath the waves. No longer does it rise above the waters of Lake Leman like a giant of tyranny, but as a sentinel of peace, bearing aloft the motto, " Liberti et Patriæ."

Berne is the capital of Switzerland, situated on the brow of a hill coiled about by the river Aar. It commands extensive views in the distance of the Oberland and Bernese Alps. The scenery from it in all directions, is enchanting and picturesque. It is true, these distant views of the Alps are not so exciting as the nearer, still they do lend to the mind a subdued and hallowing influence which, no doubt, blesses quite as long.

The streets of Berne are curious and unique, yes, odd and grotesque, bordered with architecture of the drollest and strangest designs. Along the principal highways the houses are built on arcades after the Italian style. The bears, and clock towers with their ugly pictures and ludicrous carvings, are objects of great attraction. The bear is the pet of the old and young. Nearly everybody of this city has a bear about him of some description, painted, stamped, or sculptured. The Bernese are decidedly *bearish*.

The numerous and copious fountains in the squares and at the corners of the streets, are designed, it would appear, to excite laughter. One represents an ogre in the act of devouring a child, while his pockets are full of children ready for future consumption. Below this figure is a group of bears dressed in full armor.

The city has three clock towers which are curious and attractive. One of them is sure to allure the attention of the natives, as well as foreigners. At every striking of the clock a marvellous exhibition takes place; a cock comes out, claps his wings and crows twice before, and once after the striking of the hour; then the figure of Time turns an hour-glass and keeps time with the clock-hammer by opening its mouth and swinging its scythe; while at the same time a troop of bears dance a jig. In honor of the founder of the city, several fine specimens of living bears are kept in gorgeous style at public expense. The Bernese appear almost to worship Bruin, while the Genevese adore the stork, and Luzerne reverences the lion, and other Swiss cities cherish their favorite guardian animals.

The principal building of Berne is the

cathedral, a Gothic structure of the fifteenth century. One on entering it will scarcely fail to notice the sculptures of the Last Judgment, over the main door-way, — an illustration of mediæval theology, showing the mistaken notions of Scriptural subjects then prevalent, and what the demand was for a higher order of interpretation and spirituality. The carving in the choir, and the painted windows, are remarkable works for the age in which they were produced.

The college of Berne compares well with the colleges of Geneva and Lausanne, the universities of Basle and Zurich. Its citizens manifest generally a deep interest in the cause of education. Their library of thirty-five thousand volumes, their museum of natural history, and their public-school system, afford evidence of this. Their charitable institutions are of a high order. The Bernese are fond of festive gatherings. So, in this canton, as well as in most of the others, they have their annual gatherings at which they display their characteristic costumes, manners, and habits, exhibiting their skill in archery, rifle-shooting, wrestling, and various other games. Their festive scenes are unique and unlike those of any other country.

The Swiss are a religious people, being divided into three fifths Protestants, and two fifths

Catholics. The former are still separated into Calvinists, Baptists, and Wesleyans. The religious thought is liberal and advancing. While travelling, as we observe the religious tendencies, we must be hopeful, and be impressed with the feeling of a divine cause at work for the amelioration and security of the race. As we witness the hosts moved by thought and will, and yet somehow in spite of themselves, thwarted in the wrong, and encouraged in the right, we can but recognize a Supreme Being and loving Father who is directing and controlling in the physical and spiritual realms.

On leaving this land our last reflections are quite certain to be centred upon its unsurpassed scenery which is sure to affect the mind and heart, as its works of art and forms of society cannot. In Switzerland we are meeting incessantly with the things that artists delight to paint, and poets to praise; the green valleys, the flower-bordered streams, the evergreen hills, the granite shafts, the snow-crowned peaks, and the profound solitudes in the depths below and on the heights above, — all these, and ten thousand more, come sweeping before the eye, as we ramble or muse in this land of beauty, sublimity, and grandeur.

VII.

FLORENCE, THE ART CITY.

THE love of beauty is inherent in man. The Sacred Record first presents him to the world in the Garden of Eden. This implies that he had a natural fondness for nature, and would delight in the beautiful. So has it ever been. David sung of the "green pastures" and the "still waters"; Homer was charmed with the muse from the vale and the mountain; Virgil was inspired by the land and sea; Jesus admired the lily and the sparrow. Man has been wont to seek picturesque places in which to dwell. Accordingly the Romans before the Christian era, had established considerable of a town where Florence now is, which they named Florentia, signifying it abounded in flowers and natural beauties. It is certain nature has lavished upon it munificent gifts. Mountains and valleys, hills and vales, forests and water, so commingle as to form an enchanting picture. The Apennines sweep round the east and north, rising some three thousand feet. The Tuscan Highlands press up from the south and west. The summits are bared and hoary; the sides far up are flecked with forest trees; the spurs and flanks are skirted with vineyards and olive orchards; while the extended and diversified valley in the centre, is cut in twain by the Arno, and dotted all round with eight thousand villas, having the city for a centre-piece, like a diamond in the midst of mosaics of emerald and quartz.

Standing on the heights of Fiesole, one has spread out before and around him, as inviting and enjoyable a landscape as can anywhere be found. If Rome can justly be called the sublime city; Venice, the romantic city; Naples, the pleasant city; Genoa, the mercantile city; Bologna, the musical city; Florence can properly be styled the beautiful city.

Leaving the high grounds and entering the city, we find the streets narrow and the buildings substantial, but almost destitute of ornaments. In fact, as we walk the highways and observe the grated windows and the solid masonry, we are quite inclined to feel that we are either in the midst of strong fortifications, or surrounded by numerous prisons. From the lowest to the highest story we discover little ornamentation; even the palaces have scarcely any adornment. We are naturally inclined to ask, why should this city be so shorn of beautiful finish? On examination this becomes evident.

History informs us that Florence has been subject to the severest vicissitudes; storm and sunshine, war and peace, have followed one another in quick succession. In the sixth century she was destroyed; in the eighth, was rebuilt; in the tenth, became a republic; in the fourteenth, was brought under the Catholic control; in the sixteenth, lost her freedom and did not regain her liberty till the present century. Her struggles with the Goths and Huns were terrible before she was overcome. After this subjection, followed the long centuries of strife between the nobility and the peasantry. The former could be safe only as they fortified themselves within the strongest walls. Had they decorated their buildings externally, they would have been soon defaced. So they looked out for strength and durability.

No other city of Italy has had, perhaps, so many riotous uprisings and drawbacks as Florence, yet she has continued to advance, till now she ranks as the leading art city of the world. By no means was she the first town of Italy to become interested in the fine arts. In fact she was among the last. Not until the renascent period did she turn her attention to works of art.

Rome, Ravenna, Pavia, Verona, and Pisa, in mediæval times, had become devoted to drafting, architecture, and sculpture; particularly was this true of Pisa, a sister city situated upon the Arno. Though a dead city now, it was, in the tenth and twelfth centuries, truly alive. Then her liberties astonished Italy, and her commerce was a marvel to the world; then her ships bore triumphant crusaders to Asia, and brought back gold, purple, and ivory; then pirates dreaded her gleaming lances upon the sea; then she built Campo Santo; John was its architect, Nicholas its sculptor, Giotto its painter. The kings of Judæa, the Pharaohs of Egypt, the Cæsars of Rome, the satraps of Oriental lands, had reared splendid monuments to hold their ashes and perpetuate their fame; but none of them had equalled in beauty this city of the dead. She stands as the last sad poem of the Middle Ages, or the final dirge of that dark period which was to give place to brighter and happier scenes. At that time Florence was enjoying her fullest freedom. Some of her citizens had become merchant princes. As the mantle fell from Pisa, she was prepared to take it up and put it on. Her wealthy citizens were becoming patrons of art, and were desirous that their city should become graced with enduring monuments. So, such inducements were offered as to bring some of the best artists of Pisa and other cities to live and work in Florence. At length their city was adorned with the Duomo, the Baptistry, and the Campanile, surpassing those of Pisa. These are grand structures at the present day. The dome of the cathedral is said to be the largest one in the world. The bronze doors of the Baptistry, are covered with reliefs representing Bible history. We can but examine them with admiration, when we consider the age in which they were produced, and not think strange that Michael Angelo should have said of them, "They are worthy to become the gates of Paradise." Of course the Duomo will not compare favorably, externally, with that of Milan, or internally, with St. Peter's. The latter are the outcome of the former, in part, at least; or I think we may say with truth, the last would not have been what they are, had it not been for the first. Still, if we would not be disappointed, we should visit the buildings of this city for their history, not their beauty; they should be studied, not simply looked at. However, many of the villas taken with their surroundings, are attractive and beautiful; but for the most part we search these old cities more for history than any outward expression, and so, frequently we find the ugliest places the most inviting.

In this city of a hundred and seventy thousand inhabitants, no spots are more inviting than those where some of her greatest heroes lived, wrought, and died.

The place, likely to be sought first, is the house of Michael Angelo who is to art, what Shakespeare is to literature. As we come to the humble house where he lived, we cannot easily refrain from deep emotions and serious reflections. It is natural to recall, how he early exhibited a daring spirit and signs of real genius; how at seventeen he surpassed in invention his teachers. If we have stood under the dome of St. Peter's and the frescoes of the Sistine Chapel, we can realize how it would have been difficult to teach that mind which could conceive and produce such works. Greatness of conception as a thinker, and greatness of style as an artist, render him almost peerless among peers. His deeds indue the old with sanctity and enchantment. Places which have known him, are replete with history; and history gives value to the very stones and dust which the great man touched. The old house has changed exceedingly since Angelo left it. Thus it is with matter, but not so with mind. Angelo has grown with the ages, and will continue to grow through the centuries to come. His ashes rest in a beautiful tomb in Santa Croce, but he lives in his works. How could it be otherwise? Leonardo and Raphael stood before them with admiration. Millions of hearts have caught inspiration from them: such results are blessed and pay the greatest possible reward to man. Immortal honor, but justly due to the world's greatest architect, sculptor, and painter!

Somewhere among the clustered houses Dante had his birth in 1265. It matters but little, if we cannot find just the spot, for it was in this delightful valley that he first looked out upon mortal things. It is a fit place for a poet to be born. It is full of changing beauty and sublimity. Somehow great geniuses have always found their way into this world where nature offers decided variety of scenery. The plain and desert have seldom been propitious to the poet and scholar. Here by the banks of the Arno, or on the mountain's brow, Dante found his muse that breathed into his soul the marvellous religious song of the Middle Ages. Judæa had sent forth David as the sweet singer of Israel; Greece had found a heroic bard in Homer; now Italy would have the sweetest notes drop from her lyre, and Dante is the chosen one to touch the chords. So far, these were the world's three great poets: each the greatest in his way; each singing what he felt to be truest.

Dante's youth was cheery, and favored with the best advantages of the times. But as he began to mingle in public affairs, his way became devious and thorny. His sense of duty bid him, go not with the majority. He avowed himself a Bianchi, and opposed to the Neri. On this account he was banished from his beloved city. This together with disappointed love, suffused his heart with deepest sorrow; and his countenance ever after wore the expression of angelic sadness; but out of this stricken condition at length came his " La Divina Commedia." We cannot understand, why it is, nevertheless it is true, that the highest conceptions, the clearest visions, the noblest thoughts, have been born out of tribulation and sorrow. Possibly temporal prosperity is not favorable to spiritual life and growth. Dante's pen paints the most vivid pictures of the "Inferno," "Purgatorio," and "Paradiso." No artist could be more faithful to his own ideal. We may criticise his thought as best we can, still we must allow that his poem is a marvellous production. It has served to stir the very depths of souls. Great effects come only of great causes.

Long silence had brooded over the Latin song. Some twelve centuries had elapsed since the lyres of Horace and Virgil had been laid aside. The Latin language had ceased to be spoken; and now far down in the Christian age, Dante in the Italian tongue, takes up the refrain, singing a new song to go down through the ages.

Some have said, if it had not been for prophet, Grecian bard, Latin poet, Dante never could have produced such a poem. Very likely; so we may say of Shakespeare, Tennyson, and Whittier, that they would not be what they are, had it not been for Dante and the hosts that went on before. Every stream that has flowed from the mountains of thought, has helped swell the river of life to its present fulness.

Dante died and was buried in Ravenna. In Santa Croce has been erected a monument to his memory. The Florentines have done their best to secure his mortal remains, and so have them interred in their city, but to no purpose.

The magistrates of Florence proposed in his last years that he should return, on condition of apologizing and paying a fine. His magnanimous reply was, "If I cannot return without calling myself guilty, I shall never return." He never did return, and so sealed his life with the fullest assurance that he was right; but "ungrateful Florence" has confessed her wrong by doing her utmost to bring back his mortal remains to his native city. If he died poor and oppressed, he made a record always to live. When Florence that doomed him to be burnt alive, wheresoever caught, shall have crumbled into dust, the name of Dante will be undimmed and revered by the scholar and Christian.

Go now to the Piazza del Granduca. This is a large square, surrounded on three sides by old buildings, and on the fourth with a frowning palace which was built four centuries ago. Close by it stands Angelo's colossal statue of David, triumphant in his youthful beauty; beyond this is a hideous fountain where once stood the *Tribune*, which was wont to ring with the eloquence of a free people. Not far off is the equestrian statue of Cosmo, the founder of the Medicean family. In another part under an open arcade are grouped many statues; some of them of superior merit.

Here it was in this square on the 23d of May, 1498, a riotous mob rushed together, that they might witness the death of Savonarola:

and why? Because before Luther's day, he had publicly exposed the corruptions of the priests and the Romish Church. From his dungeon of torture, as he was led forth, a roar of vengeance went up from the crowd, "Put him to death"; at the same time prayers went up from loving hearts, beseeching God to sustain the good man. The priest in charge said, "I separate thee from the church militant." "But," responded the dying man with the look of an angel, "thou canst not separate me from the church triumphant." Then they hanged him and burned his body in this very square. So the eloquent orator, the earnest teacher, and noble martyr, went out of this world; but his light was not extinguished; the truth he had uttered was not destroyed; his vile persecutors who put him to death, are forgotten, but the name of Savonarola is immortal.

Some two miles from the city proper, upon a high hill, stands a brick and stone structure showing the wear of centuries; really the stern hand of time has left many a scar upon its walls. From the hill, and, especially, from the tower, or observatory, there is an extensive outlook over one of the finest landscapes anywhere to be found. Though nature has thrown around this height such unsurpassed beauty and magnificence, still it has other and greater attractions; for here it was that a noble mind thought, studied, and looked through the first telescope into the night heavens, and then solved some of the grandest mysteries. Here and then it was that the Ptolemaic system of astronomy was dethroned, and the planetary system established. Here it was that the milky way was discovered to be made up of an inumerable number of fixed stars. I need scarcely say, this is the house where Galileo lived for years, watching and studying the phenomena of the heavens. As we mount the observatory, we can see where his telescope stood, — that first telescope, and made by his own hands. Just under the place of lookout is the studio in which the great man solved so many difficult problems; here are to be seen his chair, table, and plotting instruments, very much as he left them. Here, no doubt, he wrote his dialogues on the Ptolemaic and Copernican systems for which he was summoned to Rome, his book ordered to be burned, and he was sentenced to be imprisoned, in order to make recantation of his errors, and by way of penance, to recite once a week the seven penitential psalms. To regain his liberty, he was forced by inquisitorial authority on his knees to say, "I abjure, curse, and detest the heresy that the earth moves round the sun, and swear that for the future I will never say or assert anything which can raise a similar suspicion against me." Rising from his knees, he is said to have whispered to a friend, "It moves for all that." Regaining his liberty, he returned to this house where he continued his observations, till he became blind from intense application, and here he died in 1642, at the age of seventy-eight years, having greatly enriched the world by his productions. His "Mathematical Discourses and Demonstrations," his "Treatise on the Mundane Sphere," and many other works, are still studied by the scholar and thinker. Truth is sure to endure; error is certain to fail. Galileo's name to-day is the synonyme throughout the civilized world of genius, investigator, revealer of scientific truth and lover of humanity. His remains are entombed in Santa Croce, the Westminster Abbey of his adopted city.

Angelo, Dante, Savonarola, and Galileo, were all Protestants and republicans. This is a significant fact, when we consider the epochs in which they lived. While Florence enjoyed true freedom, she continued to flourish; but as she lost her liberty in the sixteenth century, blight came upon her, and great men ceased to be born to her. Then priestcraft multiplied its power, all the while sapping her very vitals. Thus she was languishing, till the present century, when Cavour and Garibaldi were raised up, it would seem, on purpose to rescue Italy from utter ruin and redeem her perishing cities. These heroes so roused the people that they wrenched the iron grasp of priestcraft from the land, and virtually restored a democratic form of government. Then it was, Florence took a new start, becoming for years the capital of Italy. Prosperity smiled anew upon the city; her arts were revived; her natural and artificial advantages were so improved as to become most attractive to seekers after art and beauty. Her galleries and museums were rearranged and enlarged; her Uffizi and Pitti became the galleries of Europe; and Florence was acknowledged the art city of the world.

We cannot say much in favor of the buildings containing these works. The halls and rooms are not equal to the demands; they come far short of doing justice to the paintings and sculptures. However, the piazza of the Uffizi looks very imposing, adorned with its numerous statues of distinguished Tuscans; among them we find Cosmo and Lorenzo de Medici, for statesmen; Dante, Petrarch, Boccaccio, Machiavelli, Guicciardini, for men of letters; Giotto, Orcagna, Nicholas, Angelo, Leonardo da Vinci, Cellini,

Donatello, for artists; and Galileo as the astronomer. Its works within are considered the most choice and varied of any gallery. Entering the Tribune, and as we look at the marbles and then at the pictures, we are ready to say, unsurpassed. Here is the Venus de Medici which Lord Byron said, "enchants the world." This is certainly true, if it is the sensual eye alone that is to be enchanted; for nothing of human shape was ever conceived more lovely than that sainted face, the placid forehead, the delicately refined nose, the serious mouth all ready to break into a smile, the delicate hand, the graceful arm, the yielding lines and touching beauties of the whole figure. Yes, there she stands in the attitude of gentle alarm and perfect modesty. A seraph in form cannot be any more beautiful. Surely the mind that conceived such beauty, was working for immortality. On the walls above are Raphael's "Madonna del Pozzo," " St. John in the Desert"; Titian's "Venus"; Leonardo da Vinci's "Adoration of the kings"; Rubens' "Hercules between Vice and Virtue"; and some twenty other pictures of the old masters. Of all the many rooms in the gallery, this is the one where the cultured in æsthetic art are certain to linger. Here such must catch new inspiration and thoughts of the beautiful and the spiritual.

The Pitti Gallery is very rich and extensive, containing many of the best works of Angelo, Titian, Salvator Rosa, Andrea del Sarto, Murillo, Rubens, and Raphael's celebrated "Madonna della Seggiola." The last one is sufficient to render the gallery famous. This is the sweetest of all the great artist's Madonnas; it is the expression of unsophisticated nature; as you look at it, life fresh from the divine hand seems to speak of purity, virtue, grace, innocence, spiritual charms. It is worthy to be greatly admired and extensively copied, and its beauty and influence scattered to the uttermost parts of the earth. It is a prophecy, a poem, a revelation from the All-Perfect to help perfect man. So it is not in vain that artists have labored. Theirs is a high calling, as well as that of apostle, or philosopher.

No doubt, these galleries have had not a little to do in moulding the habits and characters of the people of Florence, who exhibit refinement of manner and language which are manifest in all ranks. In fact they are deeply interested from the highest to the lowest in the fine arts, and lend their influence in every way to promote them, requiring their elements to be taught in their schools. Art and mental culture are not antagonistic, but coöperative. This truth should be felt and put into general practice. It ought to be emphasized in our own land. It is true we have done something in the way of laying out parks, cultivating gardens, beautifying cemeteries, building fine houses, and decorating hall and church.

It is said that Michael Angelo once visited Raphael's studio in his absence, and under one of his early and modest efforts, drew a heavy line, writing, "Amplius." Raphael on his return recognized that to be the criticism of Angelo, and he felt it was just; he took courage and pressed on till he became master of his calling. So we, Americans, have done enough in the line of art to give us courage to press on, and at no distant day we may feel assured that we shall have an American school of art, not inferior to the best on the other side of the Atlantic. Already we have sculptors, painters, and architects, whose names we can speak with satisfaction. Our Powers, Rogers, Story, Hosmer, as sculptors; Bierstadt, Brown, and Cooper, as painters; and others, are doing honor to our country by their works. They will bear favorable comparison with the artists of any other land. But have we appreciated them as we should? Are we cultivating the æsthetic natures of the young in our schools as we ought? Beauty has value, as well as the dollar. Ideality should not be weighed down by avarice. True culture will bless our rising generations more than mere bank stock or railroad shares.

There are many public out-door places of interest in Florence. The Boboli Gardens, named from a family that once lived in the vicinity, are considerably diversified as to surface, and are cut up into walks and drives ornamented with arbors of flowers, fountains, and statuary, so as to be very inviting to lovers of the beautiful. Joining these is the Botanic Garden which is famous for its rare plants.

The Cascine Park is the resort for those who would make a display of equestrian and fashionable equipages. It is the St. Cloud, or Hyde Park, of Florence. Here the people spend much time in driving and promenading. They hold fine horses and elegant carriages, as well as silk dresses and broadcloth coats, in high estimation. The laboring classes, as a rule, are industrious. Hands are usually busy, whether cutting the marble, setting mosaics, spinning silk, trimming vines, spading the garden, or sweeping the streets. They are obliged to be active in order to gain the necessaries of life, for living is dear, and taxes exorbitant. Since the capital was transferred to Rome, the city financially has been severely depressed. The change in a monetary sense was a great misfortune to Florence, though a good fortune to Rome. However, in a moral aspect, it may be right the reverse, as has often been the case with individuals, cities, and nations.

Just outside of the city wall on the east is a little acre of ground which cannot be easily forgotten by Americans and Englishmen; it is the English Cemetery. Now it is thickly sown with graves; many of them being the final resting-place of those who sought Florence for the sake of art, or health. The stones bear record of many familiar towns and cities in our own country. Here is the grave of Theodore Parker. It is marked by a plain marble slab with the inscription, "Theodore Parker, born at Lexington, Massachusetts, United States of America, August 24th, 1810. Died at Florence, May 10th, 1860." Though we may not accept Mr. Parker's theology in full, still we can but cherish deep feelings of respect for one who made himself a distinguished scholar, and proved himself a true philanthropist.

Another grave which must be very dear to every lover of poetry, is that of Mrs. Elizabeth Barrett Browning, who with the heart of woman, united the learning of the scholar to the genius of the poet. Over her grave is a monumental urn having upon one side her full-sized profile, and on the other, unstrung harps of exquisite designs. She passed on into the "beautiful light," beloved and lamented.

Another green mound that must seem peculiarly dear to every American, is that one containing the mortal remains of Hiram Powers. He was born in America, and was always a true American, though he lived and worked many years in a foreign land. He really possessed a genius of a high order. This early began to express itself, even while he was a boy among the green hills of his native Vermont. But his was a genius directed by moral power; so that while he lived, it kept blossoming into higher and higher conditions. All who have looked upon his "Greek Slave," or his "Christ," must feel that heaven bestowed upon him special gifts. His art expresses more than the sensuous. His marbles seem to be the embodiment of living souls; at least, they speak of the spiritual. So his works are destined to live. Whether his "Eve," "United States," " Washington," "California," '" La Penserosa," and many others, grace hall or square, they are certain to impart a benign influence; they will always breathe of high possibilities to faithful and aspiring souls.

In 1805 Hiram Powers came into this world amidst poverty and difficulties, but by his own efforts and the help of God he made life a grand success. In Cincinnati where he toiled in the museum; in Washington where he moulded clay so successfully; and in Florence where he created his models and gave the final touches to his statues, he will still be known as one faithful to God and man. Florence is glad to claim him as her inhabitant, and America is rejoiced to own him as her son. If his ashes shall serve to nourish and render more beautiful the grass and flowers of a foreign land, his life will continue to feed and beautify countless souls of his own beloved America, proving that man, noble and exalted, — that epitome of creation, that mind subject to the laws of the universe, that vegetable which connot live without air, light, and water, that animal born to be nourished like other mammalia, that microcosm whose crown is arched like the vault of heaven and whose eye kindles brighter than the stars, that being little lower than the seraphs and above all other mortals, — cannot die, but as poet, musician, artist, philosopher, scholar, or faithful servant of the Most High, is sure to live in the hearts of men and angels.

VIII.

MODERN AND ANCIENT ROME.

IN nearly the same latitude as Boston and some five thousand miles to the eastward is situated the Eternal City. It stands in the centre of undulating prairie lands, spreading out in all directions. Far away to the north are the Etrurian Hills and Sabine Mountains; to the east, the Apennines; to the south, the Alban Hills; and to the west, the Mediterranean Sea. These lands are somewhat diversified with swelling downs and woodless ravines, with grassy plats and miry bogs, with crooked streams and sandy knolls, with ancient ruins and scattered buildings.

The mountains vary from one thousand to five thousand feet in height. Their summits are bald and white; their sides are green with grass, or spotted with pine, chestnut, olive, or mulberry trees. At their bases are situated several villages of historical note. In some of these there are costly villas and elegant works of art. But the Campagna generally, is uncultivated and desolate. It is singular, it should be so, for the soil is rich and arable; still report and superstition affirm, it is unhealthy and poisoned with malaria. No doubt, the hand of industry and fortitude could change these waste places into innoxious and fruitful fields. Were it possible, I imagine American enterprise would delight to make the experiment, and I am sure, it would prove a success; so that no longer would it be poor pasturage for flocks of goats, and herds of white oxen, but would smile with fields of wheat and clover.

The city is supplied with water from the Alban Lake some twelve miles distant, and is carried in a stone aqueduct resting on heavy piers, and so adjusted as to have a gradual descent from the lake to the city. It presents a grand appearance stretching across the wide plain.

The river Tiber plays an important part, as it coils its way through the upper portion of the Campagna. Though song and story have clothed this river with fascinating charms, yet the real is almost certain to detract somewhat from the ideal. It resembles a good-sized brook in our land just after a heavy shower, washing in sand, mud, and clay, enough to make its waters thick and yellow with sediment. No wonder Virgil christened it *Flavus Tibiris*. No doubt, it was once larger than now. In ancient times it may have been navigable as far up as Rome for ships of great burdens, but it is certain, its waters are not now sufficient to float the smallest crafts from the sea.

Under the aqueous formation of these plains are found large quarries of travertine stone, which is extensively used for building purposes. It would seem, this stone must have been formed by submarine igneous agencies. The indications are, this whole region was once active with volcanoes, for many extinct craters are to be seen, and lava is cropping out on every hand, bearing ample testimony of great volcanic revolutions.

The climate of Rome is not subject to such extreme changes, as that of our own land in the same latitude. In the hottest days the mercury seldom rises above 90° Fahrenheit, or in the coldest weather, falls so low as the freezing point. In the winter months there are occasionally flurries of snow. During the cold season they have a great deal of fog, but not so much and so thick as in London, but vastly more than we have in America. As much clothing is required there, as here for comfort. Not in the future as in the past, will this city be a resort for those afflicted with chronic and lung diseases. Its cemetery for strangers bears a sad record of many who have sought it, hoping to find relief and health. Some disorders, however, which are destructive here, are harmless there. This is true of croup, scarletina, and measles; yet fevers waste there, as never here; so what is gained in some respects, is lost in others. Thus it is, when we strike the balance, we usually find the common blessings of life equally distributed.

In the centre of the Campagna once stood pagan Rome, now stands papal Rome. How significant these names! How they touch the mind with early memories! We can but recall those school-days, when with difficulty we read how Romulus founded the ancient city, and Remus lost his life while deriding its insignificance. In fancy we see them while boys nourished by a wolf. We behold earlier, Æneas and his companions landing at the mouth of the Tiber, fugitives from Troy, sending an embassy to King Latinus. Afterwards, when war broke out between the Trojans and the Romans, we see Æneas sailing up the Tiber to strike a truce with Evander, the Arcadian king, that he might gain his friendship; but in spite of his best endeavors the war raged, the contending armies grew furious, and in the heat of battle, we behold Turnus, the king of the Rutulians and the Trojan hero fiercely contending for the hand of Lavinia.

I realize these are but fables, still memory has such a hold upon them that historical criticism, however severe and just, will never be able to efface them altogether. These have clothed the seven hills with exciting romance and lasting associations. But so long as stone and brick and hills shall last, so long will pagan Rome live. However, at the present, the modern city claims our attention.

This is not so old as some towns in our own country. It is surrounded by a wall fourteen miles in length, and fifty feet high on the outside. It is made of brick and stone and crested with three hundred towers. The walls enclose the new and the site of the old city, and are penetrated by thirteen gates. Entering within the walls, we find the new city is situated to the north of the ancient in what was the Campus Martius, lying between the Tiber on the north, the Pincian hill on the east, the Capitoline on the south, and the Janiculum on the west. The Tiber runs through the northern and western portions. The city is about a mile and a half in length and a mile in width; of course the distance between the walls is greater. The first introduction to Rome is quite likely to shock the stranger's imagination, inflamed by poetical and historical descriptions. He is surprised to find modern Rome so unlike the city of the Cæsars. In one respect only is the new like the old; it is built of the same kind of stone.

Though cherished fancies meet with such disappointment, yet there is something about the present city which does attract and fascinate. There are two things within its limits, the one ancient, and the other modern,—the ruins of the Colosseum, and St. Peter's,—the sight of which will compensate one for the trouble and expense of crossing the deep seas. Like the pyramids on the Nile, they are unmatched, each the grandest work of its kind,—the Colosseum, a wonder of vastness; St. Peter's, a marvel of harmonies. The buildings of Rome are usually tall, huddled together, and ugly in their general appearance, constructed of brick and stone, but mostly of the dull yellow travertine. The houses are from two to six stories high. Some of these are spacious and elegant, containing private galleries of the finest paintings and sculptures, having spacious vestibules and court-yards adorned with marbles, flowers, and spicy trees.

The streets are narrow and crooked. The Corso which is the main one, is barely wide enough for two carriages to pass abreast. The ground story of the buildings fronting the streets, is usually divided up into little rooms for stores, shops and nurseries. It is no uncommon thing for the man of business to have his whole family close about him. Such a store, or room, is rather a stirring place, especially when the children are manipulating their heads.

The city has greatly improved since it became the capital of Italy. The beggars, priests, and swaddled babies, are not so numerous on the streets. More good horses and carriages are to be seen than formerly; still, almost everything except the fine arts, borders on the old style. The distaff is yet in use, and weaving is executed on small wooden looms, some of which have not got the length of the fly-shuttle. It seems hardly possible that the pretty Roman scarfs should be manufactured on such rude machines. Even the sculptures, pictures, mosaics, and cameos, are all produced in humble apartments; so the works of taste make no display in Rome.

The five bridges across the Tiber present no particular attraction outside of the associations connected with them.

The external appearance of the three hundred and seventy churches is not prepossessing. Many of them are unpleasantly situated and ugly shaped without, but within, are exquisitely beautiful; yet the finest of these are of little account after visiting *the church* of Rome, yes, *the church* of the world.

The eleven Egyptian columns of red granite adorning different quarters of the city, add greatly to its attractions; and then the fountains, too, of elaborate workmanship, and supplied with an abundance of pure water, are inviting blessings.

St. Peter's stands in the extreme northwestern part of the city, placed there, it is said, to commemorate the supposed burial spot of the apostle Peter. Its site is unfavorable, being too low and too much confined. It was commenced in the sixteenth century, and is not yet completed. It has cost already more than seventy millions of dollars. Raphael and Michael Angelo, the two greatest artists, were its principal architects. Its design and plan are mostly due to Angelo. On approaching it in front, one has the feeling of vastness. The portico with its numerous pillars, the Egyptian pyramid, the fountains on either side, the massive statues of St. Paul and St. Peter, and the grand entrance, all seem to excite great expectations. Stepping within the vestibule, lo, how magnificent! The marble columns and bronze doors are just where and what they should be. Passing within the church, and what vastness, beauty, richness, and harmony, reach the eye! One must feel here is a work approaching the perfect, the divine! The vast marble floors, the lofty pilasters of variegated marbles, the colossal statues, the superb mosaic pictures upon wall and ceiling, the high altar with its hundred burning lamps, the crypt below it with the most beautiful statue of Pope Clement XVI., marking the place where according to tradition, repose the remains of St. Peter, are all significant. The magnificent pictures in mosaic, looking precisely like oil paintings, are the best specimens of the art in the world. More than twenty years have been required to produce some of them, each costing, perhaps, more than twenty thousand dollars. The sleeping and waking lions in marble by Canova, are true to life. The proportions and harmonies of this church are such that one can scarcely realize its majestic size, as he walks through the nave. It seems hardly possible that it is more than six hundred feet in length, and nearly three hundred feet in width, and two hundred and fifty feet high under the rotunda. It would naturally be fancied that in such a church, there would be something of the gloom and dim religious light of the Gothic cathedrals; but in St. Peter's, there is nothing of the kind; the light comes in from its lofty windows just right. Really, it is the brightest, cleanest, lightest, and largest church in the world: it is unfortunate there should be one work of art in it, which mars instead of adding to the beauty of the place. I refer to the statue which is said to be that of St. Peter, but which, no doubt, was of pagan origin, and made in honor of Jupiter, or some other polytheistic deity. The Catholics from the pope down to the meanest beggar, as they pass it, fail not to kiss its great toe.

In ascending to the top of St. Peter's, one is sure to learn before he reaches the dome, or climbs into the bronze ball capable of holding sixteen men, which appears from the ground not to be more than a foot in diameter, that it is a lofty and massive structure. From its summit can be enjoyed an extended prospect of the whole city and the surrounding country.

Joining St. Peter's is the palace of Leo XIII., known as the Vatican. This and the Museum at the Capitol contain the chief art-treasures of Rome. In the Vatican there is a wilderness of ancient statuary, sculptures, and antiquities. It is the greatest wonder whence they all came. Room after room, and corridor after corridor, are crowded with marvellous works of art. Here is the Apollo Belvidere so strkingly beautiful; and here also is the original Laocoön so expressive of the wildest consternation. Among the pictures, the most celebrated are "The Transfiguration" and "The Madonna de Foligno," by Raphael; "The Last Communion of St. Jerome," by Domenichino; the frescos of Raphael in the Stanza, portraying Roman and Grecian history; and "The Last Judgment" in the Sistine Chapel by Michael Angelo, which occupies the whole of one end of the chapel. However much we may criticise the ideal of the picture, after studying it carefully, we cannot doubt that its conception and execution required eight long years of the closest application on the part of its most gifted author. It would require volumes to describe all the art-treasures in the Vatican.

In the Museum at the Capitol are "The Dying Gladiator" and a statue of Venus, which deserve to be counted among the great masterpieces in marble.

The success of the fine arts in Rome to-day is due to foreigners. Hundreds are there earnestly engaged in cutting the stone, and painting the canvas. Some of their works compare favorably with those of the old masters. Several of our American artists rank among the best. Though they work in a distant land, yet the result of their toil returns to adorn our galleries, halls, and public squares. Though they are abroad, still they are true to our country. They are so conditioned, they can appreciate our Republic, and with delight do labor to perpetuate its glory. The present promises that in the future, America shall be crowned with the richest treasures of painting and statuary.

The government of Rome was that of a pretended theocracy. It declared itself not human but divine, ruled by God in the person of Pio Nono. He feigned to have dominion over the temporal and spiritual, ruling bodies and minds. He admitted no one into his administration, unless he had been consecrated a priest. No one could become a member of the state, unless he had first become a member of the church. No one could truly own any property or his own life, unless he was in Catholic communion. The pope declared himself infallible, and his authority divine.

But a great change has come over the city and the papal realms, since Rome became the capital of Italy, and the king took up his abode here. Church and state are no longer ruled by the same head. The government is quite liberal, and rapidly tending towards republicanism. Victor Emanuel was a fortunate ruler for Italy; and his son, Humbert, the present king and his queen Margaret, are highly esteemed, and, no doubt, are doing their very best for their beloved Italy. They have caused striking improvements to be made in Rome. It is a clean city now compared with what it was ten years ago. Filth and beggary which were formerly so common, have been removed to a large extent, and the city is wearing the appearance of thrift, as it has not for many years past. Were the country not so embarrassed by debt and poverty, it is evident, the king would do much more in the way of improvements than it is possible for him to do at present.

The pope and his cardinals constitute rather an august-looking body. Leo XIII. would be taken to be a very sincere, earnest, and determined man. The cardinals usually have marked physical capacity; their temperaments are not the most active, still they would be taken to be men of the keenest perception, remarkably adroit in planning, and wonderfully shrewd in executing.

The state of the church in Rome is flourishing, if we estimate it by the number of priests and holy orders; for according to the last census the city had thirty-four cardinals, thirty-six bishops, fourteen hundred and fifty-seven priests, three hundred and sixty-seven seminarists, twenty-five hundred and sixty-seven monks, twenty-one hundred and thirty-one nuns, six hundred and sixty male theologians in training, nine hundred and ninety-seven Christian brethren, and others, making some ten thousand belonging to the ecclesiastical orders. This must be acknowledged a strong priestly force for a city of two hundred thousand inhabitants. It is plain to be seen that religion in Rome costs something. The holy orders must be well supported, and of necessity, it forces heavy taxation upon the Catholic subjects. They are learning that "their religion is not the cheap defence of their nation." If Leo XIII. can say, "I am the Church," the Romans are virtually saying, we can no longer support you; and so they are absenting themselves largely from all church service. Not even at St. Peter's, unless it be on some extraordinary occasion, are crowds seen joining in the worship on the Sabbath, or the week-day; and very seldom it is, that any Roman gentlemen are to be witnessed among the worshippers. They have been so grievously burdened in the past by taxation for the support of priestcraft, they are determined no longer to lend any influence in that direction. If the pope is resolved to build new churches and adorn them with the most costly works of art and precious stones, he must do it without their aid. They feel the people have been beggared altogether too much for the sake of embellishing temples of worship, and supporting multitudes of priests; and so they are looking upon Catholicism with indifference, and Protestantism, as a myth. Religion in Rome apparently has lost its former spirit, and its present devotees are clinging mostly to the letter. They reverence pictures and statues of saints; they agonize over the dead Christ; they adore the visible Virgin: they hang the picture of Mary on the infant's neck and attach it to the lottery ticket. This seems to be worship in Rome, if one kisses a church door, or a priest's hand, or crosses himself before a crucifix, or wears a rosary, or manipulates his beads. Its religion appears to savor more of the lips than of the heart, more of the flesh than of the spirit, more of earth than of heaven. Its whole structure and methods converge to this one end, to give the clergy absolute power over the people; but the Romans are no longer disposed to submit to the entire control of pope, bishops, and priests. They fully realize under such reign, the country has not advanced, and the Italians kept pace with the best civilizations. Their commerce and culture have waned during the recent centuries, and they are fully persuaded that if they are not relieved from the shackles of priesthood, there is no hope for their beloved Italy. So they rejoice that the temporal power of the pope was supplanted by the rule of Victor Emanuel, and is still held in subjection by the reign of King Humbert. They no longer bend the knee when they come into the presence of the pope; they no longer go to the confessional box; they believe in liberty of conscience and freedom of action. So the religious status of Rome is very unlike what it was in the palmy days of Pio Nono. Though Leo XIII. has anathematized Protestantism in the city of Rome, nevertheless, it promises more there than ever before. The earth moves and so does the "Eternal City." It would seem that Cavour's entreaty with reference to his cherished Italy would be fulfilled at no distant day, saying, "Give us a free church in a free state."

The cause of education in Rome has not received that attention it should, and this is made evident from the scrivini who may be seen in different parts of the city, sitting behind little tables with pen and paper, ready to do the bidding of lover, mourner, or thief, in the way of writing letters. It is necessary, there should be such helps, for not more than half of the population can read or write. Though there is such ignorance in the city, the church boasts of its numerous colleges, pronouncing them the best in the world. If this were not true, it asks, " why should students come from all the civilized countries to enter them?" It is a fact, they do have patronage from America, Scotland, England, France, Germany, and other foreign lands, but their numbers are not large. The course of studies and system of instruction in these institutions, are very loose. They have gained no fame for thorough scholarship. During the last century no standard works on medicine, law, or theology, have been produced by their professors. Had the schools depended upon Rome for text-books, there could have been no complaint of too great a multiplicity. Were it not for the name, but few students would be likely to seek an education in Rome. The special object of the church has been in its educational processes, to teach the common people they know nothing, but the priests, everything. It has allowed none but priests, or men in holy orders, to give any instruction. Its end of education has been to make all accept the infallibility of the pope, the holiness of the Virgin, and the divinity of the priesthood. But since the temporal power was taken from the pope, the public schools of Rome have changed decidedly for the better. The present king and queen are doing all in their power for them. The great obstacle in the way of general education in this city, as well as in other parts of Italy, is poverty. A large proportion of the peasantry are unable to do anything for the education of their children. Still the number of pupils in the schools has more than doubled within a few years past, and the present outlook for universal education in Rome is hopeful.

Surely Italy moves. In 1848 she struck a blow for liberty and free schools, and Tuscany and Sardinia took a forward step. In 1859 another blow was struck, and chains of tyranny dropped from Lombardy, and shouts of loyal hearts rung out, "Viva Garibaldi." In 1860 another blow was struck and the bands of Sicily and Naples were broken, and the shout was renewed by millions more, "Viva Garibaldi!" In 1867 another blow was struck and the keystone to the arches of tyranny was loosened. In 1871 the Papal states were absorbed by the Italian states, and Italy's greatest hero is resolved not to rest till Italy is blest with a "free constitution, a free conscience, and free schools."

But from the modern we turn to the ancient city. Whence the old Romans originated, it can be but vaguely conjectured; however, it would seem, at the time they settled the old city, they were a rude colony of peasants dwelling on the banks of the Tiber. Civilization was a stranger to them; hardships pressed heavily, and with the greatest difficulty they eked out a living. But somehow self-determination and undaunted courage pushed them on. Even when rent by internal feuds, and badly cut in pieces by Gauls and Carthaginians, they were not disheartened but all the more resolved upon becoming a strong and famous people. At no very distant day they were equal to great emergencies; they conquered Hannibal, Pyrrhus, and Antiochus, and overthrew Carthage, Epirus, and Greece. They extended from their great city in all directions the grandest roads. They strengthened themselves with vast armies, and marched forth conquering and to conquer, surrounding nations, not resting till Rome was mistress of the world. At the advent of Christianity, her sceptre ruled from the Clyde of Scotland to the Tropic of Cancer, a distance of two thousand miles, and from the Atlantic to the Euphrates, a distance of three thousand miles. She sat on her seven hills in queenly pomp, calling in treasures from her distant lands to adorn villas, temples, and amphitheatres. Her roads, bridges, arches, Forum, and columns, were the grandest of their kind ever built. Her civilization was being borne to the most distant lands; her legions were guarding every city, and all the frontiers throughout her vast realm. Rome could then boast of the greatest statesmen, greatest orators, greatest poets, and greatest generals. To be a Roman then was surely an honor.

But Rome that had endured adversity so triumphantly, was not to endure long the full blaze of prosperity. No sooner had she placed her foot upon the neck of Greece than she began to falter and wane. As she took to herself the luxuries and sensual pleasures of Athens and other foreign cities, internal corruptions began to pollute and destroy. Losing self-control, cruel tyrants wrenched away her sceptre, and forced upon her citizens the grossest sensualities and the fiercest cruelties; soon, half of the populace became slaves, and another large portion were adventurers of every tongue and nationality. Those who had been brave conquerors had degenerated into mere bullies; they rushed to the arena and the masses rushed after them, glorying in savagery and blood. Gladiators became the heroes; the emperors became the greatest monsters; their names beginning with Augustus and ending with Otho, savor of blood. No wonder that the "Eternal City" under the reign of Tiberius, Caligula, Claudius, and Nero, should be laid in the dust and become sublime only in its ruins.

To-day the grandest of her antiquities is the Colosseum. This was the central figure of old Rome. It was commenced by Vespasian, continued by Titus, and finished by Domitian. It occupies more than six acres of ground, being elliptical in shape, and five stories in height. When completed its exterior was grand and beautiful, embodying several different orders of architecture. Around and above its arena it had a seating capacity for eighty thousand spectators. From the top of its wall one can have a most imposing view of its stupendous grandeur. Its vaultings and sittings have been badly mutilated by the ravages of time and the hand of the despoiler. Here and there vines of ivy are hugging the walls, and crevices are thickly scattered over with shells of snails. From the nooks and crannies now and then, hooting owls swoop forth, sounding their requiems of wasting greatness. As we view these majestic ruins, we can but recall the time when it used to be crowded with the sexes of all ages and conditions, gloating upon the most horrid scenes. Men and women were delighted to hear these walls echo with the cry of "Christianos ad leones": and then to witness ravenous lions pounce from their dungeons into the arena, tearing in pieces and devouring Christian martyrs. Can it be that Titus after having loved Bernice as Antony loved Cleopatra, after having sacrificed bullocks to the god Apis under the shadow of the pyramids, and after having been pronounced divine and worshipped as a deity in most of the Syrian cities, tore up the gardens where Nero delighted to walk, clad in purple, and shod with azure buskins, with fillets of laurel on his temples and a harp in his hand, and melodious accents flowing from his tongue, and wildest passions germinating in his heart, drained from its centre, and raised this greatest amphitheatre of the world for the sole object of shedding blood? He dug up treasures from classic fields and brought the costliest spoils from Oriental cities to adorn the mighty work which had been built in three years, a work concerning which, as one looks upon it for the first time, he can scarcely refrain from asking, is it possible that this is a production of man? This is the work which required a hundred days for its dedication, and the blood of nine thousand animals to consecrate it. But did this satisfy the ambitious Titus? Nay, verily, his past was filled with remorse, and his future was terrific, and finally, as he was one day walking upon the poisonous Roman Campagna, searching for rest, he fell dead, showing, if a Cæsar builds the hugest structures of stone, adorning them with Doric, Ionic, and Corinthian graces, failing to cultivate the graces of his own heart, his monuments left behind, however grand and beautiful, serve only to magnify the wastes and ruins of his own character.

North and west from the Colosseum, not far off are the greatest of all the Roman triumphal arches, that of Constantine with its inscriptions wonderfully preserved, and that of Titus with its lettering and symbols commemorating the siege and capture of Jerusalem. Under this arch passes the Via Sacra paved with its polygonal slate stones, and wherever exposed, looking as though it were a work of yesterday, instead of having been built more than two thousand years. A little way on, are the remains of the temple of Venus and the Basilica of Constantine. These evidently were once elegant structures. Not far from these is a cluster of antiquities imposing and grand in their ruins. Here was once the Roman Forum, an irregular oblong space, about a third of a mile in length, and half of that distance in width. What associations crowd upon the mind as the eye rests upon this renowned spot! Once it was the centre and heart of the greatest city of the world! But now how changed and desolate! Now it is occupied only by relics and a few locust-trees. Clustering around it are the walls of the Basilica of Julia, the three beautiful pillars belonging to the temple of Minerva, the frontal portico of the temple of Antoninus and Faustina, the column of Phocas, the arch of Septimius Severus, the three pillars of the temple of Vespasian, inscribed in large letters with ESTITVER, the eight columns bearing testimony of a temple to Saturn, the remains of the temple of Concord commemorating the truce between the plebeians and the patricians, and the rostra of the Forum from which the Roman orators used to address the people. Here Antony pronounced his oration over the dead body of Cæsar. Here Cicero delivered his orations against Catiline. Somewhere close by was enacted the terrible tragedy of Virginia who was put to death by her father to save her from the vile hands of Appius Claudius. In the Forum it was that Manlius stood, after he had repelled the Gauls from the arena of the Capitol and saved the city when all seemed lost, wrongfully accused and about to be unjustly condemned. As the judge rose to pronounce the sentence of death, Manlius sprang to his feet, weeping and pointing to the place where duty was done; the people burst into tears, and the judge was silenced. At length the trial again proceeded, but was once more defeated as the noble man pointed to the place where duty was done; nor could he be convicted till they removed him out of sight of the Capitol.

A short distance to the northeast of the Forum is the arch of Septimius Severus under which passed the Clivus Capitolinus Way. To the rear of this arch are the remains of the temple of Concord erected to commemorate the termination of the contest between the patricians and plebeians. A little to the south of this temple is the Mamertine Prison built by Ancus Martius. It is a horrible place. It consists of deep underground dungeons walled up with vast blocks of travertine stone. Formerly, there were no steps leading to these depths; the criminals were dropped into them through holes in the roofs. In the lowest of these dismal places Jugurtha was starved to death; the accomplices of Catiline in his great conspiracy were confined and afterwards put to death. Even now, though not so terrible as formerly, it makes one's blood run cold to penetrate its dark recesses. Still farther on in this direction from the Forum, we find a mass of broken columns of granite. These are of immense size and finely cut; they bear record of the Forum and Basilica of Trajan. Here stands his famous column with its innumerable spiral carvings, commemorating his battles and victories. There is a majesty about these Roman works which is nowhere else to be found; they seem to assimilate Grecian harmony and Asiatic magnitude; if they lack the beauty of the Corinthian which took for its model the lovely form of a woman, this column does possess the colossal grandeur of a Titan.

A short distance to the west is the Pantheon, the best preserved relic of ancient Rome. It is a circular building, made of brick with a beautiful portico and dome; its front has often been pronounced by the best judges faultless. As

Rome took from Greece her religion, so she closely copied after her style of temples. The Pantheon is lighted entirely through the dome. In the seventh century it was converted into a Christian church, and in the sixteenth century, the remains of Raphael, the king of painters, were buried in it; so henceforth it is a consecrated shrine. The physical is beautiful, but the spiritual is glorious.

Not far to the south and just above the Forum is the Capitoline hill. On this hill once stood the ancient Roman Capitol and the temple of Jupiter Capitoline. Here the wise Roman senators used to meet and legislate. On its southwest side is the Tarpeian rock whence hosts of the innocent and the guilty were hurled to destruction in the stern, cruel times of the Roman Republic.

Below this hill to the west runs the Cloaca Maxima, the great sewer of old Rome, and the oldest known work of the kind in the world, dating from the time of Tarquinius Priscus. Strabo said, "It was so immense that the largest load of hay might be driven through it without any difficulty." Near by the Cloaca stands the edifice of Janus Quadrifrons with its four fronts of arches, but its two-faced deity which once crowned the work, has disappeared. Just below this monument towards the Tiber is the celebrated temple of Vesta. As we look at its columns and study its proportions, we cannot wonder that Horace and other classic scholars should extol its beauty and fairness. But a few feet behind this work flows the yellow Tiber. Certainly it is not so imposing a body of water as its history would imply. Here it was, according to the legend, that Horatius Cocles singly withstood the Etruscan army under King Porsena, until the Romans broke down the bridge from behind, and then he threw himself into the river and escaped. Here it was, too, that Clœlia, a Roman virgin, who was sent with others, as a hostage, sprang into the Tiber and swam safely to Rome.

A little to the south rising above the river, is the Aventine, the highest and the most noted of the seven hills. It was here, as the sweet singer of Mantua informs us, that King Latinus held his court with Æneas and his companions after the capture of Troy. It was here, also, that Remus stood, while his brother Romulus was stationed on the Palatine to consult the soothsayers who were to decide which of the two should be the founder of the future city. About this hill are to be seen the remains of the famous wall of Servius Tullius. Once it was graced with beautiful temples consecrated to Juno and Diana, but now its summit is crowned with modern churches and convents.

Between the Aventine and the Colosseum rests in ashes the Palatine. Its sides are steeper and more abrupt than the other hills. Its limits can be measured by a twenty minutes walk, still it contains huge masses of desolate ruins. This was the most populous part of ancient Rome. Upon it once stood the stately edifices of Catiline, Hortensius, Cicero, and Augustus. Here were the gorgeous palaces of bloody Tiberius and Caligula. This was the hill that glistened with the golden palace of Nero, whose splendor and magnificence caused it to be reckoned as one of the wonders of the world. But how fallen is Palatine now! Its beauty and grandeur have crumbled away, leaving it alone for history to tell of its former splendors.

To the south of the Palatine is the Cœlian. This has only a slight elevation, but quite an extensive area with its sides covered with shade trees. At the time of the foundation of the old city it was called Querqueta, or the city of oaks. It derived its present name from an Etruscan chieftain who controlled it in its pristine days. Tullus Hostilius had his royal residence upon it; the temples of Faunus, Bacchus, and Claudius, once adorned it; and now its southeasterly extremity is occupied by the Lateran Church and palace. This church derives its name from the Roman senator, Plautius Lateranus who was put to death by Nero. It is an imposing structure crowned with statues of the apostles and the Saviour. In this church the coronation of the popes has taken place for more than fifteen hundred years.

To the north of the Cœlian is the Esquiline, the largest of the seven hills. Its principal ruins are the baths of Titus, whose frescos on their walls are very perfect, being regarded the best specimens of painting found among the ruins of ancient Rome. A street leads from this hill to the Forum, which is reported to be the one over which Tullia rode, when she drove over the dead body of her father, Servius Tullius. It is now occupied by some of the finest buildings of modern Rome, and perhaps the chiefest among them is the church of St. Maria Maggiore; this ranks second only to St. Peter's.

To the north of the Esquiline is the Viminal. It can scarcely be called a hill, its elevation is so slight. Among its ruins are the baths of

Diocletian. Its surface principally is occupied by recently constructed buildings.

To the westward of the Viminal is the Quirinal, the last of the seven hills. The Sabines held it at the time Romulus dwelt upon the Palatine; they made it hostile to Rome and a rival with it, till Tatius effected a union between the two divisions, and ever after it was inclosed as one of the Eternal Hills.

The more these hills are examined, the more wonderful they become. Their history cannot be half told; still so long as stone and ashes shall last, they will be clothed with immortal memories!

To the north of the Quirinal is the Pincian hill, which is the most beautiful part of the modern city, being laid out as a public promenade, and tastefully ornamented with flowers and trees. Here were once the gardens of Pompey, and the palace of fabulous cost, belonging to Lucullus, the epicure, who squandered so many fortunes at banqueting.

Under the shadow of this hill to the west stood the Flaminian Gate. A little to the south of this spot is the church of St. Maria del Popolo which is believed to mark the place where cruel Nero was buried. Not far to the west is the mausoleum of Augustus, formerly the grandest monument of the Campus Martius. In it are the ashes of Augustus, Livia, and Marcellus. Virgil refers in tenderest lines to the burial of the young Marcellus in this tomb. In it, too, rest the remains of bloody Tiberius and Caligula. Across the Tiber on the bank, stands another prominent and massive structure, known as the Castle of St. Angelo, which was built for the tomb of Hadrian. Not far to the south rising somewhat abruptly from the Tiber and opposite the Capitoline, is the Janiculum, a hill whose history is intimately connected with that of ancient Rome. It is the highest ground within the walls of the city. It commands an extensive view of Rome and the whole region around. Prominent among the many buildings upon it, is the church of St. Pietro, marking the spot where tradition says the Apostle Peter was crucified. Another church of particular interest here is that of St. Onofrio, in which lies buried the poet Tasso. Joining it is his studio in which he sat when he composed the poem entitled "Jerusalem." Here are preserved his bust, portrait, chairs, tables, crucifix, autograph, and library. Near the church is Tasso's garden with its famous oak under whose shade the poet was wont to sit and gaze with delight upon the marvellous city. His name promises to be fadeless when the present city shall sleep in ashes. The mortal falls to the earth that the immortal may live forever.

A mile out on the Appian Way towards the south, are the baths of Caracalla; these constitute a vast pile of ruins. They were built on a scale of grandeur and elegance. They are eight furlongs in circumference, and were sufficient to accommodate two thousand bathers at the same time. In addition to the bathing-rooms there were others devoted to games, amusements, and instruction. Here philosophers taught, and poets sung. Here were lounges for the idle, and libraries for the learned. Nooks and corners were filled with the finest works of art, and walks were adorned with trees and fountains.

Not far beyond these baths on the same way are the tombs of the Scipios. Though their burial place is wasted, still their lives keep fresh the history of their valor and virtues, their prudence and generosity.

Farther on and without the walls are numerous objects of antiquity. Conspicuous among them are the sepulchre of Geta and the tomb of Cæcilia Metella, and in the distance stretching across the Campagna are arches of the old aqueduct built by Claudius to bring water from the Alban Lake to Rome.

But the most interesting objects near this road, only a few miles from the city, are the catacombs of St. Calixtus and St. Sebastian. These are evidently memorials of Christianity in its struggles against paganism. They consist of deep excavations and winding, underground passages. Their full history cannot be deciphered. It is thought by some they were ancient quarries whence the tufa stone was dug for buildings. Afterwards according to Horace, they were used as sepulchres for burying the poor, especially the plebeians. Still later, it is said, they became haunts for brigands. At length, under the reigns of Nero, Domitian, Trajan, Severus, and Diocletian, the Christians of Rome through persecution were driven to take refuge in these desolate crypts in order to enjoy their religious rites. Here they tarried for years while the storms of persecution raged against them. Within these recesses on walls and ceilings did they paint the Good Shepherd whose staff always supports through the dark valley, and the dove which brought the glad token of the termination of the Deluge. Here they intoned hymns, not to a Roman prætor, but to the humble Nazarene who was so ignominiously put to death. No wonder when such died, the tenderest epitaphs should be written on their tombs, as, "Arethusa sleeps in God." "Lavinia, sweeter than honey, rests in peace." "Vitellianus rests in the Lord Jesus." It is not strange that the old man, the youth, the tender maiden, with such a faith, as they were dragged hence to the arena, trembled not before the howl of the Asiatic tiger, or the roar of the African lion. While the ravenous beasts were lacerating their palpitating bodies, and Roman hosts were giving thanks to Cæsar, believing that a superstition was being destroyed and a heresy was being devoured, it was not dreamed that their blood was nourishing a life which would dethrone kings and overcome barbarities. What if Tacitus ridiculed the disciples of the Nazarene carpenter! What if Apuleius stigmatized apostles in his apologues and fables! What if Lucian scorned the sentiments which dropped from the lips of the "Beloved Son"! No longer are the muses invoked that breathed music into the souls of Horace and Virgil, or the gods appealed to, who put courage into the heart of Scipio around the walls of Carthage, or glorying into the soul of Marius as Jugurtha was dragged in chains before him! Those old divinities are dead and the Rome of the Cæsars has fallen upon their lifeless bodies!

The Forum now is a pasture where goats feed; the Colosseum stands a petrified sentinel, keeping majestic silence; the Via Sacra is sunken into an oblivious grave. The pagan has given way to the Christian. Mortal tents have become pitched on higher ground than was anticipated. A resurrection has come out of the catacombs more beautiful than the fairest Madonna, more attractive than the completest Pantheon, and more majestic than the grandest cathedral. So it is, the All-Wise leads from lower to higher orders; from polytheism to monotheism; from the Law to the Gospel.

On parting with the catacombs so fraught with significance and sublimity, the touching experience of the young student forces itself upon the mind. Prompted by an insatiable desire to seek and know, he entered these dubious, winding passages, led by a guide for the purpose of copying an inscription on a certain stone, hoping that he might be able by careful and diligent study to reveal its hidden mysteries. The desired stone was found and long the student labored to transcribe the exact lineaments. The work was so lingering, the guide wearied and felt he could tarry no longer; so he left the student alone and intent upon his work. Absorbed in his mission he thought not of being alone. At length, accidentally his taper dropped into the dust, and lo! he was enveloped in the profoundest darkness with no means of renewing his light. Immediately he began to feel his way through the zigzag passages, hoping he should ere long come into the light of day. But his labors seemed to be in vain. Finally, almost overcome with weariness and despondency, he fell prostrate, it would appear, to die; but just then his hand caught a thread placed in the winding maze, and so hand over hand he followed its leading and was safely conducted out of these strange sepulchres into the presence of the living, busy world, that he might still press on in the ways of duty. So it is, the All-Good has dropped in the way of nations and individuals providential threads which the faithful, if cast down, may gather up and follow, and they will be certain to lead above all ruins into the fadeless day and the Eternal City, whose streets will always be crowded with works of angelic art, and whose walls will reflect the paintings of faithful and sainted characters.

IX.

NAPLES AND ITS BURIED CITIES.

NAPLES and its bay once seen live in memory like a fairy dream, or an enchanting vision. The Italians say, "The Bay of Naples is a piece of Paradise let fall to the earth." Its fascinating beauties almost justify the statement.

Sailing into the bay, the island of Capri first greets the eye, rising from the mirror-surface sea like a lofty nymph, reflecting all the day long varying shadows and exquisite beauties. Looking upon it now, one is disposed to question the statement of mythology saying, "It was once the haunt of the most cruel tyrant." In front, not far off, stands Vesuvius with his crest of smoke waving as a massive plume above the steel helmet of a giant warrior. Soon is discovered a fringe of white towns circling from Posilippo on the west to Sorrento on the east, with Naples in the centre, overtopped by the castle of St. Elmo. The houses seem to rise in quick succession one above another. The hills in the distance are covered with vineyards, olive-trees, and extensive forests. Far off the Apennines shoot up their glistening spires into the sky. Everything is touched with the balmiest air and the softest light. Ships lying at anchor and sundry light crafts scattered about, complete the fascinating picture.

Though the physical is so attractive, still the deepest interest lies in the historic associations. These excite pagan and Christian memories. They tell us, these lands were once occupied by the refined Greeks who revelled in art and science, music and nature, until they were overcome by the Romans; then they passed into the hands of a succession of intruders, including Normans, Swabians, Sicilians, Austrians, French, and Spanish Bourbons. Each has left its peculiar impress, and influence. Accordingly, among the people there exists the greatest possible variety of minds, characters, complexions, dispositions, and conditions.

Entering the city one can but be delighted with the broad and beautiful street Chiaia which extends round the coast. Coming from Rome, or other cities of the Sunny Land, it is refreshing to travel this roomy highway, tastefully ornamented with works of art and nature. Penetrating into the city the streets become narrow and huddled. The houses are built upon the steepest hillsides, tier above tier, till they reach the lofty summit of St. Elmo. The buildings vary in height from one to six and seven stories. The shops, as a rule, are of the simplest construction, consisting of one small room with a wide doorway which is most always open. Here the shopkeepers work, trade, and many of them live. Those unable to secure shops, use the streets for mechanical, mercantile, and domestic purposes. It is surprising to realize how much the people here live out-doors. The number in the streets all day long and late into the night is enormous. The last part of each day is quite sure to be devoted to riding, especially upon the Chiaia. The well-to-do are furnished with elegant horses and carriages, while the poor are drawn in gigs and carts by mules and donkeys. All appear to be merry and happy; particularly is this the case with the lower classes, when fifteen or twenty of both sexes and all ages, are piled into one vehicle, and bound on a good time. The people exhibit the greatest variety of blood and culture. The majority in form are slim and tall. Many faces are handsome, others homely; some are light, and others dark; some are Grecian, some are Roman, and some are mongrel. The masses believe in little work and much play. Their motto seems to be, late to bed and late to rise, will make us jolly, if not wise. They are as impulsive and explosive as the soil on which they dwell. Then all nature serves to fire the imagination and spur the senses to rule over the reason. The tints of the sky, the luxuriance of the soil, the sublimity of the mountains, and the beauty of the sea, all have combined to mould natures, subtle and volatile, ready to sacrifice future good for present enjoyment. The Neapolitans count largely upon the climate and natural productions for their support. They believe strongly in partnership; for two unite to black a pair of boots; three or four, to wait upon one from a carriage; and a whole crew, to lift a trunk from an omnibus.

The chief manufactures are kid gloves, shoes, coral jewelry, lava trinkets, and macaroni. Though there is such a tendency to mutual aid, still the people do not look upon each other as honest and trustworthy. This is made evident by the way milk is distributed through their city. The goats and cows are driven from door to door, and the purchasers watch while the desired quantity is milked. Certainly this is practical, and should the custom be adopted in some other countries and cities, the people would be served to less water, and more cream.

In this city of six hundred thousand inhabitants, there are many church edifices, but apparently little true religion. Priests are plenty but true worshippers are few. However, the condition of things has changed wonderfully since the last Bourbon ruler was expelled from this country, and it was united to Italy under the reign of Victor Emanuel. Since that change happy advances have been made in religious and educational movements. Monasteries have been suppressed and Protestant schools have been opened in which hundreds of children from Catholic families are being educated. Some of these children are very precocious and promising. This was signally illustrated not long ago by a class of boys under fourteen years of age, who had been reading twice a day for a term of three months in Matthew's Gospel. These boys had been in school less than two years, and yet they were able to read finely any part of Matthew and John's Gospels, and some half a dozen of the class could recite from memory any passage or portion of Matthew. Could these bright boys become thoroughly educated, and then go forth as teachers in the land, what a power they would become to redeem and save their nation!

Though great improvements are being made here, nevertheless, ignorance and poverty have a strong hold. Scarcely anything is more common than to see old men with spectacles on, sitting at the corners of the streets and in public places, behind tables with pen and paper at hand, following the vocation of letter-writing. By their side may often be seen boys and girls, men and women, dictating some message of joy or sorrow, love or spite. The lower strata of society are so densely populated, there can be no hope of their speedy amelioration. If beggary is declining, squalidness is still prevalent. The poorer classes live almost wholly out of doors summer and winter. They cook in the streets and sleep on the sidewalks. Many are obliged to subsist on nothing better than raw fish and slimy macaroni. But the condition of the higher classes offers a striking contrast. They live in stately villas and grand blocks, surrounded by courts and gardens filled with orange and lemon trees laden with blossoms and fruit at the same time.

But as there are objects of equal, or greater interest outside of the city, it is natural to seek early after these. In the suburbs on the west descends from the castle of St. Elmo into the bay, the promontory of Posilippo. On its height stood more than eighteen centuries ago the villa of Mantua's sweet singer. There Virgil lived, while he composed his Eclogues, Georgics, and some of the books of the Æneid. Is it strange, that should be a cherished spot to the scholar? Who can count the number of minds that have been blest by the smooth lines dropping from the lyre of the great poet, as he lived, loved, and sung, where he enjoyed fairest views of land, sea, and sky? Not far from the site of his home, just at the entrance to the tunnel of Posilippo, is his tomb. Time has erased all inscriptions, and destructive hands of visitors have plucked up the laurel planted by Petrarch, but the ages have not been able to abrade the name of Virgil from the minds of the educated, proving that he who nobly works, is certain to become immortal in the hearts of humanity.

The tunnel of Posilippo is a wonder, when we consider that it was constructed more than two thousand years ago, and is half a mile in length, extending from Naples to the Bay of Baiæ. It was thoroughly arched with brick, paved and curiously ventilated, so that there was no inconvenience in travelling through it. We must admit, it was a grand piece of engineering in its day.

A little way from Posilippo to the west is Puzzuoli, the Puteoli at which Paul landed when on his way to Rome.. Here he found friends and tarried seven days. Puteoli was then a commodious city, furnished with magnificent buildings; but its grandeur and wealth have gone. The ruins of its amphitheatre still remain in which Nero degraded his imperial majesty by fighting with wild beasts to amuse the king of Armenia. In it also, it is said, Januarius and his disciples were forced to contend with the fiercest animals, but without injury, before their martyrdom. The cell in which the saint was imprisoned, has been converted into a chapel in his honor. Here is the white stone which turns red, so it is stated, at the instant his preserved blood in Naples is liquidized, which monkish report says, takes place three times a year.

Not far to the east of Puzzuoli, is Solfatara, a semi-dormant volcano, which Strabo christened, "Forum of Vulcan." Though it has ejected no lava since 1198, still it sends out vapors of sulphuretted hydrogen and muriate of ammonia, roaring with the noise of a thousand active blast furnaces. Not far from Solfatara is the Grotto del Cane, known to Pliny as one of "Charon's breathing holes." This is a cave whose lower portion is filled with carbonic-acid gas, so that a person standing is not injured, but a dog at his feet soon dies. It was in this vicinity Virgil pictured the descent of Æneas to the infernal regions. What could be more natural than for a people believing in mythology and polytheism, to connect these terrific prodigies with sulphurous under-ground realms, where they believed Pluto reigned to torture wicked souls?

A short distance to the west is the fabled Avernus where, the legend says, Ulysses made a visit to the Infernal Regions. But instead of its now being gloomy and fearful, it is a gem of a lake being circular and less than half a mile in diameter. Its waters are clear and alive with fish. If its name signifies birdless, the feathered tribes enjoy it now. No dense forests gloom its sides, or poisonous vapors rise from its surface, as represented by classic pens.

The Sibyl's Cave is in an inner recess leading from Avernus on the west. Probably Virgil's Sibyl had her abode in this cavern. A third of a mile from the opening is a lake of tepid water in which, it is supposed, Hannibal sacrificed to Pluto. By the order of Agrippa a tunnel of nearly three thousand feet in length was cut from this cave through a hill to the so-called Elysian Fields, which from their climate and beauty were regarded, as the home of the blessed. Now it is the most desolate region imaginable. No longer does the fabled plain lend enchantment. Its inhabitants are the most beggarly of the peasantry in Southern Italy. Surely, if they dwell in Elysium, none need despair of dwelling in "*fairy lands.*"

To the west and south of Avernus on the bay of Baiæ, once stood a delightful city bearing the name of the bay. This was a favorite resort of Horace, Cicero, Lucullus, and Cæsar. All that now remain to tell of its former beauty and grandeur, are ruined temples, baths, and tombs. The wonderful bridge which Caligula caused to be built, reaching from Baiæ to Puteoli, a distance of two miles, and the grand docks about the city, are gone except a few straggling piers. Now live among the ruins most wretched human beings, whose very presence tarnishes the works of art and the beauties of nature. When Baiæ was in its zenith, Nero had a palace here, where he was wont to spend his summers. At the time Paul landed at Puteoli, the emperor of Rome was at his summer house. About the same time the apostle sailed into the harbor, might have been seen another barge floating into this lovely bay in which was Agrippina, the mother of Nero. The son had invited the mother to visit him at Baiæ that they might reconcile certain unnatural animosities existing between them. Agrippina gladly accepted the invitation to celebrate with her son the feasts of Minerva, that all discord between them might be done away. Nero met his mother affectionately at the landing, and tenderly led her unsuspecting to a villa, where she was to take another vessel to cross the arm of the bay to the palace, where she was to be entertained during her visit. The son said "he would fain have her experience this last sail under the light of the stars, because of the vesper charms under these southern skies." So they joyfully, it would seem, tarried together till the day waned and the night waxed dark. At length the son bid the mother an apparently sweet good-by, and repaired quickly to his palace, terribly wicked and revengeful. The vessel in which Agrippina was to take passage had been fitted up with great pomp, as for an empress, but carefully adjusted so that at a given signal, the roof of the cabin burdened with lead, should drop and crush instantly all underneath. This was Nero's plan of putting an end to the difficulties with his mother without the suspicion of matricide. Those in charge of the boat were his sworn abettors. Not long after leaving the wharf, lo! a crash! The deck fell killing a servant, but so lodged as to spare the empress and Acerronia, her companion. The sailors at once cried aloud, "The barge is sinking!" The women plunged into the water, suspecting death was surely upon them. At the same time the men sprung forward to do Nero's bidding in a more certain way. But Acerronia, the faithful friend, with a woman's intuition and forgetfulness of self, saved her mistress for the time being in sacrificing her own life, by crying, "Save me, I am Nero's mother!" She was immediately beaten to death, but Agrippina floated ashore, soon, however, to be put to death.

As these facts are reviewed by land and sea, we can but feel, Acerronia died a heroine, indeed, that Agrippina was the unfortunate mother of a Cæsar, and that Nero proved himself a despicable son and tyrant!

Five miles to the east of Naples is Resina on the shore of the bay and at the base of Vesuvius. In making this distance in a carriage soon after sunrise, one can witness sights, more varied and novel than those of a balloon-fair, or an old-fashioned muster. We saw lazzaroni with head upturned and arms extended, sucking down macaroni by the yard; boys guiding donkeys by the switch, loaded with all kinds of vegetables; a woman carrying a hogshead on her head; carts drawn by single oxen; mules and cows yoked together; butcher's meat laid on the sidewalk for sale; any quantity of macaroni drying in the ditches for foreign markets; gigs crowded with peasantry in their motley costumes, and old men and children suspended in sacks under the axle-trees, riding to town; women in the doorways spinning with the distaff; barracks in one building capable of holding at the same time ten thousand soldiers; the custom-house surrounded by loaded teams waiting for a license to enter the city; and finally any number of *faccini* at Resina to wait upon us from the carriage and act as guides to Vesuvius.

From this point on horseback one can ascend, following a paved road for some two miles; then it is climbing over huge folds of black porous lava which has flowed down the sides of the mountain from time to time to the distance of seven miles. Really all now from above and below seems fearfully sublime. It is difficult to exaggerate Vesuvius. For miles now it is riding over ragged banks of lava, barren and desolate. After six miles of hard climbing the Hermitage and Observatory are reached which are situated twenty-two hundred feet above the sea. The professor in charge of the observatories has carefully watched and noted the phenomena of the mountain, until it is now believed, he can tell when there is to be an eruption some days before it will take place. He has observed that previous to an outflow, the water of the bay recedes from the strand, the wells dry up around its base, the earth trembles by spells, and the air is likely to become lurid and oppressive. Science has proved a great blessing to those dwelling about this mountain. These buildings stand upon a portion of land which has remained undisturbed since the destruction of Pompeii and Herculaneum. Lava has been poured all round, still it has been spared to smile with oaks, olives, vines, and fig-trees. It is now connected with Resina by a carriage-road. From the Hermitage on for three miles, it is passing over old and new formations of lava. At this extent the cone of the mountain begins to rise very abruptly. Now there is an opportunity to ascend either by rail, or on foot, to the crater. If the decision is in favor of the latter, then it is climbing, scrambling, and wading through sand under difficulties to the height of some sixteen hundred feet to the summit which is in altitude more than three thousand feet above the sea. As the rim of the crater is now reached which is circular and a third of a mile in diameter, the sight at once becomes sublimely exciting! As often, as every minute, a large quantity of molten lava is hurled many hundred feet into the air, and then it soon comes rattling back into the basin of the crater. The scene is truly wild and furious, and yet somehow it does fascinate and hold one spellbound to its awful grandeur! We gathered up forty varieties of lava from the crater.

The prospect from this height is enchanting. The bay, fringed with its white belt of towns, is lost in beauty, or glorified by distance. On all sides save that looking upon the sea, are mountains rising billowy into the air of every type — conical, abrupt, craggy, verdant, and far off, crested with glistening snow. The only regret the visitor can have on leaving Vesuvius is, that he has not more time to see and admire, and better means afforded for carrying off more and larger specimens from this realm of fiery sublimity. Descending, the eye is delighted with all below and around, and the heart is made glad to Him who created the sea, the mountain and sky, so varied and so expressive of All-Wisdom and All-Power.

In the seventy-ninth year of the Christian era from the top of Vesuvius a thousand feet in depth were lifted and thrown upon Pompeii situated to the southeast some nine miles distant, and then liquid lava flowed from the crater to the southwest burying Herculaneum deep out of sight. These overwhelmed cities remained for centuries undiscovered. Resina stands over Herculaneum. The ruins of this city were discovered in 1709 by digging a well. The lava covering it is exceedingly hard and a hundred feet deep. Descending a long flight of stairs cut out of the lava, we come to a Roman open-air theatre. It has been excavated so that all parts of the stage can be seen, — the orchestra, the stand for the crier, and the frescoings on the walls. The lava ran into every crevice and nook, still enough has been removed to show that the theatre was immense. Some distance south of this, explorations have been made where the destruction was by showers of ashes and sand. A prison and several other buildings have been unearthed, still for the most part Herculaneum is sealed, as in solid rock. But seven miles from Resina to the eastward, a little way from the bay, is Pompeii. This city lay concealed till as late as 1750. It was revealed by an accidental discovery of painted relics. This city was covered with ashes and loose lava which composed the upper portion of Vesuvius. It has been nearly all removed, so that the city and the walls can be seen without any obstruction. The roofs of most of the houses are broken in; otherwise the city is remarkably well preserved. It can be studied in detail on its own site, or in the museum at Naples. On its site remain the streets, temples, theatres, houses, shops, baths, and tombs. Most that was movable has been transported to the National Museum at Naples. The houses are one and two stories high. The streets are narrow, and the pavements are deeply rutted from the wear of chariot wheels. The buildings were made of brick and faced with stucco. The larger mansions must have been truly magnificent.

The walls bearing the names of Sallust, Pansa, and Diomede, indicate that their residences were elegant. The shops and stores were small, and are to be distinguished by their marble counters and signs cut into the front walls. Ovens, corn-mills, wine-vessels, and oil-jars, remain just as they were last used. The temples are of Corinthian style and of very elaborate workmanship. The amphitheatre is almost entire, having a capacity sufficient to seat ten thousand spectators at the same time. Over mantels and awnings, there are many exquisite paintings and mosaics, but on the walls of some of their common rooms, are voluptuous pictures which must have been constantly before the eyes of whole families, and which now would be tolerated only in the lowest haunts of profligacy. This implies, if the city was a favorite resort for scholars and artists, its people were vitiated and sensual.

It would seem before Pompeii was buried, there had been warnings of impending dangers sufficient to drive most of the inhabitants from the city; so that but few lives were destroyed in it; probably not more than two or three hundred out of a population of ten thousand. The remains of these have been found in such conditions as to show, they were frightened and overcome in an unsuspecting hour. It appears as though these were after treasures in the city; for in the hands of some were found bags of gold and precious things. The bodies are well preserved. Rings are upon their fingers and ornaments about their necks. Some of these relics are to be seen in rooms near the gate of the old city, while others are in the museum at Naples, where now are to be witnessed more of Pompeii than among its roofless walls. On visting that remarkable collection of antiquities, one can but be deeply interested in the numerous rolls of charred papyrus which are being unravelled and made legible, so that the history of that people is being revealed. These shrivelled scrolls serve to bring us near their writers and times; but certainly they do not strike the mind more vividly than the preserved articles of food ready for the table, — such as baked bread, roasted fowls, cracked nuts, spices, loaf sugar, dates, olives, and various grains. In the culinary department are to be seen, kettles, spiders, ladles, graters, moulds and forms for pastry, representing chickens, pigs, and hearts. Several elaborate cooking stoves have been discovered, furnished with bronze ware, plated inside with silver. The Pompeians cooked their eggs on their breakfast-tables in boilers capacitated to hold twenty-four. These utensils are similar in shape to those of modern dates. From the shops have been collected scales and steelyards, evidently nicely adjusted; compasses, measures of length, liquids, and grains. The measures are in the form of pretty vases; the weights are busts of gods, emperors, and figures of animals. The lamps and candelabra are graceful in design and beautiful in finish. In the baths have been found bathing-tubs, mirrors, combs, dressing-cases, musical instruments, locks, keys, bells, and door-knobs. From the stables have been gathered harnesses and carriages which must have been airy and beautiful. In the workshops have been discovered hatchets, saws, hammers, and garden tools, not inferior to those of the present day. The collection of surgical instruments is extensive, throwing much light upon surgery, proving the antiquity of the profession. Some of the instruments surpass even many of the best in modern practice. The workmanship in jewelry and personal ornaments, is of a high order and not inappropriate for present use. The mosaics and frescos in style have never been surpassed. The statuary in marble and bronze is very choice. Surveying the many figures of every possible design, one can but feel they are true to life and nature. Those taken from the temples and altars, show that their religion was polytheistic. This region must have been to the ancients, what Rome now is to the papist world. Here were their Elysian Fields and their awful Avernus. Is it strange that from these wastes, should come forth at the present time a mild form of deism, or pantheism? The inhabitants have always believed much in Egypt and Greece. But their ancient faith did not save them from sin and destruction. We have little reason to suppose that their modern atheistic views can render them honest and determined for the right. Their recuperation, or reformation, is to come from the west.

Their present school system has been transplanted from America. Since Garibaldi trod this soil, moved by the principles of Washington, striking a death-blow to Bourbon tyranny, this whole region has experienced a great awakening. Let free education do its perfect work, and Christianity will surely let fall her richest benedictions upon this fair land. Then here nature, art, and the spiritual, will combine to perfect human souls.

Just outside the walls of Pompeii, close by the main entrance, is a stone sentry-box in which was found, as the city was being uncovered, a petrified sentinel with sword by his side, standing as one faithful to duty in the midst of the most threatening dangers. No other object among the ruins, or sights of that land is so suggestive. It is full of thrilling inspiration. It foretells the sublimest victory.

X.

GREECE AND ATHENS.

GRECIAN soil and seas are rich in natural beauty and classic story. As we have sailed among the islands south and east of Attica, we have found them like emerald gems dropped upon the sapphire bosom of the Ægean Sea. Were the legend true that Icarus, the son of Dædalus, being offended at Minos, made wings and feathers of wax for himself and son, so as to escape from Crete, and while soaring too high the sun melted off their wings and they fell into the sea, producing these islands, we should say that fall and death were timely and fortunate, yielding such results of beauty and durability.

Rhodes has told us of her colossal statue which once spanned the entrance to her main harbor, and how the knights of St. John on her soil fought for Christianity. We have seen Selos which rises like a pyramid of purest green, and Syme which looks as though it might have produced Nereus who after Achilles was the handsomest man among all the Greeks at the siege of old Troy. We have anchored by Cos, the birthplace of Apelles, the greatest painter of ancient times. We have examined the barren and rocky Patmos which still repeats its sad tale of the banishment of St. John. Chios has offered us her claims, as being the birthplace of Homer, and assured us that Ion, the tragic poet, and Theopompus, the historian, were born upon her soil. Lesbos has smiled upon us and taught us of the sweet singers, Alceus and Sappho, of the Ionians and Æolians, so fond of music and poetry. We have gazed upon Trojan fields made enchanting by the epics of Homer and Virgil. Tenos, Andros, and Syros, have all spoken to us of the past and the present, inspiring the feeling, there is something peculiar and charming about Grecian lands and Grecian character.

At early morning our steamer is ploughing its way into the Saronic Gulf. The sky is of the clearest ruby; the air is like crystal; the glimmering water is shooting off in every direction the fire and silver of the sunlight. Almost encircling us in fairest outlines are sharp and lofty peaks painted on the sky. As the steamer approaches the shore, the village of Piræus and the white-crested Acropolis meet the eye.

They do not appear to be more than five miles away, yet they are ten or twenty miles distant. Our steamer winds its course among the islands, and at length whirls into a narrow channel between the island of Salamis and a peninsula of the mainland. Upon the right only a few rods from us, just upon the shore, is a plain marble slab purporting to mark the grave of brave Themistocles. Memory would fain linger here and worship at the shrine of the great warrior. It is pleasant to recall how, when a boy, he was full of spirit and fire, — how he spent his hours of leisure and vacation not in idleness, or play, but in composing declamations, — how his master was wont to say, "Boy, you will be nothing common, or indifferent, you will either be a blessing, or a curse to the community," — how he said, as he became the head of a family, that "He had rather his daughter would marry a man without money than money without a man."

Upon our left is the island of Salamis, and around it the bay of the same name. Strange deeds now begin to haunt the mind. We can scarcely conceive how the old Athenians once found security on that island of a few miles in extent, when the Persian hosts invaded their land. As we pass into the roadstead of Piræus, anchors are dropped, and lo! we are resting where once was moored the vast fleet of Xerxes, waiting for battle. On the shore a little way off rises up some five hundred feet, the grassy mound on which that Persian king sat, ready to rejoice in the defeat of the Greeks and the success of the Persians. Fancy now pictures that foreign fleet of fifteen hundred galleys crowded with men from more than fifty nations. How striking their armor and costume! There are Persians clad in tiaras, tunics, and trousers, thickly set with scales of iron, having in hand glistening spears and daggers; Assyrians, with helmets and steel-headed clubs; Scythians, with weapons of iron and stone; Indians, arrayed in cotton, having bows and arrows of cane; Æthiopians, with bodies painted, and only half covered with the skins of lions and leopards; Thracians, attired in bushy fox-skins, and armed with long-bladed spears tipped with poison.

The morning was fair, and out from behind the island of Salamis sailed the humble fleet of Themistocles consisting of only five hundred small galleys. The fleets came in contact; spears flashed; blades rattled; and men fell. Xerxes sat on his elevated throne sure of victory. High noon came and the Greeks had held their own. As the sun dipped to the west, Persian ships were sinking, Persian ships were fleeing, and as the stars shone out, Xerxes was a conquered king; his army was routed and disgraced; victory was shouted for the Greeks, and Themistocles was crowned with lasting glory.

Leaving our steamer we are conveyed in small boats to the shore. No sooner are we on land than we are beset with hackmen who sputter out the modern Greek so fast, it becomes almost a question whether they can understand themselves. They lay special stress upon drachmas and numerals. They commence bidding on a high key and at high rates, but they keep dropping in price, while we keep silent, till we begin to think they will give us something to ride with them to Athens, a distance of five miles; but as one offers to carry us for a shilling apiece, stepping into his hack we are at once rolling through the streets of Piræus. This modern village impresses a stranger favorably. The place shows signs of considerable enterprise.

Our hackman does not drive so fast as to make us feel that he is in great haste for his fee. But we have no disposition to find fault with the rate of speed. We are crossing the Attic Plain. Every foot of ground is classic. Upon the right we see now and then remnants of the ancient walls which used to extend from Athens to the Saronic Gulf. It is marvellous, how the fingers of Time will pick away solid rock. Soon we are in the midst of autumn fields of grain and grass and groves of olives. As we reach the half-way house which is a sort of tavern, our driver comes to a dead halt, and out rushes a Greek boy with bottle and glass in hand planting himself directly in front of us; filling a glass with wine he passes it to us, but his dark eye flashes with astonishment, as we refuse to drink. After urging in vain, he turns to the driver, giving him his share and ours too, and then turns back, asking us to foot the bill. As we move on, the wine, or something else, has given renewed force to the whip, and increased velocity to our carraige.

The marble relics of the Acropolis now appear as though they hung in the air. All conspires to make us feel, we are in a land where poets, artists, philosophers, and scholars, have been born and have died. The fairy plain, the shady hills, the white-crested mountains, and the deep azure sky, fill the mind with inexpressible delight! Almost too soon we are riding through the city of Athens.

The new city is to the north of the old, and, therefore, to the north of the Acropolis. We count less than sixty years since this city was commenced. It has a population of some fifty thousand. Its extent north and south is two miles, and a mile east and west. It is a fine city for the East. Coming from Turkish towns it seems almost an elysium. The buildings are not grand or imposing, but they bear marks of Grecian taste and style. There are no flat roofs here as in Cairo, Jerusalem, or Constantinople. The houses are built of stone and most of them are two stories high. The main streets are Hermes and Æolus, adorned with the papyræ-tree which resembles the weeping willow in form, but is an evergreen, very graceful and fragrant. On these streets are several first-class hotels which will compare favorably with the best in our country. The churches are constructed of variegated marbles, not massive but unique. The palace which stands on rising ground in the eastern part of the city, quite under the shadows of Lycabettus and Hymettus, makes a fine appearance. The gardens about it are extensive and tastefully laid out. It was somewhere here that trees thrived, and Aristotle was wont to walk and deliver at the same time his dissertations to his disciples. We would naturally infer that King George with his queenly consort might be happy, dwelling where nature smiles so propitiously, and associations are so suggestive of wisdom and learning.

The University outwardly is conspicuous and attractive on account of its proportions and harmony. As we examine it internally, we find it stands for substance and not mere show. Surely it is a bright light in this new city.

To the south of the modern, we can here and there discover remnants of the walls of the old city which encircled the Acropolis, and extended down to the sea. But the new city shows wisdom in not girdling itself with stone and mortar piled up like a huge prison, shutting out the free air and light, and shutting in impurities and death.

We find the people generally intelligent, ambitious, slightly self-conceited, living more on the past than the present, or future. Their leading idea seems to be to obtain an education, and this in their opinion consists in possessing a thorough knowledge of the Greek language. Even among the poorest classes Greek grammar is sure to come before work. So education in this city is universal. All the children from six to sixteen years old are in their schools. So little urchins in rags, and youths without shoes to their feet, and in many instances without garments to their backs, are bound to have an education, as well as the children of the better classes. The sexes are not educated together; the laws of the country will not allow of this. The girls advance from the primary school to the normal. Probably, there is no other city on the eastern continent, where woman is so highly educated, as in Athens. As we meet some of the young women on the street, or in the school-room, who read Homer and Xenophon with the sweetest intonation and euphonic rhythm, we are ready to admit they would furnish to modern Phidiases fit subjects for modern Minervas and Venuses.

The boys go from the primary school to the gymnasium, and from the latter to the University. The University is flourishing; its students number more than sixteen hundred. These come from all parts of the country, and are really young men. They look as though they might have a good deal of the old Athenian and Spartan blood coursing their veins. Many of them would make fine models for an Apollo or a Jupiter. This institution has a medical, legal, theological, and philosophical, department. The instruction is given in lectures. The professors are masters of what they teach.

They love their vocation. As we listen to a professor while he discourses upon the life and works of Xenophon, to another while he treats upon Homer's Iliad, to another as he discusses hydrostatics, and to another while he expounds the law, though we cannot understand all they say, still we really enjoy the lectures, the speakers are so animated, their tones are so musical, and the students are so enthusiastic and intently devoted to taking notes. Frequently some clear statement, or impassioned strain of eloquence, will take the scholars right off their seats. They read Homer, Socrates, Plato, and Thucydides, as we read Whittier, Longfellow, and Bancroft. The modern Athenians are emulating the spirit of their ancestors. They are rapidly gaining in influence. They are sending out many teachers and physicians, not only into the rural districts of their own country, but into Turkey, Asia Minor, and Persia. Athens may justly be said to produce the best physicians and female teachers found in Oriental towns or cities.

If we step into the House of Parliament, we find an assembly of men similar to our legislative bodies. Most of the members are dressed in the European costume; a few from the Highland districts still hold to the ancient style of dress. These are attired in the white frock and trousers, girdled with the red sash, and the black tunic loosely falling from the shoulders. They look airy, stylish, and comfortable. The assembly, as a body, is orderly and dignified. Some of the members exhibit striking talent and eloquence. At times exciting and patriotic speeches are made. Turkey is the bane of Greece, and were the latter rich, Turkey in Europe would soon be driven the other side of the Bosphorus, and Crete would be set free.

The scenery about Athens is exceedingly varied. It possesses the elements of beauty, grandeur, and picturesqueness. Its plains of smiling fields and shady olive-trees, constantly guarded by sea and land, present a picture which attracts the eye and pleases the taste. It is really just the place in which to grow men of ability and genius. What a long line of noble characters originated here,—Thucydides, Xenophon, Pericles, Isocrates, Demosthenes, Sophocles, Æschylus, Longinus, oh! we cannot recall half of the names of the famous ones who opened their eyes amidst this profusion of nature's charms! Here, too, they became students of nature and philosophy, adding countless attractions to their nativity.

A wide belt of olive-trees almost encircles

the city. Somewhere among these, it cannot be decided just where, Plato had his academy. Here he was teaching, when he defined man as "a two-legged animal with his feathers picked off"; and Diogenes catching a cock and stripping him of his feathers, threw him into Plato's school, saying, "See Plato's man."

It is afternoon. The long shadows begin to fall. The air is clear as a diamond of the first water. It is a fit time to climb the steep rocky sides of Lycabettus and enjoy a sunset scene in this classic land. Lycabettus bears about the same relation to Athens, Vesuvius does to Naples; or Arthur's Seat, to Edinburgh. As the summit is reached, we find we have been climbing with our might for an hour; but the first sweep of the eye more than compensates for all the toiling and sweating. The broadest sheet of clearest light illuminates land and sky. To the west lofty Cyllene and Taygetus cast their deep shadows into the valleys and plains; to the north the wooded sides and white-crested tops of Parnes are burnished with emerald and tipped with silver; to the east the rosy pyramid of Pentelicus and the violet and heather-sided Hymettus, give us their warmest greeting. All around are spread out the plains of Athens, not far reaching but beautiful in outline and every feature. Sunlight and shadow are kissing the trembling waves of the Saronic Gulf. The green waters of the Ægean Sea sparkle and glow. The marble columns and high-piled ruins of the Acropolis like fairy lace-work, hang in the air. The city and the fields around seem to be bathing in a lake of light and glory, wrapping themselves in flaming gold and mellowest shades. At length the sun falls behind the Delphian cliffs, dropping deepest shadows upon all below, while the pinnacles of the mountains, the minarets of nature's temple, blaze for a little, and then send out the voice, day is gone, twilight has come; and in the still quiet rest of parting day, one star after another looks down through these Grecian skies, till the whole azure is all aglow. Ah, these are the same lights of God that smiled when Homer sung and Plato taught and Phidias carved! Nature here wears the investiture of kingly honors, woven from the beauties of nature and dyed in the wonderful reflections of heaven. The task of climbing is compensated a thousand-fold by the joy of seeing.

Attica is not extensive in area, its greatest length being fifty, and breadth thirty miles. Still all civilized lands are breathed upon by Attica. Its influence touches the best thoughts and words of men, and ever will. It quickens the inspiration of the poet, the orator, and scholar. It is the parent of the most beautiful creations of art. The painter and sculptor of every nation have inherited from Attica. The galleries of princes and nations tell of Attica. The temples and council chambers of capital cities bespeak the praises of Attica. In the providence of God when Christianity came, the city of Minerva alone was prepared to picture in perfect language the beauties of the Eternal City.

We will now take a walk of ten miles across the Attic Plain northeast from Athens to Mount Pentelicus. Our way leads among fields of wheat and groves of olives and oaks. We pass through the villages in which Pericles, Aristides, Plato, and Socrates, lived. There is nothing attractive in them now but association and suggestions of the past. We are here reminded of the reply of Diogenes to Plato who sent the cynic a large cluster of grapes, when a request was made for only three. On receiving them Diogenes said, "Just like some philosophers, you ask them a question which could be answered by three words, and they will give you a thousand."

Occasionally we see peasants ploughing in

their wheat which has just been sown. Seeing their farming utensils, we would not judge, we were treading classic soil. We are surprised at the number of old people we observe by the roadside and in the hamlets. We are reminded of Theophrastus and Georgius who seemed to be in their prime, when about a hundred years old. Ah! there is something about this Grecian air which is favorable to health and longevity. In the House of Parliament we saw several very aged members. Some of their teachers in their schools must have experienced more than threescore and ten summers and winters. While walking at a rapid pace, we do not become weary, as we would in France or Holland. Now when we have reached the base of the mountain, we feel just prepared for a climb of three miles to the height of three and a half thousand feet above the sea. Here we enter a monastery and inquire of the monks the best way to the top of Pentelicus. We find them pleasant and cordial. One of them offers to accompany us to the summit free of charge, but we choose to be our own guide. Here it becomes us to say, we feel very different towards the monks of the Greek and Roman churches from what we did, before we had any acquaintance with them. We are forced in spite of former prejudices to acknowledge that the majority of them are earnest and devoted Christians. In the past we have known more of their faults than of their virtues.

At the foot of the mountain it is like summer, even now that the sun at noonday is touching the lowest point in his annual course. The oaks, lindens, and osiers, have scarcely let fall a leaf from their boughs. The acorns still hold fast to their cups, and the locust pods dangle on the limbs. The birds are thick and merry. When half-way up the mountain, it is like spring. The heather is in full bloom, nearly covering the surface, while it is as completely covered with honey bees. The air is tinged with purple hues and filled with humming music.

Here we come to the two great marble quarries. The larger one is open to the light. Its perpendicular walls are immense. At its base and on one side, is a wide cavern hung and set with stalactites and stalagmites of marble and alabaster, tinged with a variety of hues. The mouth of the grotto is fringed with ivy and heather. This marble resembles that of Paros in whiteness, surpassing it in fineness, and eclipses the Carraran in lustre and purity of color.

About twenty-two hundred and ninety years ago this quarry, which is now as silent as death, resounded with the din of hammers and the creaking of cordage and pulleys, as huge blocks were lifted from their massive beds.

We cannot help looking upon the spots, where great men were born, with feelings of respect and love. So the old homes of Burns, Scott, Washington, Schiller, and Humboldt, are objects of admiration. We are willing to journey far away to see a philosopher, or to look upon a poet, or to be greeted by a saint; and how can we stand in this silent quarry, the birthplace of so many grand structures and beautiful statues, without feelings of veneration? He must be emotionless, who could look upon this vast chamber, so suggestive of immortal fabrics, without enthusiasm and profoundest gratitude.

On the summit of Pentelicus, we experience a winter climate without any snow. The air is sharp and bracing. It is marvellous how far the eye can reach. Almost the whole of Greece can be surveyed from this point. Our vision ranges over plains, hills, rivers, bays, straits, seas, and mountains, whose names are immortal in song and history.

The physical character of this country is

strangely diversified. The elements spread out before the eye, combine to offer every conceivable variety of landscape views. The mountains are numerous and lofty in proportion to the extent of surface. Their crests of marble and snow, their sides belted with grass and herbage, present in the sunlight the pictures of interchanging silver, emerald and amethyst.

To the westward rise up eight thousand feet Arcadian Cyllene, and Parnassus so long believed to be the home of the muses. To the north the classic peaks of Ossa and Pelion tower high, and still higher is giant Olympus which once rocked the gods in his snowy cradle. It is impossible to represent fully the enchanting beauty and grandeur of these mountains. It is not strange this air, this climate, this diversified scenery, should have resulted in bringing forth, exhilarating, and exalting an intellectual and æsthetic race.

At the foot of Pentelicus to the north and east, lies in calmest silence along the seashore the plain of Marathon. With our glass we can easily trace its surface of six miles long and two wide. It is completely shut in by mountains and sea. Can it be, that is the plain on which four hundred and ninety years before Christ the ten thousand Greeks met in deadly conflict the hundred thousand Persians? That was a terrible struggle; the few against the many, the right against the wrong. The Persians were routed and driven to their ships, leaving six thousand dead, while the Athenians lost less than two hundred men. Miltiades and Callimachus won lasting glory; Datis and Artaphernes experienced lasting shame. All that now remains on that renowned field to tell of Grecian valor and Persian cowardice, is the little mound marking the spot where the Athenian dead were tenderly buried. Yes, it was on that mound that Pericles stood not long after the brave heroes had fallen and pronounced eloquent eulogies upon their life and memory. He pointed out the virtues and merits of the fallen, showing that they should be held in everlasting remembrance. " Emulous of men like these," he said, turning to the Athenians, " do you also, placing your happiness in liberty, and your liberty in courage, shrink from no warlike dangers in defence of your country."

We can but admire the ancient Grecian character. It is so simple and true to nature. They felt as we feel in our normal state. They wrote perfect poems, essays, and speeches; they produced perfect vases, statues, and temples. They wrought as we now work; they do not seem to be twenty-five centuries off, but close by our side, as we take in their thought and work. They were wont to cast bouquets at the feet of their statesmen, and decorate the graves of their patriots with flowers. The thoughts that stirred the souls of Plato, Phidias, and Solon, thrill souls still. It matters little when and where we live, if we are only true to highest conditions and opportunities; for then we shall be like the royally true everywhere.

Let us now return to the city and survey the site of ancient Athens. As we take our position upon the Acropolis, in fancy we see the old city proudly embracing this rocky height which was crowned with the completest works of art and beauty, as an altar where the immortals delighted to dwell. Here the Athenian might stand on this platform of solid rock three hundred feet high, one thousand feet long, and five hundred feet wide, and survey his fatherland. Yonder to the south and west lay the harbors of his city, thronged with ships from all parts of the world. A short distance to the east flowed the sacred Ilissus, and to the west, the famous river Cephisus. Well might the Athenian then be proud of his inheritance of thrilling memories, of valorous deeds, of inimitable arts, of unequalled landscape pictures.

As we tarry in this city of Themistocles and Phidias, Cimon and Miltiades, we can scarcely be too grateful to the mother of many of our arts and sciences. She bequeathed them to Rome and to England and to America. Really we have no beautiful work of art, no finish of church, or hall, but that points to some relic scattered about the Acropolis. We are made to realize, as we look and think, that this is the ideal country of art, genius, poetry, and romance. Here voices speak, telling us as nowhere else, how Plato mused, Socrates taught, Pericles ruled, Aristides won virtue, Æschylus called forth tears, Euripides melted hearts, Phidias carved, and Demosthenes spellbound the passions and set on fire the genius of his countrymen. At every step we touch some memorial of the past. How enchanting must have been the city, whose relics are now strewn about us, when it rose up in its perfectness with its gleamings of marble and glistenings of precious metals, kissing the balmy air and clear sunlight of these Grecian skies! Ancient Athens will live forever and remain young and beautiful in the imagination of the scholar and the poet. Her Acropolis shall be the proudest pedestal crowned with the most perfect statues of cultured genius.

The summit of this hill can be approached only from the west. The gateway which the Greeks called Propylæa, is inviting as well as imposing. Its stones are immense and the workmanship unique. It was intended to be for a defence and a monument of beauty. It was all this. The Athenians were delighted with it, and national foes tried to imitate it. It had five openings through which the periodic throngs of jubilant Pantheists were wont to move. The grooves of the chariot wheels are still visible on the entrance floor. These stones have been worn by the tread of the most gifted sons of Athens. A trifle within the Propylæa is the restored temple of the Wingless Victory. Pausanias informs us that he gave no wings to Victory, because the Athenians would not allow her to fly from their city.

Near the centre of this elevation and in the most prominent place, stands what remains of the Parthenon, — that temple of all temples, ordered by Pericles, built by Ictinus, and adorned by Phidias. Its grand columns, its vast blocks of marble, its fragments of statues and relievos, indicate that it was once a perfect building. Simplicity and majesty of mass and proportion were its striking characteristics. The eye is fascinated even in studying the outlines of its ruins. If it has been mutilated by Venetian bombs, by the mines of Morosini, by the hammer of Theodore, by the artillery of Turk and Greek; if hosts of its statues and treasures have been captured by Lord Elgin and King Ludwig, and borne away to Rome, Munich, Paris, and London, yet plenty remains to assure the inspector that in its completeness, it was a perfect poem cut in stone; that it was a monument of petrified light, reflecting the genius and art of a refined people. What an advanced civilization that could produce a Pericles to order, a Phidias to design, an Ictinus to execute, numerous sculptors to decorate, large means to defray expenses, and minds to admire and appreciate such a temple! When will another such edifice be built? Not while Gothic architecture holds the sway. The Gothic is sombre and beautiful, but the Greek is full of order and light, — heaven's first and last factors of perfect creations!

The Parthenon was constructed entirely of Pentelican marble. It was surrounded by a peristyle of forty-six columns; each column was over six feet in diameter at the base and nearly thirty-six high. At each end of the temple stood a portico of six columns. The edifice was two hundred and twenty-eight feet in length; one hundred feet in breadth; and forty-seven feet in height.

To the north of the Parthenon are the remains of the Erechtheum, a beautiful Ionic temple. Some of its adornments are well preserved, showing that it was deserving a place near the temple of Minerva.

There are foundations and relics of other temples and monuments which once graced this height. Looking over the wall to the south, almost under us, we discover the ruins of the Odeum of Atticus Herodes which was built in honor of his wife Regilla, that songs might be sung to delight the Athenians. To the east of this are some of the marble seats, still visible, of the Dionysiac Theatre where the elite of Athens were wont to listen to the plays and tragedies of Æschylus, Sophocles, and Euripides.

Still farther to the east and at the foot of the Acropolis, we see the unique memorial of Lysicrates, known as the Lantern of Demosthenes. A hundred rods farther east, we observe the arch of Hadrian which opens to the Olympieum which was once the superb temple of Jupiter. The thirteen columns of Corinthian style now standing, out of the hundred and twenty-four, give evidence that it must have been grand, indeed.

To the west from the Acropolis, not far off, do we see the best preserved work of antiquity in Athens,—the temple of Theseus. The building is now quite complete. Its style and architecture are modelled after the Parthenon. In it are preserved some of the fragments of the statuary which adorned the old city. But among the whole collection there is not an entire statue, or piece of art work. The better specimens, or complete productions, saved from the ravages of war, or dug from the ruins, have all been shipped to foreign cities, so that modern Athens must go abroad to witness the best works extant of its ancient city.

Turning the eye across the Agora, which is the valley leading to the Propylæa, is the Pnyx Hill. Its front is somewhat abrupt and portions of its ledges are cut away so as to form steps, seats, and a bema. Here the multitudes used to assemble, to listen to the eloquence of Grecian orators. From that stony platform Demosthenes delivered his speeches which thrilled and delighted the gathered hosts. Can it be that the living orator even dreamed that, as his smooth tones fell upon listening ears, his words would descend through the ages to stimulate youthful declaimers with patriotic ambition, and gratify the profoundest minds?

A little way to the south of the Pnyx, in the solid stone of the Museum Hill, is the prison of Socrates. From the top of the ledge an opening was cut, and deep down in the rock three cells were hewn out; in one of these the great philosopher was confined on account of his free thought and free expression; but he was honest and his philosophy was dearer to him than his life. He was ready to suffer at the hands of sophists, because he believed in the durability of justice, the instability of wickedness, the happiness of virtue, and the punishment of sin. No wonder the passionate Alcibiades should say, "When I listen to Socrates my heart leaps, and tears rush to my eyes. I have heard Pericles and other able orators, but they do not move me like this Marsyas. Within he is full of earnestness and the sweetest virtue." It is not singular that such a one should endure, when passion raged and Pantheistic force locked him in prison walls. His firmness to the right enabled him without flinching to drink the deadly hemlock, and then resignedly lay himself on his pallet of straw to die. As we witness in imagination the noble man departing this life, that gloomy prison becomes lighted up with a halo of glory, and the dying Socrates becomes the greatest hero of all Greece, and the wisest philosopher of old Athens.

Once more look down just below us, only a short distance to the right of the Propylæa upon that pile of ledges shaped by the hand of nature, save the stairs which are cut into the rock, leading from the Agora to the summit. That is Areopagus, or Mars Hill, where the Greek Tribunal used to be held. That is really a sacred relic of ancient Athens. Around and upon those rocks the highest councils have assembled, the gravest charges been given, and the severest judgments been passed. Up those time-worn steps centuries after Socrates had been led as a prisoner, the Apostle Paul walked as one arraigned before the highest dignitaries. Before Stoic and Epicurean philosophers, and the most learned men of Greece, he delivered a bold, searching, and eloquent address. Then Athens was in her glory. The Acropolis was rife in beauty and magnificence. As Paul looked upon those altars and temples around him, consecrated to false worship, and as he recalled the inscription, "To the unknown God," what spiritual language fell from his lips! His words moved hearts there, as they never had been moved before. His logic seemed more potent than that of the wisest sophists, his eloquence, more searching than that of Pericles, and his philosophy, deeper than that of Plato.

The glory of old Athens has faded and greatly wasted under the ravages of time. The wisdom of Greece has grown dim, as it has travelled down through the centuries, but the glory of Paul blazes as never before. While the doctrines of the Stoics and Epicureans have waned, the teachings of the Apostle have waxed strong. While through nature, history, and relics, we are led to admire old Athens, through Paul we are induced to adore the city of our God. Let us rejoice that we can look back to Socrates, as the grandest hero of classic Athens, and to Paul, as the glorified saint of Attica.

XI.

LOWER EGYPT AND CAIRO.

WE took passage from the Queen City of the Adriatic for Alexandria. The sun was dipping close to the horizon, as our steamer slowly pressed its way along the serpentine channel into the deep sea. The city reflected silver and gold as the sunlight played upon roof, dome, and tower. The water was smooth as glass, and the sky, of the deepest blue. Our departure from that quaint city seemed signally fortunate. The mind had been interested in its novelties, its streets of water, its gondolas and boats for hacks and coaches, its palaces and churches, its Bridge of Sighs and Ducal Palace, its paintings and sculptures, its doves and beads. As we cast lingering looks upon the vanishing city, we could but think of other days and olden times, when artist, hero, and scholar, ruled this land and sea, when ships from all climes were bearing heavy burdens to and fro across these waters, and Venice was the pride of regal doges, ruling the world in commerce.

A prosperous passage through the night brought us the next morning into the harbor of Brindisi, once ancient Brundusium, the terminus of the Appian Way, and rendered forever memorable by the death of Virgil. As we go on shore, we find here and there a relic of the old city, reminding us of that eventful convention in which Horace and Mæcenas acted such a conspicuous part; and of that siege which Pompey sustained with the consuls and senators of Rome against Julius Cæsar.

We found but little in the modern to remind us of the Milanese, the Romans, or the Venetians. The people have lost much of the ancient civilization, and learned little of the modern. They look hard and homely. Most of them go barefooted and with unwashen faces.

At sunset we leave this city. The wind is blowing strong from the east, and it is not long before some of the passengers are ready to pay homage to Neptune. On the following day we catch sight of Grecian highlands near sandy Pylos, and are strongly reminded of classic scenes and heroic deeds. In imagination we see Telemachus hastening to inquire of Nestor concerning the fate of his dear father. Day by day, and night by night, we are riding under the same sun and stars that shone upon Cadmus and Jason, upon lawgiver and prophet.

On the fifth day of sailing from Brindisi from the bow of our steamer, we spy a small object far ahead and just above the waves of the sea; and in half an hour more, a long range of sandy coast is presented, dotted with numerous windmills, and in the centre of the crescent-shaped shore stands the city of Alexandria overtopped with its numerous domes and minarets. At once we discover that to be a peculiar city, unlike any in western lands. Soon anchors are dropped in the roadstead, a mile from the shore, and immediately a score, or more, of small boats crowded with yellow faces in the midst of blue and white shirts, red caps, and variegated turbans, are rapidly approaching our vessel, and almost as quick as thought they are on deck here and everywhere, clutching at this valise and that umbrella, this bundle and that trunk. The passengers are amazed and enraged; some must laugh and others scold. In such a crisis coolness could hardly be considered a virtue. As we stand guarding our effects, it is pleasant to feel, there must be an end to all mortal fusses; and at length the rage is over, and a tall, straight, and well dressed

Arab accosts us, asking, if we would like a dragoman. This means, would you like a courier, a valet, an adviser, in short, one who is to speak for you, and provide for you? He is dressed in loose trousers, a tight jacket of light blue broadcloth, and a red cap. He conducts himself gentlemanly, and is careful not to present any claims, but begins to talk at once about America and England, evidently being at loss to decide whether we are from the new, or old world. He presently informs us, if we wish, we can go on shore in his boat. In these Eastern ports, there are no wharves; so the ships are obliged to anchor out some distance from shore, receiving and discharging their passengers and cargoes in small boats. We accept of the kindly offer and are soon on shore, and in front of the custom-house having for the most part sand for its flooring and the open sky for its roofing. A barefooted official soon demands our passports, hurriedly scans them over and returns them, requesting the gate to be opened that we may be ushered into the city of Alexandria. As we search for our baggage, we find it is undergoing examination; great brawny hands are fumbling it over and piercing eyes are penetrating every crevice and nook, expecting to find some "tobac," or "vino," which will be subject to heavy duties, and will be quite certain to place in their hands much bukshish.

But disappointment is pictured on the officer's face as he comes to the last parcel and discovers nothing subject to taxation. By no means are all the other voyagers so fortunate. Now as we advance into the city what a variety of costumes and complexions meets us on every hand! What a mingling of the strange and the familiar! Surely the oriental and occidental have met here, and are apparently forming unions for life. Here are to be seen French, English, Italians, Copts, Moors, Bedouins, Turks, and Nubians. We hear as many different tongues spoken on the sidewalk, as we see different faces. The contrast of dress is singularly striking. The Frenchman looks as though he had just come out of the drawer; the Arab as though he had just crawled out of the mud. The little donkeys which are flying about the streets so lively, are novelties, indeed! It seems strange how such tiny legs and small bodies can bear up so large burdens. Here comes along one with a fat old Arab upon his back with his long legs dangling almost to the ground. It is plain, the rider would pull down more pounds avoirdupois than the animal under him. Yonder we see half a dozen gentlemen, perhaps, clerks from the stores, galloping off upon the backs of these little creatures with boys running close to their heels, spurring them up. In another direction we discover a whole street full of donkeys with naked boys upon their backs, seated between bags of water; close upon them are several sailors from some ship just anchored in the harbor, taking their first ride upon the Egyptian tramwāy. They all turn down a street crowded with camels and dromedaries, laded with merchandise. They rush together pell-mell, and are very soon strangely mixed together and brought to a stand-still. Donkeys keep rushing in from all quarters; it at once becomes a monstrous jumble. Now begins the Moslem's chorus of pulling, whipping, and kicking; at length, the Gordian knot begins to unloose, and by some mysterious means all are set free and go on their way as though nothing strange had happened.

In the eastern part of the city we come to the Pillar of Pompey which towers above all surrounding objects. This consists of a pedestal ten feet square and fifteen feet high, with a round column of solid granite, seventy feet high and six feet in diameter, crowned with a beautiful capital. This reminds us of another city which once stood where the modern now stands. History and memory enable us to look across the sea to Greece. Some three hundred and thirty-two years before the Christian era, in imagination we see a youth full of promise and ambition; he had been for a long while under the instruction of the wise Aristotle. His father Philip who had proved himself a wise general, was suddenly cut off in the midst of great undertakings. The son at once stepped forth to carry out the plans of his father. So we discover the youthful Alexander crossing the Ægean Sea with Grecian forces and marching through Asia Minor and Syria, conquering city after city, till at length he reaches the mouth of the Nile, where he founds a city taking his own name, which in less than two centuries becomes opulent and cultured. About the time the Ptolemies succeeded the Pharaohs, when Memphis was old and Thebes crumbling into ruins, Alexandria was in its greatest splendor. Then the city had a population of some six hundred thousand inhabitants instead of sixty thousand, as at present. Then there was a broad street extending from Lake Mareotis to the Mediterranean. In the central part of this thoroughfare stood the Serapeum surrounded by its four hundred columns, of which Pompey's

Pillar was one. In connection with this temple was that great Alexandrian library of seven hundred thousand volumes in manuscript after four hundred thousand volumes had been destroyed. Here, too, was a university in which were assembled fifteen thousand students at the same time, to listen to the lectures of Origen, Philo, Euclid, Manetho, Aristophanes, Apollonius, and Apelles. Theology, science, art, and history, received special attention. This city then was the centre of civilization and learning. Scholars came hither from all parts of the world for instruction. Grecian and Egyptian skill united to adorn it with the grandest works of art. As we go upon the sea-shore, we can witness the site where that first lighthouse was built, rising up five hundred feet above the sea, and from whose summit the nightly fires were kept burning that safe passage might be made far away upon calm, or troubled waters. The lighthouse of Pharos constructed out of the whitest marble, was worthy to be counted among the seven wonders of the world.

Close upon the sea stood one of the Needles of Cleopatra, a monolith of syenitic granite, being seventy feet high, and dating back fully twelve centuries before the Christian era. This obelisk is one of many which once adorned the city of Heliopolis. As the stranger gazes upon its tapering spire and its quaint hieroglyphics, his mind must thrill with stirring associations. He can but recall the name of Rameses III., in whose honor it was erected, and the dusky queen of Egypt, whose name it bears at the present time. It is an enduring monument of pathos and wildest history. Shakespeare has verily made it a poem in stone. Now it is the property of our country, and graces Central Park, New York. How it kindles the imagination and lights up the past! How expressive the union of the oldest and the youngest, the marriage of the ancient to the modern!

A little way from Pompey's Pillar on the east, we come into a grove of palm-trees. These are growing indigenous to the soil; they are quite unlike the trees of our groves, or forests. They have not the grace of the elm, or the strength of the oak, or the conical beauty of the maple. They will average about fifty feet high and a foot in diameter. Their leaves are all at the top, spread out like an umbrella reversed. Under these are thickly clustered the dates. There are six or eight bunches on each tree, and each bunch contains something like a bushel of fruit. A native comes out to gather dates; so fastening a rope round his body and clasping it about the trunk of the tree, adjusts it in such a manner that, as his feet are braced against the tree, the rope upon his back sustains him. By springing and lifting the rope at the same time on the tree, he ascends quickly to the fruit. There high from the ground he rests composedly, picking out the ripe dates till his basket is full; and then lets himself down as strangely as he ascended. Certainly, education does accomplish wonders.

Passing to the market-place, we find it is a favorable time to visit it, for it is Saturday, the special day for sales. A large number of cattle have lately arrived from far up the Nile, and many sheep have recently come in from the Lebanon hills. The grounds are not divided into compartments, but everything is just where it happens to be. All seems to be marvellously mixed up. How strange the animals look! The oxen have giant frames and little flesh. They have large humps above their shoulders and monstrous spreading horns; their color is that of the mouse; and they are valued at sixty dollars a pair. The sheep have evidently been where the grass was plenty and sweet. These are larger than the Swiss, the Scotch, or New England sheep. Their wool is long and fine.

The cows are few and very coarse. They afford no signs of filling a twelve-quart, or even a six-quart pail, at one milking. The people here rely largely upon goats for milk, and these are almost countless and of several varieties. We see some fine horses looking as though they had just been led out of English, or American stalls. A good horse will bring here from three to five hundred dollars. The inevitable donkeys are present in large numbers, and full of their pranks, keeping the boys in charge of them on a constant lookout. The poultry are well represented. The fowls are not caged but tied together in bunches by their legs. How unmerciful is such treatment! But custom sanctions it, and custom sanctions also woman's killing them. The wheat, beans, pease, cotton, millet, dates, pomegranates, are strewn round in great confusion. Disorder appears to be the law of the place.

Not far from the market we enter a Moslem cemetery containing forty acres in area. It is thickly crowded with mounds from one to three feet high; the larger are graves of men, and the smaller, of women. The Mohammedan regards woman as inferior when she comes into this world, and as inferior when she goes out of it, and so he emphasizes this feeling by burying her in an insignificant grave. The only vegetation in the yard consists of sunburnt cactuses and half a dozen locust-trees. It is a most desolate burial ground. While wandering among the graves, we observe a funeral procession advancing. It is led by a dozen women dressed in black and white; then come two bearers with the corpse on their heads, followed by forty men as mourners; no female kindred are allowed to be present. The women leading are hired to wail and lament. Oh! what noises they make as they are approaching the grave! When this is reached, the corpse is laid upon the ground and a priest performs a short service, and then the body is placed in the grave, in a partly sitting position with the face turned towards Mecca. The mourners now withdraw to a locust-tree and are seated under its shade, smoking their pipes and apparently not discomforted, while the hired servants are doing their best in the way of weeping. Thus they tarry till the grave is covered, and when this is done they leave the yard with quick steps and light hearts, as though they had not been disturbed by any great grief, or rendered lonely by the departure of a dear friend.

Near Pompey's Pillar we descend into deep cavities. As we go down, we find the dirt or earth as solid as stone; when some fifty feet from the surface our tapers are lighted, and we follow winding passages; as we advance we find remnants of pottery, fragments of tombstones, and pieces of human bones. These cells and vaults were once filled with mummies which were deposited here long centuries ago. Many of them have been taken out of these dark recesses well preserved. Some of them may now be seen in the museums of Paris, London, and New York. Now and then we discover niches in the sides of the cavities, where, no doubt, vases were placed, and lamps were kept burning. The relics plainly show that these were burial places of ancient Greeks and Romans. Many of the urns and vases taken from these tombs, are beautiful in style and finish, showing that the dwellers here did excel in moulding the clay. While searching among these relics, we can but have the feeling, the world is old. It is evident, the land here has been sinking during past ages, and this will account for these tombs being buried deep beneath the modern city.

Is it asked, how we like the government of this country? We can say, we find it exceedingly Turkish. The governor, or pacha, has things his own way. In name only is he subject to the sultan of Constantinople. The past history of the country shows that it has been controlled by a succession of more than three hundred kings. Its record breathes of bloody tyranny. The present ruler holds the life and death of his subjects in his own hands. Without any trial he has caused many to be put to death. All who take part in his government must be his sworn friends. It is true that in his realm, progress is being made in the way of railroads and steamboats, but this is mainly due to foreign pressure and the necessity of the age. Most of the wealth and enterprise of Alexandria at the present time is due to foreigners. Good fortune now seems to be smiling somewhat propitiously upon the city of the great warrior whose name it perpetuates. Perchance, when western cities shall have grown old and wise, and shall be wasting away, Alexandria shall grow again into a city of fifteen miles in circumference, becoming once more the centre of art and learning.

But we must bid adieu to this city; so taking the train for Cairo, we are soon moving across a wide and level stretch of country. Looking out of the car-windows, we see canals of water bordered with rushes and covered in places with white lilies having blossoms a foot in diameter, and pads exposing a much larger surface. How we wish, we might pick some of these surprising beauties and send them across the great sea to the loved ones who delight so much in the works of nature. On either hand are to be seen fields of cotton, rice, millet, and Indian corn. It is now the last of September, and in places camels and donkeys are yoked together ploughing the ground for sowing the wheat. In some parts of the country three crops a year are taken from the same field. These may be wheat, rice, and Indian corn. As we examine the rich soil, we can realize, how the land is the gift of the Nile. We frequently pass villages with houses huddled together, and built out of sun-burnt brick. Their appearance is far from being inviting. Still as we stop at their depots, it is pleasant, to witness men, women, and children, offering cold water to passengers, hoping to receive in return some bukshish. Probably, there are no other people living, who are so temperate as to their drink, as the Mohammedans.

The valley of the Nile varies in width from five to ten miles. Its waters are now falling; they began to rise about the first of June, reaching their height the last of August. The land rises from the river in terraces; and as the water withdraws from the highest and most distant, the peasant goes forth often sowing the wheat upon the soft mud; and by the time the water has receded from the second terrace, making it ready for sowing, the grain of the first sowing is up some inches; and by the time the seed is up on the land close by the river, that which was first sown, is ready for harvest. So here we have a beautiful illustration of that Scripture saying, "First the blade, then the ear, after that the full corn in the ear"; or as we witness them casting the grain upon the shallow water, as it is leaving the field, we are reminded of another passage saying, "Cast thy bread upon the waters, and after many days, it shall return unto thee." In places we notice oxen turning the windlass and so raising water from lower to higher ditches; we also see men lifting it by means of the old-fashioned well-sweep, or standing on opposite sides of the ditches, swinging tight woven baskets by ropes attached to the handles, so as to throw it upon the elevation above them; in this way they keep the fields irrigated.

At length we are crossing the Nile; we find it a wide river at this season of the year; though its natural embankments cannot be a mile apart. Not far below us the Delta begins, and the river commences to divide into numerous branches, so that at its mouth there are many rivers emptying its waters into the sea. In the distance we can see the desert, and now we are reminded of the warfare which has been going on for ages between the sand and water. The Nile speaks of life, and the desert of death. So far the river has borne off the palm. No wonder, it has been an object of worship. It breathes of mystery, and yet is full of hope. To the Egyptians it is a good power, while the desert is an evil one. No wonder, it should give rise to the allegory of the burial of Osiris in its sacred waters, whence he rose once a year, to scatter fresh blessings over the earth. Its annual overflow which has occurred within a few hours of the same time for centuries, presents a problem in physical science which has not yet been solved. Here in Lower Egypt it rises from twenty-five to thirty feet. Should it come short even a few inches of twenty-five feet at Cairo, the people would expect a famine; or should it rise but little above its ordinary height, they would fear great devastation from floods. So they have watched and worshipped the Nile. In all the cities along the banks, there have been priests whose exclusive service has been devoted to the god, Nilus. Then, too, its plants and vegetation have been regarded divine; and so they have been expressed in works of art. Everywhere in their tombs and temples are to be seen the graceful outlines of the rose-colored lotus. As friends have died, they have regarded it a blessing, if their bodies could be borne across the Nile to the silent city. They have cherished the feeling that the god Anubis watched over all such burials. Are we aware, when we speak of the darkling stream, and crossing the river of death, we are using images which originated by the mysterious Nile?

Now that we are over the river, we are reminded, we are on the western border of the land of Goshen. Here imagination cannot fail of presenting pictures of the old Israelites, as they were settled in this country. At first they were only a little handful of Abrahamic descendants, providentially, it would seem, brought into the land and so guarded, that for more than two hundred years they multiplied in numbers and advanced in civilization, till they became a mighty power in Egypt. In cultivating the soil, in working stone and wood, and moulding the clay, they took the lead. At length the original inhabitants began to fear their influence, and Pharaoh set in operation forces which soon ground them down into the most abject slavery. At that time a few miles to the east of us stood the city of On, better known as Heliopolis. It was then the seat of wisdom and culture, the Oxford of Egypt, filled with temples and colleges. Here it was that Joseph married his beautiful Asenath; here Moses was schooled, laying the foundation, deep and strong, for a noble life and character. Still later Plato resided here for some twelve years as a student; no doubt, it was here that he became initiated into the great doctrine of immortality which afterwards flamed out in his classic Phædon. The only relic left of that grand old city is a single obelisk similar in shape and size to the Needles of Cleopatra. Could we only solve the mysteries of its curious hieroglyphics, what strange histories of past ages would be revealed! But now we must leave it a mystery amidst a cluster of date and acacia trees.

After riding some eight hours in the cars from Alexandria, we find ourselves at the station just outside of Cairo. The first look upon this city assures us, it is altogether Oriental. Here again we are beset with the donkey boys; they are determined we shall have a ride into the city upon their quaint tramway; but we decline all offers, and push our way into the city of tall houses, numerous mosques overtopped with still more numerous domes and minarets, and along streets crowded with countless men, women, and children. As we look up, it seems odd to see the roofs on the opposite sides of the streets drawing in towards each other, and frequently meeting so as to shut out the sunlight. We step into a hotel and inquire the price of board and lodging per day, and we are informed, six dollars in gold; thinking this too high, we pass on to another and make the same inquiry, and are informed, four dollars in gold, which is the cheapest house in the city for its conveniences. So here we take up our abode and fare well as to all necessary comforts.

As we go out into this city of more than six hundred thousand inhabitants, we find the houses huddled together, the streets everywhere narrow and shut in, and all the day long, hosts of people crowding the thoroughfares, as though all had been turned out of doors. As we watch their movements, they do not appear to have any special object in view except that of simply killing time. Now and then the monotony will be broken by some Arab whipping his wife, because she has let the veil covering the lower part of her face drop so as to expose her mouth and chin; still he delights to have her make exhibition of her nude breast, especially, if it is prominently developed. The stores are on a small scale. The goods in the average store might be placed all at once upon the back of a donkey, and he would bear them away with ease. We discover some manufactures going on here and there, though on a small scale. It is stated, there are those engaged in work all the way from picking up refuse in the streets to constructing a watch. As we are passing along, our attention is attracted to a school by the roadside. The building has for its flooring the sand and for its roofing the open sky. As we stop to look in upon them, the two masters and forty pupils from the ages of six to ten years old, spring to their feet and advance towards us, sharply gazing at the strangers, as much as to say, it is our privilege to look, as well as yours. For five minutes, or more, the mutual staring is kept up; and then teachers and children assume their sitting positions right in the sand, and begin to move their lips and swing their bodies back and forth; we inquire of our dragoman what they are doing. He says, "They are learning a Mohammedan prayer, and, when they shall have committed a few prayers to memory and learned a little smattering of numbers, so as to calculate bukshish, then their schooling will be completed." How sad for children to be thus conditioned! They have apparently good physiques and intelligent faces. Could they only be educated in our own country, what men they would be likely to make! But their religion binds them as with iron chains in ignorance. In this land the priest and the sword have the mightiest sway.

At length we come into the quarter of the bazaars. As the eye reaches on, it would seem, there must be more than half a mile of stores clustering together. Entering them we find all kinds of productions of the country for sale, and a great variety of articles from the far east, and a few from the far west. The merchants are very polite, and proffer us at once little cups of coffee, which it is expected we will drink without hesitancy, whether we are disposed to trade with them or not. As we sip the coffee, we soon feel it tingling to the very ends of our fingers, convincing us, if the quantity is small, the quality is large. Some of the shawls, shoes, and silks, are beautiful, but costly. If one has money in abundance, here is a good chance to spend it.

Leaving the bazaars our attention is soon attracted by a band of music, so called; but it strikes us their instruments must be the same as the Israelites used in blowing down the walls of Jericho. At least, the noise is tremendous. On inquiry we learn that a wedding is being celebrated. So we watch the movements, and soon discover a carriage in front of a house with bunches of money attached to the covering; this is the bride's dowry. It is not long before the front door opens and a piece of carpeting is stretched to the carriage, and an object completely wrapped in white raiment is led to it and helped within, and the door is shut. We are informed this is the bride, but we ask, where is the bridegroom? "Oh," it is stated, "he has gone off in some other direction, and, perhaps, will not meet this wife for weeks." It seems somewhat singular to us that the bride should have her first ride after her marriage alone. Just before the carriage starts, two long-legged fellows with rods in hand, dart away swinging them and crying out to the top of their voices, "Clear the way, clear the way," and the carriage follows on. The bride is bound for the public baths; she is pursued by a band of half-naked singers who make the air crazy with the most horrid discords and barbaric howls and screeches. Soon they are out of sight, leaving us with the impression that marriage in this country does not tend to elevate woman, or ennoble man.

As we look around, we behold a motley crowd. Here are Arabs, Turks, Numidians, and all sorts of human species from that of a puny, sore-eyed urchin with its face literally covered with flies, to those of handsome men. Some of the faces are yellow, others tawny, and others of darkest bronze. The costume of the better classes consists of trousers fastened about the body by a cord with silk tassels at the ends, a frock reaching down to the heels with full flowing sleeves; and on their heads the turban, or tarboosh. The lower orders wear generally, only a loose shirt, and many of the children are entirely nude. The manner in which affairs move on, conveys the idea that they are pretty well satisfied with this kind of life.

We now ascend to the citadel, and as we pass within the walls, we are soon made conscious, we are in the stronghold of the pacha of Cairo. The walls are massive about it. On the east side is a splendid mosque, and on the south a superb palace. Before we can walk on their polished floors, we must exchange our shoes for slippers, that no damage may be done the marbles as we pass over them. In the mosque the ceiling and walls are decorated with lively frescos. The side towards Mecca is inlaid with the richest red and white alabaster. To the right of the entrance is the sarcophagus of Mehemet Ali. Here we see no statuary, or paintings. The Koran forbids such ornaments to be in a Mohammedan church; however, in a few instances we have seen carvings of unknown plants and animals, called arabesques; these seem poor substitutes for the wonderful creations of Raphael, Angelo, and Rubens, which adorn the churches of Western Europe.

In the palace we find a large suite of rooms frescoed and carpeted with light and sombre colors. The dancing hall of the pacha's Circassian wives is strikingly gay. It is sufficiently large to accommodate two hundred at the same time; however, we make no effort to ascertain whether he has so many wives, or not.

From the palace we go to the well of Jacob and look down into a hole twenty feet in diameter and two hundred and seventy feet deep. Tradition says the Israelites were wont to draw water here. Certainly the well bears marks of age.

Now we seek the most favorable spot for prospecting, and lo, what a panorama lies spread out before us! To the north and east we can see the obelisk of Heliopolis; still nearer are the tombs of the Mamelukes; to the south are the lofty quarries whence the stone was cut out for the building of the city, and on their heights may be seen ruined castles and crumbling edifices. To the westward are the wasting ruins of old Cairo, the famous island of Rhoda, green with its groves of palms, and still farther on, the gigantic pyramids of Gizeh and Sahara. To the north and west along the banks of the Nile, are fields of waving corn; while close about and under us is the city of Cairo with its four hundred mosques of glistening spires and domes. From this place of look-off we would judge the city to be three miles in extent east and west, and a mile north and south. The buildings look as though they were all joined together. The roofs are mostly flat and evidently used for domestic purposes. They serve as sleeping apartments in the hottest seasons. Would it not be a strange sight to look at six hundred thousand people sleeping upon these house-tops! The sunset is fast approaching. The Moslems are expecting the calls all over the city of the muezzins from the lofty galleries of the minarets, bidding them worship Mohammed and their God. There are no bells here, as in America, to strike the hour of worship, or trumpets, as in Jerusalem, to proclaim the season of prayer.

In this vast city, there is no public library. In fact, we have seen no books in the shops, or stores, except a few copies of "The Arabian Nights," and a small work on geometry; neither is there any museum in which are gathered up treasures of antiquity. It seems as though the people are not living, but only staying here. We can but ask, how long is this order of things to continue? Why should the old civilization which was once so rife in this land, be suffered to dwindle into the present low state? All this region once was occupied by a prosperous and cultured people. Here were the haunts of poets, philosophers, and scholars. In those ancient days to be an Egyptian was an honor. Then countless hammers were ringing in the quarries; brickyards were busy with stirring hands and feet; potteries were turning out the most beautiful vases; grand temples were being built, and gorgeous palaces were adorning the banks of the Nile. But how fallen the glory of the past! Refinement has been supplanted by vulgarity; erudition, by ignorance; the beautiful, by the ugly; the palace, by the hut; progress, by deterioration. As we bid adieu to the city of Saladin and the Arabian Nights, we must think of it, as an ever-changing panorama of life and death, of the caressings of the Nile and the blastings of the Desert.

A donkey ride of twelve miles to the southwest takes us to the great pyramids. As we are borne away upon the little animals, we are forced to regard them strange anomalies of patience and endurance. On our way we pass through old Cairo, which we find a filthy and desolate place. We cross the Nile on the crudest raft to the island of Rhoda where stands the tall column bearing the records of the rise and fall of the river for many centuries; here the palm-trees are thriving, but the people dwelling among them are wretched indeed. From this land we are ferried once more, donkeys and all, across another branch of the river. By this time we begin to realize that the Nile is really a great institution, deserving to be called the mother of Egypt. It is many times the width of the Thames at London Bridge, or the Hudson at New York City. From this point we are hurried upon the gallop for miles over a level stretch of country to within a few hundred rods of the mighty wonders of the desert. Here we dismount, and wade through the sand, nearly knee-deep, to Cheops, and lo, right before us are the vast objects which inspired such amazement and mystery in our boyhood! How familiar they have been made to us by books and pictures! Like weird necromancers they invoke hosts of spectres from the shadowy graves of the past. Somehow as we gaze, we feel, they cannot well be exaggerated, any more than the Alps, or Niagara Falls. Ah! they had a history before history began — when the world's "gray forefathers" roamed at will over the earth, and angels made frequent visits to the children of men. Perchance, Abraham was familiar with their massive forms, and Joseph frequently rested under their extended shadows. Generations have lived and died; empires have risen and fallen; arts and sciences have flourished and decayed; still on the partings of the desert and the Nile, stand as of old these huge structures of unknown time, challenging the greatnesses of to-day!

But here we are, and the Bedouins, also. Like Hamlet's ghosts, they come and go in quick succession. We purchase the privilege from the pacha of the Bedouin tribe to ascend to the top of the largest pyramid by paying seventy-five cents each; and now we proceed at once for the climb, but as we attempt to leap to the top of the first layer of stone, behold, twenty hands are behind us, and we come back more quickly than we went up. Two, or three trials more, convince us, it is no use, we must employ two of these great brawny fellows to assist and defend us. As we strike a bargain with them, at once they clasp our wrists and leap up the huge blocks, pulling us after them, and in a few minutes we are on the top of Cheops at Gizeh. This was four hundred and eighty-four feet high, but several layers of stone have been thrown from the summit. It covers over thirteen and a half acres of ground, and its sides are precisely adjusted to the four cardinal points; the length of one side of the base is as many cubits, as there are days and parts of a day in a year; the height of the pyramid bears the same relation to the perimeter of the base, which the radius of a circle bears to the circumference. It is evident that the architects who planned it, were scientists, being familiar with astronomy and mathematics. According to Pliny, some three hundred and sixty thousand men were employed thirty years in building it. It is evident, a part of the stones were taken from quarries close at hand, and the rest were brought from far up the Nile. This pyramid, and also the next two largest, Chepren and Mycerinus, and the Sphinx, are built upon a range of Lybian ledge about one hundred feet above the river.

We enjoy a fine view from this height; the Nile can be seen for a long distance; and we can look far out upon the African desert; the pyramids of Sahara are readily seen. It is said, there are more than seventy of these pyramids in Egypt; some of them are constructed of brick and others of stone. Cheops is built entirely of stone having two hundred and seventy-two courses. As we complete our prospecting and commence to descend, our assistants clasp our wrists again, and shrewdly peering into the face, ask, if we know Jack and Jill, and begin to chant,

> " Jack and Gill went up the hill,
>   To draw a pail of water,
>   Jack fell down and broke his crown,
>   And Jill came tumbling after,
> Crying give bukshish, give bukshish,
> Goody American give much bukshish, much bukshish ! "

At length we are safe on the sand once more; and now we pass round to the north side, and enter a passage descending on an angle of twenty-six degrees, nearly four feet high and more than three feet wide, and three hundred and twenty feet long; at the end of this there is a horizontal passage leading to the mortuary room. Sixty-three feet from the entrance is an ascending passage for a hundred and twenty-five feet on an angle of twenty-six degrees; at this point is a horizontal passage to the left, one hundred and ten feet long, ending in the Queen's Chamber which is some eighteen feet long, seventeen feet wide and twenty high. Returning to the ascending passage and following its course, we soon come to the Great Gallery which is a hundred and fifty feet long, twenty-eight high, and seven wide. At the upper end of this we enter the King's Chamber which is thirty feet long, seventeen wide, and nineteen high. This, as well as the other chambers, or rooms, is lined, floored, and ceiled with syenitic granite, highly polished. In the walling of this room has been discovered a sarcophagus some twelve feet long, three wide, and three deep. Above this chamber are still other rooms. After examining the vast pile, it appears evident that it was designed as a tomb and memorial of the vain monarch who caused it to be built. Its workmanship is the perfection of art. The mind that conceived it must have been grand. For ages it has stood, and through the centuries to come it will stand, revealing its wondrous story to millions yet unborn.

Some rods in front of the pyramids of Gizeh

rises above the wavy sand, as from a petrified sea, a massive figure with a human face and a lion's body which the natives call Aboohol, signifying the father of terrors, or immensity. It is a monster of strange repose and indescribable meaning. It is couched, as it has been couched for unknown ages, with open eyes gazing into duration. Hither the Pharaohs, the old Hebrews, the ancient Persians, the classic Greeks, the brave Cæsars, Arab warriors, Christian believers, scientific savans, and curiosity seekers, have come in long procession and wondrously stared into that face, so expressive, and yet so unchanging. We may mock at it as we will, yet there is something grand in its unchangeableness.

A short distance to the southeast of these imposing monuments and closer upon the bank of the Nile, have been opened up from the wastes of sand, the ruins of old Memphis. If the name does not take hold of the heart at first like the name of New York, London, or Rome, still it had a brilliant history long before these modern cities were even dreamed of. Memphis had a splendid court, when Attic soil was roamed over by barbarians, and wildest savages were holding in their possession Latium. Hither came the great Alexander, looked and admired. During the reign of the Ptolemies, it was the city of civilization, and so it continued till it was conquered by Amrou and buried in the sands with all its pomp and glory of forty centuries.

Now, as its great temple is being uncovered, and its avenue of sphinxes revealed, we can but wonder at its magnificence, and cease to question that Memphis had once a circuit of sixteen miles. In the Louvre at Paris are to be seen some twelve hundred votive and sepulchral tablets taken from its Serapeum and its Apeum. The apis was the sacred animal of this city, and whenever it died, or was killed, it was carefully embalmed and sacredly interred in the Apeum whence four hundred mummies of this animal have been discovered within the last thirty years. These temples are lined and faced with polished red granite from Syene. Here are symbols and hieroglyphics telling of a people highly educated before Moses taught, or Homer sung; here are relics of art which had fulfilled their mission of cultivated taste and beauty long before the temple of Solomon glistened with gold, or the Parthenon reflected its silvery charms. Here are representations of ships somewhat like those now-a-days seen in Boston Harbor; of glass-blowers at work like those we saw in Venice; of flax-dressers toiling as they toil in Ireland to-day; of weavers reminding us of those producing the Roman scarfs; of potters turning off as elegant results as those now so celebrated at Sèvres; of painters who were masters before the canvas; of statuaries who possibly paved the way for Phidias and Angelo; and of gymnasts who evidently understood how to pitch the quoit, hurl the javelin, and throw the ball. In how many ways the history of Egypt marks the history of civilization! It was in Egypt the Hebrews first learned their lessons of fortitude and endurance. Here was called out the grand heroism of Joseph; here Moses was made the great lawgiver, and Joshua trained to his royal generalship. It was to this country the sages of Greece repaired for instruction. Rome stood abashed in the presence of Cleopatra. Christianity suffered no loss in the Alexandrian school of philosophy. Through whatever vista we look, the continuity of human history carries us back to the banks of the Nile, as the source of philosophy, science, and art. The course of civilization has been, Egypt, Greece, Rome, Modern Europe, America. Man is the heir of the ages; and step by step, his progress has been from the far East to the far West. If the sun of his fortunes rose in beauty, it promises to set in glory.

XII.

MODERN AND ANCIENT JERUSALEM.

IT is the last of October; the air is mild; the sun is dipping close to the western horizon; and the sky is reflecting opal and gold. Here we are, two thousand feet above the waters of the Mediterranean, still we are surrounded by hills upon which once stood cities that could not be hid. On our right is Mizpah crowned with its white mosque, wearing the appearance of departed greatness. Just under its shadow lies Gibeon thickly belted with trees of fig and olive. To the left is Gibeah, the birthplace and home of Saul. To the east is Ramah, now clothed in dust and ashes. Near at hand are wheat-fields generally covered with loose stones. Here and there are patches being sown, and others becoming green with growing wheat. Close by is a peasant hurrying up his little oxen, that he may plough in before sunset the wheat which he has sown, for should he leave it uncovered during the night, the birds would be likely to capture it, before he should return to his work on the morrow. As we survey the farmer, we discover that he is an Arab, some forty years of age, being five feet and eight inches tall, having a piercing eye, a broad chest and strong limbs. Outwardly he is a fine specimen of a man, but as our dragoman informs us that his education was limited to memorizing a few Mohammedan prayers and learning to count bukshish, we could but feel how unfortunate that mind should be thus oppressed. His oxen, though six years old, seem inferior, when compared with the cattle of England, or America. The yoke consists of a rough stick cut from an olive branch, made fast to the necks of the oxen by withes. The plough is evidently patterned after the one used in Noah's time; it cuts a furrow about four inches in depth and width. The sowing in Judæa is done before the ploughing, for there is scarcely any sod to be broken. As we look at the fields we can but wonder, how it is possible for vegetation to thrive here; everything looks scorched and dried up; for the past four or five months there has been no rain, but as the winter shall set in and the ground become watered, it will give forth abundantly. At first it appeared strange that fields should be so completely covered with stones, but on examination we can understand why it is proper and necessary; for the outcropping rock is of lime formation and, when pulverized, forms just the nutriment for grass and wheat; so these stones, as they lie all the long summer exposed to the burning sunlight and corroding gases, crumble in pieces and become suited to nourish grain and plants. It is singular how crisped and sunburnt almost everything is at this season, except where the wheat is just coming up, and now and then little clusters of crocus blossoms smile out from the rocks. As we dismount from our horses and pluck these flowers, how we wish, we might send bouquets of them far away over the seas to dear friends, because they would be so significant and clothed with the richest associations. Bevies of larks and sparrows are flying in every direction. No wonder, if the little birds were so plenteous in the time of Christ, that four should have been sold for a farthing. Then, too, the birds are full of sweetest song, certainly doing their utmost to overcome the weird appearance of desolation which is widely prevailing.

As we bend round a spur of the mountains, our dragoman exclaims, "There is Jerusalem!" and lo! three miles southward is Jerusalem, the city of which we have read and dreamed from our childhood. Our imagination has placed it above all other cities; we have regarded it as the home of the wisest men; as the spot where the saddest and greatest deeds have been wrought; as the place where prophets have lived, where apostles have taught, and the Son of man suffered, died, and was raised from the dead. In thought it is a marvellous city. The old seems infinitely superior to the new; though we must acknowledge, the modern city with its walls, battlements, minarets, domes, and towers, presents a grand appearance. Hills and mountains encircle it; yet it stands upon a cluster of hills. We can but feel, we are now everywhere treading sacred ground. All the way from Joppa, we have been following the path of the prophets, and now we are on the way which apostles travelled passing from Galilee to Mount Zion. The surface is greatly diversified. It is plain that the whole country is of volcanic origin; the surface rock is porous; and the rounded summits bear marks of aqueous, as well as igneous agencies. It would be difficult to find a more broken landscape. The road we are following is no more than a goat-path, still it has been the highway from Jerusalem to Samaria and Galilee for thousands of years. When within a mile of the city, we are informed that upon our right are the tombs of the Judges and the Kings, cut out of the native ledges, but we cannot stop to examine them at present. Soon we are under the shadows of the lofty walls and before the Damascus Gate of the city. We cannot gain entrance here, because the pacha has sent forth a mandate that no luggage shall enter this gate-way, so we are forced to turn our course round to the Jaffa Gate. On the north side of the city we find no buildings; the vacant space appears wild and forsaken; at the northwest corner we pass over a spur of the mountains which divides the waters of the Kedron from the valley of Gihon; on the west side we find the Russian Hospice consisting of a large cluster of buildings for the accommodation of pilgrims from that country, and a long block of dwellings for the accommodation of Jews who are unable to secure tenements inside the walls. At length, we find ourselves in front of the gate on the west. Our dragoman informs us that here we will be obliged to have our baggage examined, unless we buy off the custom-officers; so, as they present themselves ready for duty, we slip some bukshish into their hands, and they are very cordial and perfectly willing, we should enter the city without any further trouble. So in single file each horse steps his length into the gate-way, and then to the left his length, and then to the right his length, and behold! we are within the city of Jerusalem. Now, as we look around, we are ready to say distance does lend charms; for the immediate does not equal the remote view. But here we are within walls two and a fourth miles in extent, and from thirty to sixty feet in height. Their crests are irregular and broken by battlements and gate-towers. At first sight these walls appear formidable, but on examination we are satisfied, it would not require a long time for an American, or a Prussian battery of guns, if favorably adjusted, to raze them to the ground. We see remnants of other walls within the present one, showing that other cities have stood here. Some of the stones composing them are immense, and, no doubt, bear chisel-marks which were made more than two thousand years ago. These walls were constructed as a defence to the city. Through them open five gates: the Damascus, on the north; St. Stephen's, on the east; the African and Mount Zion, on the south; and the Jaffa, on the west.

The site on which the city is built, inclines to the east, and the houses are strangely huddled together, varying in height from one to two, three, and four stories. These are built out of gray limestone, having flat roofs for the most part. In fact, the only convenient places for walking within the city, are found upon the tops of the buildings. From the size and scarcity of the windows, we would infer that the people do not believe in sunshine and good air. Though their houses are joined so closely together, still there is much vacant space within the walls of the city.

Such streets we have never witnessed in any other town; they are devoid of all plan, or convenience. As we pass down St. David's, the main street, we find it paved with stones which were laid, perchance, before the time of the Crusades. They are worn so smooth, it is with difficulty our horses can move over them. They are too uneven and irregular, it is certain, for carriages to pass over them. For quite a distance this street is arched and overtopped with houses, and on each side are shops and stores having rooms from six to eight feet square, and six feet high. In a store is usually kept but one kind of goods, and not so much in quantity but they might all be packed with ease into a Saratoga trunk. The merchants are evidently pleased with their calling, and feel that they are doing business on a large scale.

The Turkish and Arabic tradesmen are generally sitting in the midst of their goods, so as to be able to reach handily any article kept for sale, and are usually anxious to sell, unless it be at the hour of prayer which comes five times a day. If you should be striking a bargain with them, and the muezzin should send down the call from the minaret, saying, "It is the hour to worship Allah," your trading would be sure to stop till the prayers were ended, and when these should be completed, the merchants would delight to drive a sharp bargain.

At length, while advancing on this street we are brought up against a dingy wall which intercepts the way, bearing the marks of age. This is supposed to be a wall that belonged to the ancient city. As we turn from this to Christ's Street towards Damascus Gate, we observe many changers, brokers, dry-goods and hardware merchants, engaged in trade on no larger scale than those on St. David's Street. While passing along almost every merchant beckons us, or holds out some article, hoping to induce us to buy. They tease foreigners, as though they believed, their pockets were full of sovereigns.

But what are we after in particular so near the close of the day? An abiding place while we may sojourn in Jerusalem. Are there hotels here? Yes, two, but their rates are so exorbitant that we are searching for the Prussian Hospice, where our dragoman informs us, we can be comfortably cared for by paying a dollar a day. Soon on Christ's Street we halt before an iron door; the bell is rung, and immediately the key is turned and a Prussian gentleman presents himself; our passports are examined, and then we are invited to ascend upon the house-top, and there above the rest of the buildings we are shown into a room which we can occupy, when we wish, during our stay in the city. It is proper to state here, that we find this a Christian home and our wants are well supplied. Of course, we do not see any beefsteak on the table, nor much mutton, still we have chicken, eggs, tea and coffee, and good wheat bread which is occasionally somewhat gritty for the reason, it is threshed upon the ground and winnowed as of old, and usually ground by hand; however, in Jerusalem they have one grist-mill driven by mules. The water, as it comes upon the table in glass bottles, is likely at this season of the year, to be somewhat disturbed, as we look through it towards the light; at least, we prefer to have it boiled some time before we attempt to drink it. On the whole, we have no reason to complain of the living in this city.

Before exploring farther, it is proper, we should look at the people, and study somewhat their characteristics. We learn, there are in the city twenty-five thousand inhabitants. Fifteen thousand of these are Jews; five thousand, Moslems; two thousand, Greeks; fifteen hundred, Latins; four hundred, Armenians; eleven hundred, Protestants and Copts.

The Jews are mostly immigrants from foreign countries, and thoroughly consecrated to their faith. In their habits they are peculiar. The men have their hair shingled behind, but hanging in tresses in front of their ears. They wear for their outer garment a kind of dressing-gown faced with fur, and caps edged with fur. Their women are attired after the European style. The Jews are the most enterprising class in the city. Nearly all the business is carried on by them. They are as expert here in shaving money, as in New York, or London. Their leading characteristic everywhere is persistency.

The Moslems are Turks and Arabs. The men are well formed and muscular, but the women are deformed and abject looking beings, as a rule. The wives are regarded as inferior to their husbands, and generally treated as slaves. Their religion teaches, woman was fashioned out of the great toe of man, and therefore, should submit to his authority in this life, and rest in a diminutive grave after death.

The Greeks have mainly come from Grecian colonies. Not a few of them look as though they might have some of the old Athenian and Spartan blood coursing their veins. The sharp features and keen eye indicate mind and culture, yet we are informed, ignorance prevails among them, and that even some of their priests are unable to read, or write.

The Latins are mostly Italians, and appear as though they came from the Sunny Land. They are devoted Catholics. As a whole they are superior to the Greeks here, and far in advance of the Arabs. Their priests are generally monks wearing the cowl and the long brown frock banded to the body by a rope and beads.

The Protestants are of all tongues and nations. The mass of them are Europeans, ranking, perhaps, in this order, Germans, French, English, and Russians, though more speak the English, than any other language.

The modern, like the ancient city, is divided into four quarters, named after the sites which they occupy. Mount Akra is the northwestern; Mount Zion, the southwestern; Mount Moriah, the southeastern; and Mount Bazetha, the northeastern. We would scarcely think of calling them mounts, their elevation is so slight. Still they must have been greatly changed since the time of the first city. Several cities have been built above them and destroyed, and the stones and mortar out of which they were made, compose the foundation of the present city. So this vast accumulation of *débris* must have greatly changed their original condition. In places the waste must be thirty, or forty feet deep.

Going upon Akra, we at once realize this to be the Christian quarter. In fact, this is the cleanest part of the city. Here the foreign ministers and consuls reside. Here are the Christian churches. As we inspect these, we find the Latin burdened with pictures of the crucifixion and the Virgin. The outward is expressive of religion. In the Greek church we meet with few pictures and statues. The edifice is in the form of the Greek cross, and exquisitely simple and beautiful in all its adjustments. The Protestant church is plain but convenient. These different sects here appear to live and work in the most perfect harmony. No doubt, they agree to disagree, and this always results in peace. While wandering about, we are troubled with the narrowness of the streets, and marvel, how people can suffer themselves to dwell in such close relations; for we should not think of calling the highways, streets; because they are too narrow for that, being not more than three feet wide; however, St. David's and Christ's, are possibly nine, or ten feet in width.

In the centre of Akra we come to a huge structure; it is the pool of Hezekiah; it must be two hundred and fifty feet long, one hundred and fifty feet wide, and fifty, or sixty feet deep. This bears the marks of age. It is said to have been built in Solomon's time. Looking at the sides, we can but ask, where did they quarry those vast blocks of stone, and how did they place many of them so high? It is a perfect piece of masonry to-day. It has every indication of enduring for the ages to come. Looking at this pool, we would judge, if it should be filled with water, it would supply the whole city with this essential element for more than a year, and yet we are informed that nearly every private house is supplied with a cistern to catch water during the winter, that they may not suffer for the want of it during the long drought of summer.

Leaving this quarter, we will direct our way to Mount Zion, over which the Armenians hold sway. This is the highest part of the city, and the inhabitants here would be pleased to have you regard it the aristocratic portion. We first come to an open space of some rods in extent; this is the exchange and parliament house of this nomadic people who want no other roofing than the open sky, and no other flooring than these rough stones. It is also the marketplace where we see several caravans of camels; one of which has just come in from Jaffa, loaded with wheat and olives; another came in yesterday from Hebron, bearing grapes, figs, and pomegranates. The camels and dromedaries look wearied and forlorn. Even some of them that came in yesterday have their loads on their backs, and as likely as not, they have had no food for the last twenty-four hours. It is evident, the buyers are not numerous, or anxious to trade. All business here is done on a slow and small scale. The owners of the produce are forced to keep a sharp lookout, for hungry dogs, and more hungry beggars, are watching an opportunity to practise substraction on the eatables. Under the shadow of a wall close by, we notice some dervishes and bedouins sitting, or lying on the ground, while two or three of them are sleeping; those awake are busily engaged transplanting fleas from their own garments to those of their dreamy companions. They show themselves experts in this business, for only experts could be successful in capturing such undiscoverable tormentors. Even Yankees fail in this undertaking after much practice.

A short distance to the west near the Jaffa Gate, is the tower of Hippicus, or, perhaps, as often called, the tower of David. We obtain a permit of a half-dozen Turkish soldiers guarding the entrance by giving them liberally of bukshish, to ascend it. Apparently these guardsmen feel their responsibilities are great. Their uniforms consist of blue Turkish spencers and trousers striped with yellow braid. They are armed with flint lock-guns, and clumsy, broad-bladed swords. We climb a hundred irregular steps, and we stand upon the top of the tower, whence we have a fine view of the city, and an extended prospect of the surrounding scenery. With delight we gaze upon Olivet, Bethlehem, and portions of the Kedron. Thrilling associations crowd the mind, as we stand here, and inquire, where were King David's palace, Solomon's Temple, Calvary, Golgotha, that Judgment Hall, that Communion

Chamber, and the almost countless places made memorable by noble and ignoble deeds? As we descend and are leaving the vestibule, we notice a little girl of sparkling eyes and fairest complexion, sitting on the pavement and rocking her little body back and forth. She has, perhaps, experienced eight summers, and as many winters. But what is she now doing? We are told she is memorizing Mohammedan prayers. Who is she, and whence did she come? She is a slave belonging to one of these officers, and was purchased in the land of Moab of her parents. What! do they raise children there at the present day to sell, as we do our cattle and sheep? Certainly, and what was paid for her? Our dragoman says "some three hundred dollars." What is to become of her? Oh, she is to learn a few prayers, and possibly be taught to play on some rude instrument, and by the time she is ten, or eleven years old, her master will take her as a wife, or concubine! We can no longer doubt that civilization has journeyed westward, or be too thankful for our homes and the sacredness of the family ties.

In the Arabic language, or the language of the country, they never call this monument, tower, but needle; so they would say, "The needle of David." Through the basement there is a passage-way closed by a door; still they do not say door, but eye. The opening leads into a yard, or court where horses and camels can be kept in safety from robbers. Now, if a camel has been unloaded, and the cameleer wishes to leave his caravan, to search for some buyer of his unsold goods, he dares not leave the unburdened animal, unless there is some one to guard it. So if he is alone, he will take the camel that is free from any burden and lead it through the eye of the needle into the court referred to. Now a horse can go through the passage without any difficulty, but the camel must crouch and rub its way through. No doubt, this needle was here in the time of our Saviour. Hence, how forcible his language becomes, when he was addressing those rich Pharisees and Sadducees, saying, "It is more difficult for a rich man to enter the kingdom of heaven than for a camel to go through the eye of a needle."

As we are walking over this sacred ground, our attention is attracted by pitiable looking objects on the tops of the houses; some of them with eyes gone, noses wanting, and arms, handless; these are lepers. As we approach the buildings, those who are able to come down into the street approach us entreating for bukshish, bukshish, with such tones as pierce the heart, and force the hands of pilgrims deep into their pockets, causing them to bestow generously upon these unfortunate beings. Here is a lad near us who has, perhaps, seen six or seven bitter winters; his eyes are red and his bare limbs all covered with whitish scales; his very look seems to say, "I am a leper, and am to die a leper; my life is worse than death." Here is another who has suffered with the disease for more than twenty years. He appears still more wretched; his skin is of a darker color; his countenance wears a sadder expression; he has evidently not the least hope of recovery; he is dragging out the most miserable existence. By the wayside is another abject-looking being. It would seem, she is unable to walk; a part of her face is eaten away; she no longer lifts her eyes but keeps them fixed upon the ground; she is apparently longing to die. But have we not reason to fear in the presence of such a loathsome disease? As the lepers approach, they are very careful not to touch us, for, if there was danger of this, the cry would ring through the city, as of old, "Unclean! unclean!" The lepers are not allowed to lean against a post, or touch anything which would be likely to expose those free from the disease. No doubt, the leprosy is imparted by contact; and so in this respect the greatest caution is taken to guard against its spread. But how does it originate? It would appear, as a general thing, from filthiness and improper food. Are they ever cured of it? Yes, there are instances, where those afflicted with it have been fully restored; this has been done only under the most skilful treatment.

Had we time it would be interesting to enter the Armenian Convent and Temple and witness a service, or look upon the many treasures garnered up in this sacred place.

The only two synagogues of the city are upon Mount Zion. These are crowded to overflowing at their Sabbath worship. The Jews here are devoutly religious, and strict observers of their creeds and ceremonies. Many of the aged remind us of the ancient scribes and patriarchs. They are a peculiar people and decidedly consecrated to their church. They seem to believe, their lost tribes will ere long be restored to their beloved land, and once more Israel will be strong in the Lord.

Here David had his beautiful palace, when Jerusalem was in its glory; and here tradition points out the sepulchre where the ashes of the inspired poet repose.

A little to the north of this quarter towards the centre of the city is the Church of the Holy Sepulchre which at the present time is the most contentious place within Jerusalem. The Romans, the Greeks, and the Armenians, all lay claim to this church. So necessity has divided it up into three compartments, and assigned a certain portion to each of these religious bodies; still, there is no reconciliation among them; they despitefully treat and persecute one another. Each claims to have possession of Calvary, and to understand many things connected with the crucifixion and burial of Jesus. The spirit that pervades this place certainly does not savor of peace and brotherly love. The building itself is not particularly inviting, or imposing, though it has been very costly. Perhaps, it is sought after more than any other structure within the city by strangers, yet by the Christian scholars who have devoted the most attention to the topography of historical places here, it is not felt that this church marks the place where the Saviour was crucified. No doubt, if the *débris* could be removed from the site of the old city, the locality of many places of special interest would be readily discovered, which are now involved in mystery and uncertainty.

Crossing the Tyropæan Valley to the east,

we are on the most sacred Moslem ground in the world save that at Mecca where they believe their prophet lies buried. We are now on Mount Moriah. This is a cherished spot to the Jew and the Christian. Here we find a large space, in whose centre stands the mosque of Omar crowned with its massive dome glistening in the sunlight like gold and precious stones. Around it are extensive mosaic pavings of choice marbles. The Mohammedans claim that it stands on the exact site of Solomon's Temple. We gain admittance to it by paying an exorbitant fee, and find within but little of striking interest. Of course, we have the privilege of looking into the "Well of the Leaf," and the "Hole" where tradition says, "The Ark of the Lord rested." There are no pews, or seats in this temple. The Moslems worship sitting, or lying on the floor. Should we be here on Friday which is their Sunday, we would have the privilege of witnessing a service. So we can enjoy three Sabbaths a week in this city: Friday is the Mohammedan; Saturday, the Jewish; and Sunday, the Christian.

As we leave the mosque, we hear the cries of the muezzin from the lofty minaret, announcing the hour of prayer; and at once the Mos lems drop upon their knees, bowing their heads and moving their lips as though in devoutest worship, reminding us of the time when this place was disturbed on Sabbath days by the bleating of sheep, as the knife was put to their throats; by the lowing of bulls and heifers, as they were led out to slaughter; by the tramping of soldiers on guard; by the marching of priests in long processions; and by the clamors of worshippers around altars flaming with many costly sacrifices. When the Jewish horn was blown from the temple wall, announcing the Sabbath, all labor ceased. No one was suffered to kindle a fire, make a bed, boil a pot, pull a dumb beast from the ditch, or raise an arm in self-defence. So when Jesus came teaching that it was lawful to do good on the Sabbath, what an uproar was made! Hearts were enraged and hands were lifted to slay him; but Pharisaic valor was not equal to Christian fortitude.

Near the mosque of Omar is another large building which is the principal harem of the city, where the wives of the Turkish officers and nobility reside. Soon after sunrise and during the last part of the day, may be seen moving among the marble columns around the structure white figures of veiled women who appear as mysterious as Hamlet's ghost, or the weird sisters of Macbeth.

Let us now turn our attention to an Arab family who are preparing for supper. The members consist of a husband, wife, son, and daughter. The man is a peasant who has just returned from the field where he has been sowing and ploughing in the wheat; the wife has been to the public fire of the city and obtained a few live coals; the children have come in from the outside of the city with little handfuls of kindling. The mother places the coals on an elevated paving-stone one side of the travelled way, and supplies them with the scanty fuel, kindling the fire into a blaze; then she puts into an earthen dish a pint of sweet oil, a pint of legumes, and a pint of olive fruit; these she stirs up with her fingers, and holds the vessel over the flames, moving it back and forth, at the same time bending over the dish, so as to catch any odor rising from the food; when her olfactories are perfectly satisfied that the mess is cooked, she removes it and puts it directly in front of her husband who is sitting on the pavement, while she and her children stand, or sit in his rear; for a Moslem husband and father never eats with his family; he must be served first; so he soon begins to take from the dish with the first knives and forks ever made the olives and legumes, holding his fingers long in his mouth to suck off the oil. When he has despatched about half of the quantity, the dish is removed, and his "hobble-bobble" pipe is set in front of him and the wife puts into its bowl some new Lebanon tobacco and supplies it with a fresh coal; then the husband winds the serpentine stem round his body, adjusting the mouth-piece so that he is at once taking his comfort. Now the mother and children repair to the food and soon dispose of the rest. After this, the goat-skin bottle of water is brought forward and all partake of the universal beverage among Mohammedans. The meal is now ended and the family soon go into their house which is close by. The Arabs and Turks are seldom out after sunset. As we look into their home, we find, it consists of a single room, some twelve feet square. We discover no chairs, no bed, no clothing in it, nothing in the way of furniture except the rudest apology for a stove. But where do they sleep? Why, of course upon the floor! We notice on one side of the room, there is an elevation of stone-work something like a flat German oven; well, this is the husband's bed, and when the weather is cold, a fire is built under it, to keep him warm as he retires, but the wife and children can endure sleeping on the cold sand. This is the average Moslem's home.

As we proceed to the north, leaving Mount Moriah, we come to the rise of ground called Bezetha. This is the Mohammedan quarter, and is thickly occupied with buildings. Here, too, we find St. Stephen's Gate and the pool of Bethesda; no doubt, this pool is one of the ancient works; there is no water in it now. As we pass along the Via Dolorosa, we notice in the walls fragments of porphyry columns and plinths of verde-antique, projecting over doors and windows, telling of other cities and older civilizations.

Turning from the Via Dolorosa towards the centre of the city, we are among the shops of shoemakers, blacksmiths, and wooden-ware workers. These are not on a large scale. Shoemaking seems to take the lead. The ground everywhere is so stony, there is the greatest demand for shoes; but the shoes, how they look! They would be curiosities and unaccountables in the shop windows of France or America. The street is the blacksmith's shop; and to shoe a horse, it takes three men, one to hold him, and another to hold up his foot, and still another to fit the shoe and drive the nails.

In some of the shops, quite a business is being carried on in the way of making boxes, inkstands, rules, and numerous curiosities from wood brought from different parts of the country.

Leaving the shops, we come to an open court around which are many men and women offering for sale chaplets, rosaries, and crosses, made from olive wood; pebbles from the Dead Sea; apples of Sodom from beyond the Jordan; oak from Mamre; relics from Bethany and Bethlehem; souvenirs from Samaria and Galilee. But we are soon beyond the clamor of these greedy merchants, and are again surrounded by Turkish soldiers armed with pistols and sabres, who are guarding the Holy Sepulchre.

It is Friday afternoon, and we must not fail to visit the Jewish Wailing Place which is to the rear of the Mosque of Omar towards the centre of the city. It consists of a triangular space, overshadowed on the east by an ancient wall which is reputed to be a portion of the wall existing in the days of King Solomon. At least, it bears marks of great antiquity. At three o'clock in the afternoon the Israelites begin to assemble here. They have purchased the right of the Turkish government to occupy these grounds every Friday afternoon from three to five o'clock. The Jews have fared hard here, and still do; they have been smitten on every hand, but their pride, their trust, and their hope, are undaunted. Hither they come, old men with snow-white beard and trembling steps; young men, the pride of their nation; women dressed in linen and sackcloth; and little children; all press to this spot so sacred to them, with their parchment Bibles in hand, desirous to commune with the past and hope in the future. On reaching this place they hold their faces to the old walls in silent prayer; this service continues for several minutes in perfect silence. Then the aged are seated on the stone flooring, and some rabbi recites a passage from Lamentations, and soon all voices are joined with his in pathetic tones, repeating the wailings of their departed prophets and wise men. It is not long before they are worked up into intense anguish, wringing their hands, swinging their bodies, beating their breasts, and weeping copious tears. We cannot question their sincerity. After this experience which lasts nearly half an hour, an aged rabbi rises, who reminds us of the patriarchs, and addresses the assembly, paying deference to the past and speaking most encouraging words as to the future, entreating his people never to falter but always press forward, and the Lord will restore once more their beloved Mount Zion, and rebuild their wondrous temple. At the conclusion of his remarks another priest recites a promise, and quickly all voices are repeating in unison stirring words of Jewish sage and seer. The faces are now lighted up with joy, and all hearts seem to be sure a good time is coming to the lost children of Israel; and now the benediction comes, consisting in shaking hands warmly throughout the large assembly, bidding each other a God-speed in their religious work. Having witnessed this affecting service and others of this religious body, we cannot doubt that great changes are yet to come to this city through the Jews. They are flocking hither from all quarters of the world. They are willing to undergo any hardships, if they can only die in Jerusalem and be buried by the brook Kedron.

Passing outside of the walls to the northwest, we find a spur of the mountains extending close down to the city, which divides the Kedron from the valley of Gihon. As we follow the latter, we soon come to a pool of Gihon which is another immense cistern, being in a state of decay. As we descend, the valley keeps drawing in towards the city, and soon we are under the shadows of Mount Zion. As we look up towards the city, we discover the hillside is very steep and stony. Here we come to the second pool of Gihon which is about six hundred feet long, four hundred wide, and fifty, or sixty feet deep. These pools were built, it is thought, in the time of Solomon. Just above, to the west, is an aqueduct leading along the mountain-sides to Bethlehem, and three miles beyond to the pools of Solomon, consisting of three vast cisterns graded one above the other like steps, which are five hundred feet long, three hundred wide, and fifty deep. These are all grand works telling of a people living more than two and a half thousand years ago, who were skilled in quarrying stone and piling them into massive structures. A little below the large pool of Gihon the valley turns to the east. Here the severe image of Moloch stood at the time the Jews were wont to worship that deity. Here, when that monster was fired to red heat, they would place women and children in his consuming grasp, to appease his wrath, and secure their salvation. Because of the cries and groans of the dying, they would beat drums to stifle and drown the agonizing tumult, and so the Israelites named the place Tophet. After this, as the Jews returned to the service of the true God, they despised the place and its surroundings, hurling into it the offal of the city. The Greeks called it Gehenna, and to protect the city, a fire was kept constantly burning, to consume the waste and filth; and so Christ referred to it as the place "where the worm dieth not and the fire is not quenched."

In this valley on the south, the ledges are cropping out in many places, and these are honey-combed, as receptacles for the dead; some of the openings are large enough to contain one corpse; others, two, or three, or many. It would seem, in olden times they did not believe in burying the dead in loose soil, but must inter them in the solid rock; and, moreover, before they could be laid away in these silent recesses, they must be carefully embalmed. As we climb up the ledges on the south a short distance before reaching the brook Kedron, we come to the spot which tradition points out as the "Potter's Field," or Aceldama, which the priests purchased with the "thirty pieces of silver" received from Judas, as the price of our Saviour's blood; but we do not find it a field; it is a cavern in the ledges being partly natural and partly artificial. Really, it is a room from fifteen to twenty feet square. We have little reason to doubt that this is the place purchased for the burial of strangers with the money that became so despicable in the sight of Judas. Descending and crossing the valley up towards the city, we stand by the pool of Siloam. Here the water is gushing out in quite a large stream from the sidehill, and where it trickles down into the valley, "the lily grows" and "Sharon's dewy rose" does still smile.

Leaving this spring and descending a short distance to the east, we are by the brook Kedron and in the valley of Jehoshaphat. In this autumn-time there is no water running in the brook. Should we be here in April, there would be a large stream of water. Its bed now is full of stones. Close upon its banks and far up the sides of Olivet are Jewish graves thickly sown. Now and then may be seen an aged Israelite walking in this silent city, or resting upon some grave, as in the act of praying that, when he dies, he may be buried among the graves of his fathers. This is truly a sacred spot to the Jew.

If we follow the Kedron down half a mile from the city, we come to an opening made in search of antiquities. Being let down into this some fifteen feet, we find ourselves in a canal cut out of the solid rock, six feet high and five feet wide. As we examine the sides, we see where the water had worn out creases, showing that it must have flowed through this channel for a long period. Before advancing towards the city very far, we come to a stairway leading to the surface; the steps themselves have been wholly worn away. When the stairs were first opened up, keys and pieces of pottery were found at their junction with the canal, implying that formerly multitudes used to come here for water. We do not ascend much farther before we discover another similar stairway. Then we come out of this dark recess, and pass to the southeast corner of the city, just outside of the walls, and are let down by the means of a rope eighty feet, and then following an opening, out towards Mount Zion for a considerable distance, we come to the sides of a building constructed of marble, or fine limestone; the stones are accurately bevelled and firmly cemented together, so that a penknife blade cannot be pressed between them; yet what building this was, or who piled it up, no one can guess. Could all the waste of the city be removed, what discoveries would be brought to light! Could we look upon them, we would be ready to admit that the oldest things are the newest. Following the Kedron which draws in toward the walls of the city, we soon find ourselves in the most sacred place. This is Gethsemane, forever consecrated by that divinest of prayers, "Not my will, but thine be done." Here are olive-trees growing, as they grew, when the disciples rested here, waiting for the Master, while he went out to pray. Here Jesus was betrayed by that deceitful kiss into the hands of a raging, priestly mob crying, "Crucify him, crucify him."! How can this be otherwise than an affecting and cherished spot to all Christian hearts? We have such emotions here, as we never have had before. Often, perchance, we have had joyful feelings, while visiting some grove, or spot, once frequented by poet, or scholar; or while climbing to the top of castle walls redolent with tales and legends of bravest heroism; or while visiting the homes of Scott, Shakespeare, and Bryant; or while standing by the tombs of Von Humboldt, Harriet Browning, Raphael, Virgil, and Abraham Lincoln. It is sweet to visit places where great souls played in childhood, nobly wrought at life's noon, and were gloriously translated, as the mortal dimmed and wasted away. Here in Gethsemane we think not of poet, artist, or scholar, but of Him who was infinitely more than all these, who journeyed through this land, looking upon these hills and valleys, stones and flowers, birds and stars, men and angels, that He might forever bless the human race. In Him we see divinity; and, if we walk in His light, we shall evermore enjoy the New Jerusalem.

INDEX.

	PAGE
Augsburg and Protestantism	133
Alpine Waterfalls	173
American Artists in Rome	222
Ancient Rome	230
Aventine Hill	238
Avernus and Sibyl's Cave	256
Ascent of Vesuvius	260
Ascent of Lycabettus	280
Attica and its Influence	281
Acropolis, its Relics	288
Alexandrian Library	304
A Wedding Scene in Cairo	319
Ascending Cheops	325
At the Damascus Gate	336
An Arab Family and Mode of Living	354
Aceldama	361
British Museum and its Wonders	44
Bank of England	50
Bread Street, Birthplace of Milton	61
Broadest and Finest Street in Europe	72
Boulevards of Paris	86
Burgos and its Cathedral	107
Bavarian Statue at Munich	147
Berlin, its Places of Interest	152
Berne and its Bears	185
Berne Cathedral and College	187
Boboli Gardens of Florence	206
Buildings and Streets of Rome	216

INDEX.

	PAGE
Bridges across the Tiber	217
Baths of Caracalla	243
Bay of Baiæ	257
Battle of Salamis	271
Bezetha and Via Dolorosa	356
Business of Jerusalem	356
Clyde and its Shipbuilding	3
Cathedral and Necropolis of Glasgow	6
Calton Hill and its Monuments	18
Castle Rock	21
Cleopatra's Needle on the Thames	56
Cannon Street and the Romans	58
Cheapside and Guildhall	61
Cornhill and the Poet Gray	62
Churches and Preachers of London	64
Champs Elysées and its Gardens	74
Conservatory of Measures	79
Churches of Paris and Religious Status	82
Columbus in Spain	100
Cervantes and his "Don Quixote"	107
Cordova, the Oxford of Spain	108
Cologne Cathedral	126
Calvin, the Reformer	180
Castle of Chillon	184
Campagna, its Desolation	211
Climate of Rome	213
Churches of Rome	218
Colosseum and its History	231
Capitoline Hill and Tarpeian Rock	237
Cloaca Maxima	237
Cœlian Hill	239
Catacombs of St. Calixtus and St. Sebastian	244
Castle of St. Elmo	254
Catacombs of Alexandria	309
Citadel of Cairo	320
Course of Civilization	331
Church of the Holy Sepulchre	351

INDEX.

	PAGE
Dresden Gallery, its Madonna del Sisto	144
Duomo of Florence, and other Noted Buildings	193
Dante, his Life and Work	195
Destruction of Pompeii	263
Donkey Ride to Pyramids	324
Descent into Excavations near Mount Zion	363
Edinburgh and its History	15
Edinburgh Schools	28
English House of Parliament	52
Education and Benevolent Institutions of Paris	89
Escurial, Palace of Philip II	109
English Cemetery of Florence	207
Egyptian Columns in Rome	218
Esquiline and Viminal Hills	240
Education and Schools in Greece	276
Egypt and Cairo	297
Experiences in Cairo	315
Egyptian School	317
Entrance into Jerusalem	336
Experience at the Prussian Hospice	340
Fingal's Cave	1
Fleet Street and its Associations	59
France and Early History	67
French Artists	78
From France into Spain	106
Florence, its Natural Beauties	189
Florence and its History	191
Forum and Basilica of Trajan	236
Founding of Alexandria	303
Fields in Judæa	333
First View of Jerusalem	334
Greenock and James Watt	3
Glasgow	5
Glasgow and Physical Condition	5

370   INDEX.

	PAGE
George's Square and its Statues	6
George Street and its Monuments	21
Grassmarket and Covenanters	24
Greyfriars Church and Churchyard	25
Gladstone and Northcote	52
Grenada and the Alhambra	108
Germany, its Situation and History	119
Germans, their early Religion	125
Graves of Luther and Melancthon	131
German Music	140
German Art and Artists	142
Glacial Wonders	175
Geneva Cathedral and College	180
Genevese Scholars	182
Galileo, his Tower and Works	199
Galleries of Florence	202
Government of Rome	222
Greece and its Island Views	269
Government of Egypt	309
Goshen and the Israelites	314
Gethsemane	364
Highlands of Scotland	13
Holyrood Palace and Edinburgh Castle	22
High Street, Past and Present	22
Heriot Hospital	25
Hotel de Cluny and its Relics	79
Hotel des Invalides and Museum	80
Hebrews in Egypt	331
Harem and Veiled Women	353
Iona and Scotch Kings	1
Illustrations of Scripture	312
Janiculum Hill and Tasso's Garden	242
Jerusalem, Modern and Ancient	332
Jewish Wailing Place	357

INDEX.

	PAGE
Kensington Museum, its Treasures	46
King Street and Spenser	62
Kedron, its Recent Excavations	362
Legend of Robert Bruce and Spider	2
London and its History	33
London Tower	37
London National Gallery	53
London Parks	54
Luxemburg Palace, its Treasures	79
Libraries of Paris	88
Leipsic, Musical Centre of Germany	142
Luzerne, its Attractions	168
Lake Leman, its Classic Spots	179
Lausanne, Resort of Gibbon	183
Leo XIII. and his Cardinals	223
Landing at Alexandria	299
Lepers on Mount Zion	348
Madeleine, a Grecian Church	85
Means of Traffic in Paris	87
Moors in Spain	98
Madrid, its Past and Present	111
Madrid Museum and Art Galleries	116
Munich and its Pinakothek	143
Munich, its Glyptothek	145
Museum and Bronze Foundry of Munich	146
Madame de Staël's Home and Grave	183
Michael Angelo's Home and Tomb	194
Museum on the Capitoline Hill	221
Mamertine Prison	235
Museum at Naples	264
Modern Athens	274
Mount Pentelicus, its Marble Quarries	284
Mars Hill and St. Paul	295
Market of Alexandria	306
Memphis, its Sepulchres	330
Mount Akra	342

	PAGE
Mount Zion	345
Mount Moriah and Mosque of Omar	352
Notre Dame, dedicated to St. Genevieve	69
Notre Dame, its History	83
Notre Dame as it now is	84
Naples, its Past and Present	248
Nero and his Mother	258
Needle of David	347
Oxford and Regent Streets	63
Origin of the Romans	229
Olivet and Jewish Graves	362
Princes Street and Monument of Scott	20
People of Edinburgh	27
Prince Albert's Monument	57
Paternoster Row	62
People beyond the Rhine	69
Paris, its First Name	69
Paris Six Hundred Years ago	70
Paris University and its Teachers	70
Place de la Concorde, its History	74
Pantheon and Tombs	85
Priesthood in Spain	105
Potsdam, Birthplace of Humboldt	138
Powers's Life and Sculptures	208
Pagan Rome and its Hills	214
Progress in Italy	228
Pantheon of Rome	236
Palatine Hill	239
Pincian and Quirinal Hills	241
Puteoli and St. Paul	255
Petrified Sentinel	268
People of Greece	276
Plain of Marathon	286
Parthenon and other Temples	290
Pnyx Hill and Demosthenes	293

INDEX.

	PAGE
Pillar of Pompey	302
Palm-Trees, gathering of Fruit	305
People of Jerusalem	341
Pool of Siloam	362
Robert Burns and Ayr	7
Reformation in Spain	103
Rhine, its Castles and Legends	122
Religious Expression of German Cathedrals	128
Religion in Germany	151
Rhigi, its Ascent and Charms	171
Rousseau's Garden	181
Religion in Geneva	182
Rome, its Situation	211
Rome, the Capital of Italy	217
Roman Triumphal Arches	233
Roman Forum	234
Relics of the Buried Cities	266
Ride to Cairo	310
Rise and Fall of the Nile	313
Roads of Judæa	335
Russian Hospice	336
Scotland	1
Scotch Lakes	14
St. Giles's Church and John Knox	24
Scott and Abbotsford	31
St. Paul's Cathedral	42
Smithfield and its Jousts	62
Schools of London	64
St. Chapelle, its Beauty and Use	84
Spain, its First Inhabitants	95
Spain Three Centuries Ago	101
Seville and First Inquisition	107
Strasburg Cathedral	127
Schools and Universities of Germany	147
Switzerland, Natural and Historical	157
Switzerland, its Government	167

INDEX.

	PAGE
Swiss Life	168
Swiss Highways	173
Savonarola and his Martyrdom	198
St. Peter's, its Wonders	218
State of the Church in Rome	223
Schools and Education in Rome	227
Schools of Naples	252
Solfatara and Forum of Vulcan	255
Scenes from Naples to Resina	259
Scenery about Athens	279
Socrates and his Prison	294
Scenes in Alexandria	301
Sowing and Ploughing in Judæa	332
Site, Streets, and Buildings of Jerusalem	338
Stores and Tradesmen of Jerusalem	338
Tower Hill and Penn	62
The City where Paris now stands	69
The City of Paris and its Characteristics	71
The View from Arc de l'Etoile	71
Tuileries and their History	75
The Louvre and its Galleries of Art	76
Tomb of Napoleon I.	81
Tell and Gessler	162
The Tiber, Past and Present	212
Travertine Stone	213
Temple of Vesta	238
Tombs of the Scipios	243
Tomb of Cæcilia Metella	243
Thrilling Experience in a Catacomb	246
Tunnel of Posilippo	254
Temple of Theseus	293
The Sphinx	329
Tower of Hippicus, and Touching Incident	346
Tophet and Moloch	360
Valladolid and its Places of Interest	107
Vatican and its Art Treasures	220

INDEX. 375

	PAGE
Virgil's Home and Tomb	254
Valley of the Nile	311
Views from the Pyramid	327
Valley and Pools of Gihon	359
Wallace's Tower and Dunglace Castle	4
Westminster Abbey, its Monuments	39
Wittenberg, Home of Luther	129
Worms in the Reformation	132
Weimar, its Poets	136
Within the Pyramid of Cheops	327
Walls of Jerusalem	336
Zwingle, his Noble Death	165

www.ingramcontent.com/pod-product-compliance
Lightning Source LLC
Chambersburg PA
CBHW030349230426
43664CB00007BB/586